COMPELLING INTEREST

COMPELLING INTEREST.

The Real Story behind *Roe v. Wade*

ROGER RESLER

eChristianBooks

Published by eChristian, Inc.
Escondido, California

Compelling Interest: The Real Story behind *Roe v. Wade*

First printing in 2012 by eChristian, Inc.

eChristian, Inc.
2235 Enterprise Street, Suite 140
Escondido, CA 92029
http://echristian.com

ISBN: 978-1-61843-113-4

Cover design by John Wollinka.

Interior design by Larry Taylor.

Produced with the assistance of Livingstone, the Publishing Services Division of eChristian, Inc. Project staff includes: Dan Balow, Afton Rorvik, Linda Taylor, Ashley Taylor, Tom Shumaker, Lois Jackson, Joel Bartlett, and Sheila Urban. Index prepared by Sandi Frank.

Printed in the United States of America

19 18 17 16 15 14 13 12 8 7 6 5 4 3 2 1

To Marcia,
the love of my life, and our two, now fully grown
"compelling interests," Stephanie & David.
You make life an adventure.
Thank you for allowing me to
spend way too much time in the man cave.

Contents

Preface

The year was 1981—at least if memory serves correctly. I was a junior in high school attending a concert featuring the brother-sister trio: The Second Chapter of Acts. Annie Herring—of Easter Song fame—sang a song that stood out from the rest. The chorus included this refrain:

My God, we're killing thousands, believing the lie.
My God, we're killing thousands without blinking an eye.

Given my sheltered life, it was a mystery, at the time, what she was singing about. Over the ensuing months and years the term "abortion" came up from time to time and, to my shock, I gradually began to realize that what Annie had been singing about was not occurring in some far-off land or in some barbaric past. It was reality, despite the clean streets and white picket fences I was accustomed to. The notion that mothers would voluntarily go to a clinic for the express purpose of "terminating an unwanted pregnancy" was a rude awakening. Abortion was *literally* killing thousands here and now. But thousands of *what?* Fetuses? Babies? Human beings? Persons? Blobs of tissue? Products of conception?

In addition to examining the landmark Supreme Court case that made abortion legal, this book will attempt to answer that and other related questions—recognizing, that easy, black-and-white answers are not always available—or at least obvious.

One thing should be noted from the outset. In the original audio version of this book (2007)—which was actually produced five years *before* this newer print version (which, admittedly, is not the typical course of events)—I made an effort to use the term "pro-choice" as much as possible to describe those who oppose most legal restrictions on abortion. One of the reasons I made that decision was an effort to appease people on that side of the debate. My logic, which seemed reasonable at the time, was that since it is the term *they* prefer, I should, in good faith and in attempting to carry on a civil discourse, honor their wishes.

In the interim, however, I have come to the conclusion that this decision was a mistake for several reasons. First, it gives unwarranted emphasis to exactly what the pro-abortion movement wants to emphasize (which is illegitimate) while simultaneously de-emphasizing precisely what they wish to de-emphasize (which is what the controversy is all about). In short, simply using the term (even in good faith) is akin to validating their logic, which, I will argue in this book, is seriously flawed.

Second, one rarely hears prominent pro-abortion/pro-choice advocates respectfully using the term "pro-life advocates" or "right-to-life proponents." Instead, we are nearly always characterized as being "anti-choice" or, at best, "anti-abortion." The former is simply inaccurate, since the public battle is not against "choice" but against abortion. The converse, however, does not follow. While you almost never hear pro-abortion proponents publicly admitting they are, in fact, pro-abortion, the fact is the choice they emphasize is not available without it. You cannot argue for the validity of a choice unless you think *each option* in the choice is morally acceptable. The pro-life community has no problem with the choice *not* to abort. It is only the choice to abort (in the absence of dire circumstances) that we reject. It is not the fault of the pro-life community that one "option" in the choice is morally unacceptable. So the public fight is over abortion, not the ability to choose it over not aborting. It is therefore at least as accurate to use the term "pro-abortion" to describe one side as it is to use the term "anti-abortion" to describe the other. Given all these factors, and considering that it is not a perfect world so some compromise is in order, I have made the decision in this edition to use both terms "pro-abortion" and "pro-choice" as interchangeable. I also use the terms "pro-life" and "anti-abortion" as interchangeable and I reject the term "anti-choice" as inaccurate and propagandistic, just as I also reject the term "pro-death."

Background

In 2005–2006 I conducted a series of interviews which were digitally recorded in audio format with leaders in the pro-life community. They included:

1. Sociology professor at St. Louis University and pro-life author, Dr. William

Brennan. Some of his published works include: *The Abortion Holocaust,* and *Dehumanizing the Vulnerable: When Word Games Take Lives.*

2. Professor of Bioethics at St. Louis University, Dr. Gerard Magill. Dr. Magill currently serves as Vernon F. Gallagher Chair for the Integration of Science, Theology, Philosophy and Law at Duquesne University and is the author of numerous articles and books.

3. The late Dr. Mildred Jefferson. Dr. Jefferson is distinguished as the first black woman to graduate from Harvard Medical School. She was a practicing physician for many years and was also a cofounder of the National Right to Life Committee. Her contributions to the pro-life movement are numerous, and her eloquence in defending life is greatly missed.

4. Dr. Carolyn Gerster is a retired family practitioner and surgeon and also cofounded the National Right to Life Committee with Dr. Jefferson. Dr. Gerster is still active within the pro-life community.

5. Dr. Jim Thorp is a practicing perinatologist (a specialist in high-risk pregnancies). Dr. Thorp has spoken authoritatively on fetal development and high-risk pregnancies before Congress.

6. Prolific author and speaker Randy Alcorn, whose commonsense approach to the subject of abortion is unmatched.

7. Photojournalist Michael Clancy. In 1999, Clancy took a series of photographs that changed his life, and one in particular that still receives national attention. The subject of his photo was the then unborn Samuel Armas who decided to reach out of his mother's womb during fetal surgery only halfway through pregnancy. Clancy was present and caught the baby's actions in a series of high-speed photos.

The content of these interviews in combination with the original audio recordings of the *Roe v. Wade* oral arguments obtained from the National Archives was used along with quotes from other sources and my own narrative to produce the original audio version of this work. The majority of that material is retained for this edition while some has been revised for easier reading. Updated material has also been added.

As you read this book the main message I hope to convey is that the "logic" that was necessary in order to legalize abortion on demand in 1973 in the

United States was flawed, and the historical view of abortion presented to and adopted by the *Roe* Supreme Court was lopsided and inaccurate.

Moreover, the current prevailing notion that the pro-choice position is neutral while the pro-life position is a religious imposition is also inaccurate. In fact, I argue that this notion is completely backward.

The greatest flaw of *Roe v. Wade*—and the competition is stiff—is that the decision formally and unapologetically rests on the notion that the morality of abortion is appropriately founded on an appeal to ignorance.

Acknowledgments

There are a lot of people who could be thanked in connection with this project, starting with my mom and dad, of course, who not only gave me life but made it a good one. Then, of course, there is my kindergarten teacher ... okay, you get the point. I had a lot of help along the way! No doubt I will miss someone I shouldn't but in the hopes of giving credit where credit is due: Special thanks, of course, to my wife, Marcia, who put up with many hours of me buried behind a computer and even did some voice work for the original audio version. Thanks also to my daughter, Stephanie, and my son, David, for some great voice work. Mark Flint helped with music production for the original version and also provided a voice, as did his wife, Lindsey. Other voices included Shawn and Jodene Saavedra, Jim Berger, Sam and Cathy Norris, Tammy Smith, Laura Riley, Mark Curtis, Michelle Lebert, Kindelly Ferreira, and Shannon Maples. Special thanks to Steve Morgan for helping me track down difficult-to-find law articles.

Special thanks to Dan Balow at eChristian for believing in this project, and Afton Rorvik and Linda Taylor for helping me sound like a real author. Thanks also to John Wollinka and Larry Taylor for great cover and interior designs.

And special thanks also to the guests who were willing to donate some of their time for interviews and offer their unique insights into this perplexing problem. And thanks to those who took the time to read and endorse this manuscript.

Finally, thank you to all who labor daily, in one capacity or another, for the cause of life. Your efforts are not in vain.

—Roger Resler
Phoenix, Arizona
2012

Cast of Characters in *Compelling Interest*

Alcorn, Randy – Pro-life pastor, speaker and best-selling author.

Balkin, Jack, Ph.D. – Pro-choice law professor at Yale Law School. Professor Balkin wrote a fascinating book with the rewriting of *Roe v. Wade* as a premise in *What Roe v. Wade Should Have Said* in which he played the role of the chief justice.

Blackmun, Harry – Supreme Court Justice from 1970 to 1994. Justice Blackmun was a newly appointed justice when he crafted the *Roe* majority opinion. As a Nixon appointee, Justice Blackmun was not expected to support abortion, given Nixon's opposition to abortion. After the opinion began to receive criticism, Blackmun became an increasingly staunch defender of abortion.

Brennan, William C., Ph.D. – Professor at the School of Social Service at St. Louis University. Author of several pro-life books including *Dehumanizing the Vulnerable: When Word Games Take Lives.* Dr. William C. Brennan, who is pro-life, should not be confused with pro-choice Supreme Court Justice William J. Brennan.

Brennan, William J. – Supreme Court Justice from 1956 to 1990. Justice Brennan was one of the less vocal supporters of *Roe v. Wade* but a passionate supporter, nonetheless, voting with the majority. Pro-choice Justice William J. Brennan Jr. should not be confused with pro-life author and professor, Dr. William C. Brennan, who is a sociology professor at St. Louis State University.

Brinker, Nancy – Susan G. Komen Foundation founder and CEO Brinker found herself embroiled in controversy in early 2012 for her response to media accusations that Komen was pulling its funding of Planned Parenthood grants because of that organization's reputation as a provider of abortions. In the end, Brinker acquiesced to pro-abortion pressure and resumed Komen's funding of Planned Parenthood, losing support from both sides in the abortion debate.

Burger, Warren E. – Chief Justice of the Supreme Court during *Roe v. Wade*. Appointed by Republican, Richard Nixon, Burger was originally thought to have been a long shot by Sarah Weddington. Disappointing many pro-lifers, however, Burger voted with the majority in *Roe v. Wade*. Burger was chief justice from 1969 to 1986.

Clancy, Michael – Freelance photographer who considered himself pro-choice until he witnessed the prenatal surgery of Samuel Armas and captured a series of photos showing Samuel reaching from his mother's womb and grasping the finger of the surgeon. Clancy is now a pro-life speaker.

Coffee, Linda – Sarah Weddington's partner in developing and arguing *Roe v. Wade*. A classmate of Weddington's. It was through a friend of Coffee's that the pair discovered Norma McCorvey (Jane Roe).

Dellapenna, Joseph W. – Villanova law professor and author of *Dispelling the Myths of Abortion History*. While Professor Dellapenna may be characterized as pro-life, his views on abortion are more liberal than that term generally indicates. Nevertheless, his 1,200+-page book clearly refutes the logic that was used by Sarah Weddington and Harry Blackmun to justify the legalization of abortion on demand.

Douglas, William O. – Supreme Court Justice from 1939 to 1975. Perhaps the most adamantly pro-abortion justice on the bench during the *Roe v. Wade* hearings, Douglas voted with the majority.

Edelin, Kenneth, M.D. – A Boston area ob-gyn and National Chairman for Planned Parenthood from 1990 to 1992. In 1975, while working at Boston City Hospital, Dr. Edelin was convicted of manslaughter of an aborted fetus who, according to evidence, breathed outside the womb. The jury conviction was later overturned by a judge.

Faux, Marian – Pro-choice proponent and author of the book *Roe v. Wade, The Untold Story of the Landmark Supreme Court Decision That Made Abortion Legal*.

Finkbine, Sherri – A Phoenix children's T.V. personality and mother of four. Without realizing the potential harm to her unborn fifth child, Finkbine took headache medication during pregnancy in 1962 that contained thalidomide, a drug harmful to a developing fetus. Upon learning of the potential harm and confirming it, she sought an abortion in Arizona and was denied. She eventually traveled to Sweden to obtain a legal abortion there. The resulting controversy contributed to the public outcry to liberalize U.S. abortion laws to include exceptions for fetal abnormalities.

Flowers, Robert – Texas Attorney who argued the pro-life position against Sarah Weddington during the second hearing in *Roe v. Wade*, October 1972.

Floyd, Jay – Texas attorney who argued in favor of the pro-life position against Sarah Weddington in the first hearing of *Roe v. Wade*, December 1971.

Gerster, Carolyn, M.D. – Dr. Gerster is one of the cofounders of NRLC, the National Right to Life Committee. She is an outspoken pro-life proponent and a retired medical doctor.

Guibilini, Alberto, Ph.D. – A bioethicist from the University of Milan. A supporter of both abortion and infanticide. Coauthor of a highly controversial article in the *Journal of Medical Ethics* titled, "After-birth abortion: Why should the baby live?"

Guttmacher, Alan – A pro-abortion gynecologist and a past president of Planned Parenthood. Ironically Guttmacher was originally opposed to abortion in the early years of the birth-control movement. Like Margaret Sanger, the founder of Planned Parenthood, Guttmacher then espoused birth control as a means of eliminating abortion. Nevertheless, as the pro-abortion movement began to take shape in the 1960s Guttmacher became a prominent abortion advocate. He founded the Association for the Study of Abortion in 1964.

Hames, Margie Pitts – Pro-abortion Georgia attorney who filed suit against the Georgia reform law (even though it allowed exceptions for rape and health) resulting in *Doe v. Bolton*. Like Weddington, Hames won the case at the Supreme Court.

Handel, Karen – Pro-life former Senior Vice President for Public Policy at the Susan G. Komen Foundation. Handel resigned amidst pressure from pro-abortion proponents during the Susan G. Komen/Planned Parenthood funding controversy of early 2012.

Harrison, Beverly Wildung – Pro-abortion professor of ethics at Union Theological Seminary in New York. (Ret.) She has been described as a "Christian feminist ethicist" by Marian Faux.

Hodge, Hugh Lenox – Pro-life professor of obstetrics at the University of Pennsylvania in the mid-1800s.

Hughes, Sarah – A dominant personality on the three-judge panel who heard the original oral arguments in *Roe v. Wade* at a federal court in Dallas, Texas, before the case went to the U.S. Supreme Court. Linda Coffee had clerked for Hughes before *Roe* came before the federal court, and Weddington and Coffee had done their best to ensure that the case would be brought before Hughes's court, whom they were confident would be sympathetic to their cause. Their efforts were successful and their confidence in Hughes turned out to be correct. Hughes is also famous for swearing in Lyndon Johnson aboard Air Force One following the Kennedy assassination.

Jefferson, Mildred, M.D. – One of the cofounders of the NRLC, the National Right to Life Committee. Dr. Jefferson was also the first black woman to graduate from Harvard Medical School and became the first female doctor at the Boston University Medical Center. In addition to her private medical practice, Dr. Jefferson was an outspoken pro-life advocate. She is credited for changing Ronald Reagan's position on abortion from pro-choice to pro-life. In a personal letter to Dr. Jefferson, Reagan wrote:

> You have made it irrefutably clear that an abortion is the taking of a human life, I am grateful to you. (see: http://en.wikipedia.org/wiki/Mildred_Fay_Jefferson)

Lee, Patrick, Ph.D. – Dr. Lee is the Director of the Institute of Bioethics at Franciscan University in Steubenville, Ohio. He is also a professor of bioethics and philosophy. Dr. Lee is the author of several books including *Abortion & Unborn Human Life*, which is a particularly cogent and succinct defense of human life in its earliest stages.

Leonard, John Preston – Pro-life Rhode Island physician in the mid-1800s.

Live Action – Pro-life group started by Lila Rose most famous for producing undercover videos exposing unethical and potentially illegal activities at Planned Parenthood clinics.

Lucas, Roy – A pro-abortion attorney who is not well known but is largely responsible for the idea that abortion is a Constitutional right that falls under the banner of "privacy." Lucas was the first to articulate this idea in a 1968 *North Carolina Law Review* article. The concept of the right to have an abortion protected by "privacy" was radical at the time and considered a long shot even by other pro-abortion proponents. But Lucas's radical idea was eventually adopted by Sarah Weddington and finally the U.S. Supreme Court in *Roe v. Wade.*

Marshall, Thurgood – Supreme Court Justice from 1967 to 1991. Marshall was a very pro-abortion justice and consequently sided with the pro-choice majority. On more than one occasion Marshall expressed his point of view that *not funding* abortions for poor women amounted to an attempt to impose pro-life and/or religious values on society.

McCorvey, Norma – aka "Jane Roe." The plaintiff in *Roe v. Wade.* Although the lawsuit couldn't have been brought to court without McCorvey (or someone) as a plaintiff, Norma never attended any of the proceedings in *Roe v. Wade.* She played no active role in the conception, development, and strategy of the case and at times couldn't be located by her attorneys. In the years following *Roe,* McCorvey was an outspoken advocate for abortion. In recent years, however, she has converted to a pro-life position, even publicly advocating for the reversal of *Roe.*

Means, Cyril, Jr. – Pro-abortion New York University law professor who was an attorney for the pro-abortion group NARAL in the years leading up to *Roe v. Wade.* Sarah Weddington developed a friendship with Professor Means as she was typing the key briefs submitted with the case in favor of legalizing abortion. Weddington drew heavily on Means's ideas and, just before oral arguments began, presented each justice with copies of two pro-abortion law articles written by Professor Means. The logic and history presented in these articles is now generally rejected on the basis of inaccuracy.

Minerva, Francecsa, Ph.D. – Australian philosopher and medical ethicist. A supporter of both abortion and infanticide. Coauthor of a highly controversial article in the *Journal of Medical Ethics* entitled: "After-birth abortion: Why should the baby live?"

Mohr, James – Author of *Abortion in America*. Much of the logic in Mohr's book is self-contradictory and inaccurate. For example, Mohr implies that abortion methods were commonly employed and effective in the centuries leading up to the nineteenth. Historian Joseph Dellapenna demonstrates in his book, *Dispelling the Myths of Abortion History,* that the opposite is true: Abortion was rarely attempted, dangerous to the mother, and largely ineffective until modern antiseptic practices revolutionized medicine in the late nineteenth century. Unfortunately, Mohr's inaccurate thesis has been widely accepted.

NARAL – Originally this acronym stood for the National Association for the Repeal of Abortion Laws. Currently it stands for the National Abortion Rights Action League, Pro-choice America.

Nathanson, Bernard, M.D. – One of the cofounders of NARAL. In the early 1970s, Dr. Nathanson operated the largest abortion clinic in the world. But an increasing awareness of fetal development caused Dr. Nathanson to radically change his position to solidly pro-life. In his later years, he became more outspoken in favor of life than he had been as a pro-abortion proponent.

Noonan, John T., Jr. – Attorney and later a Senior Circuit Judge on the United States Court of Appeals for the Ninth Circuit. Noonan is the author of numerous books including, *A Private Choice: Abortion in America in the Seventies* (1979), which is a particularly eloquent and logically powerful book defending the pro-life position and exposing the fallacies of pro-choice logic.

NRLC – National Right to Life Committee. The largest pro-life organization in the United States.

Paulsen, Michael Stokes – Pro-life attorney and law professor at the University of St. Thomas School of Law. Paulsen participated in a mock re-write of *Roe v. Wade* in Jack Balkin's book, *What Roe v. Wade Should Have Said.*

Powell, Lewis – Supreme Court Justice from 1972 to 1987. Powell voted with the majority in *Roe v. Wade.* Recent evidence indicates that Powell may have been responsible for the *Roe* emphasis on viability as a key cut-off point for abortion. (See: http://www.davidgarrow-com.hb2hosting.net/File/DJG%20 2000%20AmLawRoevWadeLFP.pdf)

Rehnquist, William - Supreme Court Justice from 1972 to 2005. Justice Rehnquist was a newly appointed justice when *Roe* was decided. He joined Byron White's dissent and also wrote a brief dissent of his own. In his later years, Justice Rehnquist served as Chief Justice.

Richards, Cecile – Planned Parenthood president from 2006 to the present. She is the daughter of former Texas Governor Ann Richards.

Rose, Lila – Pro-life activist who is famous for producing undercover "sting" videos that show Planned Parenthood employees engaging in unethical and potentially illegal activity.

Rubenfeld, Jed – Pro-choice Yale law professor and participant with Jack Balkin in Balkin's mock rewrite of *Roe v. Wade* in his book *What Roe v. Wade Should Have Said.*

Singer, Peter, Ph. D. – Australian philosopher. Professor of ethics at Princeton University. Argues in favor of abortion and infanticide on the basis that neither fetuses nor newborns are "persons."

Stevens, John V., Sr. – Pro-abortion pastor who argues that life is in breath and that fetuses are not alive because they do not breathe through their lungs until birth.

Stewart, Potter – Justice of the Supreme Court from 1958 to 1981. Stewart sided with the pro-abortion majority in *Roe v. Wade* and was perhaps the most vocal justice during oral arguments.

Storer, David Humphreys - Professor of Obstetrics and Medical Jurisprudence at the Harvard Medical School in the mid-1800s. An early pro-life advocate and father of his more famous son, Horatio Robinson Storer.

Storer, Horatio Robinson, M.D. – A Boston gynecologist and early pro-life/anti-abortion crusader. Dr. Storer was the leading physician in the late nineteenth-century doctors' crusade against abortion. He was also a prominent member of the American Medical Association.

Thorp, James, M.D. – Pro-life perinatologist (a surgeon who provides medical care, including surgeries, to fetuses in the womb to save or improve their lives in cases of high-risk pregnancies).

Tooley, Michael, Ph.D. – Philosophy professor at the University of Colorado.

Tooley argues in favor of abortion and infanticide on the basis that neither the fetus nor the newborn are "persons."

Tundermann, David - Pro-choice Yale law student who worked with Roy Lucas in the early 1970s in an effort to repeal abortion laws.

Wade, Henry – Dallas District Attorney responsible for enforcing the laws of Texas. Although he is the "Wade" in *Roe v. Wade*, he did not argue the case. That duty fell to employees at the Texas Attorney General's Office, Jay Floyd and Robert Flowers. Wade is also famous for his part in the prosecution of Jack Ruby for the killing of Lee Harvey Oswald.

Wattleton, Faye – President of Planned Parenthood from 1978 to 1992. On a 1991 *Phil Donahue Show* she proclaimed: "I do not accept that a fetus is a baby; it is a fetus."

Weddington, Ron – Law school classmate, fellow attorney, and husband of Sarah Ragle Weddington. Father of her aborted child. The couple are now divorced.

Weddington, Sarah – Pro-abortion attorney most famous for devising, developing, arguing, and eventually winning *Roe v. Wade*.

White, Byron Raymond "Whizzer" – Supreme Court Justice from 1962 to 1993. Justice White was the only justice to articulate a fairly compelling pro-life dissent of the majority opinion in *Roe v. Wade*, although still lacking in forceful defense of the unborn. Justice White had already achieved fame as both a football and baseball star in the 1930s and 1940s.

Wolf, Naomi – Pro-choice feminist who wrote a highly controversial article on abortion in 1996. The article was controversial primarily among her pro-abortion peers because it candidly admitted that unborn humans are babies, yet she still advocated for abortion on demand.

PART 1.

How Did the Court Become Involved in the Abortion Debate?

CHAPTER 1

Mrs. Weddington Goes to Washington

I've noticed that everybody that is for abortion has already been born.
—Ronald Reagan, Presidential Debate in Baltimore, Sept. 21, 1980

In 1967, an apprehensive, 21-year-old, University of Texas law student named Sarah Ragle discovered she was pregnant. One of only a handful of women majoring in law at a time when females were discouraged from such male-dominated endeavors but determined to pursue a career, Ragle was not interested in motherhood. Not married at the time, Ragle was "seriously dating" (Sarah Weddington, *A Question of Choice*, Penguin Books, 1993, 12, hereafter "Weddington") Ron Weddington. Ron was also a devoted law student and also not ready for parenthood. The couple concluded that a baby would interfere with their career plans and, though abortion was illegal in Texas, determined to find a doctor who would accommodate their wishes.

Until 1970, the law in Texas made it a crime to "procure an abortion" or to attempt one except with respect to "an abortion procured or attempted by medical advice for the purpose of saving the life of the mother" (Texas Penal Code, Articles, 1191–1196).

Unable to locate a doctor willing to perform an abortion for them in Texas, the young couple eventually decided to travel to Piedras Negras, Mexico, just across the Texas border at Eagle Pass, to obtain the desired abortion. Although abortion was also against the law in Mexico, doctors there were often more willing to overlook legal technicalities. After cautiously walking across the border, they met a man at a prearranged location who quietly led them to a small white building housing an abortion clinic. In spite of the secrecy, stigma, and inherent danger in what they were doing, Sarah was, nonetheless, determined to go through with the abortion.

With the "pregnancy" out of the way, both Ron and Sarah would be free to continue their law studies. After anesthesia, the doctor performed a D and C (dilation and curettage) abortion while Ron waited in the lobby. The couple returned to Austin and their studies the next day. They married in 1968. Though graduating at the top of her class, Sarah Weddington had a difficult time finding employment in her chosen field. The legal profession was still dominated and tightly controlled by men. After some unsuccessful searching, she eventually found employment through a college professor with the American Bar Association in Austin, Texas.

Discouraged with the lack of opportunities, Weddington found support from a "consciousness raising" group mostly made up of fellow University of Texas classmates. The group had ties with an "underground counterculture" (Weddington, p. 25) newspaper called the *Rag*.

Among concerns typical in the late sixties, such as "what to do if a person was arrested in a protest" or "where to find the best music in town" (Weddington, p. 26) abortion was a frequent topic of discussion in the *Rag*. In addition to articles on contraception, Weddington's friends at the *Rag* began publishing information on where to obtain legal abortions and which methods they determined to be safe. As a result, the publishers increasingly began to receive questions from women seeking abortions, and an underground abortion referral group began to develop. This caused some concern since abortion was still illegal in Texas. Although Weddington contends that she never personally recommended anything illegal in those pre-*Roe* days, she did do research for the group in an effort to determine whether or not their activities were legal.

Over time, Weddington began to immerse herself into her research and eventually, with encouragement from the referral group, came to the conclusion that the Texas abortion law could and should be challenged. Along with Linda Coffee, a Rice University graduate and former law school classmate, Weddington set out to challenge the law.

These two young lawyers knew that judges don't take up valuable court time listening to random concerns about how the law *might* affect their constituents. In order to bring a matter before a court there must be a "genuine case or controversy." So, in order to challenge the Texas abortion law, Weddington and Coffee needed to find someone who could show a direct and significant impact from the law. Ideally, they needed to find a pregnant woman who wanted an abortion but couldn't obtain one.

This proved to be a challenge. Even their connections with the *Rag* provided little assistance in finding the right plaintiff, although some of Weddington's supporters toyed with the idea of becoming pregnant just to help the cause.

Yet the referral group did have contact with pregnant women who were seeking abortions and, according to Weddington, some of them indicated their willingness to help:

> ... but they were all at an early stage of pregnancy and had the money to get a prompt abortion—certainly the safest route for them. We did not know how long it would take us to get the case filed or how long after that it would take for a court to act. It was best for them to go ahead and have an abortion. Our search would have to continue. (Weddington, 51)

Eventually, through an attorney friend of Coffee's who handled adoptions, the lady lawyers managed to find what they were looking for. Divorced and pregnant for the third time, Norma McCorvey had no steady income or home, living for months at a time with friends or family members.

McCorvey's first child, a daughter, had been taken by the state when McCorvey's mother determined she was not fit to be a mother. Through a difficult turn of events, the girl was eventually raised by McCorvey's own mother. But Norma soon found herself pregnant again. This second child was given up for adoption. In the winter of 1970, McCorvey, already struggling emotionally and financially, was once again pregnant with her third child:

> I was damaged goods. For the moment I had control of myself and knew where my next meal was coming from. But I also knew there was something dark and scary waiting for me—or maybe already inside me. Something drugs or beer or running couldn't make go away. There was a baby. No, not a baby. I couldn't even bear to think of it as that. There was this thing growing inside of me, getting bigger every day, and I couldn't push the terrible fact of it out of my mind. This wasn't like the other times. I didn't want to give birth to another unwanted child. I didn't want to give up another child. I didn't want a child to be born with me as its mother. There was no good reason

to bring this poor thing into the world. I simply didn't want to be pregnant. *I didn't want to be pregnant.* (Norma McCorvey, *I Am Roe: My Life, Roe v. Wade, and Freedom of Choice,* Harpercollins, 1994, 103–4)

It was in this state of mind that McCorvey agreed to meet with Weddington and Coffee at Columbo's Pizza parlor in Dallas. Apprehensive, but curious to see if these lawyers could help her, McCorvey agreed to be the plaintiff in court. But the courts were also sensitive to the fact that some plaintiffs would not want their names to become public knowledge, so they allowed for pseudonyms. In an effort to remain anonymous, McCorvey decided to be known as Jane Roe. The *Wade* in the case was Dallas District Attorney Henry Wade, the individual legally responsible for enforcing the law.

Of course at this point, no one had any idea how far *Roe v. Wade* would go, or how famous "Jane Roe" would eventually become despite the desire for anonymity. None of the players in this unfolding drama had fame in mind. Weddington and Coffee simply wanted to change the Texas abortion law. And McCorvey merely wanted out of her pregnancy.

And so it began. *Roe v. Wade,* a case involving an attorney who had had an illegal abortion with a client who wanted but couldn't get one because the case required an active pregnancy. Pro-choice writer, Debbie Nathan, wrote of this irony in the *Texas Observer:*

> By not effectively informing [Norma] of [where she could get an abortion], the feminists who put together *Roe v. Wade* turned McCorvey into Choice's sacrificial lamb—a necessary one, perhaps, but a sacrifice even so. (*Texas Observer,* Sept. 25, 1995 as quoted in: Norma McCorvey, *Won by Love,* Thomas Nelson, Inc., 1998, 29)

Running concurrent to *Roe* was another case which similarly attacked a Georgia abortion law called *Doe v. Bolton.* The Georgia law dated to 1876 but, unlike Texas, permitted abortion in cases of rape, birth defects, or even when the health of the mother was determined to be threatened. This law was challenged by an attorney in Georgia named Margie Pitts Hames. These cases eventually merged at the Supreme Court level and came to be known collectively as "The Abortion Cases" but *Roe* has overshadowed *Doe* in the public arena.

Though it had been a difficult endeavor to find the right Jane Roe, and even though Norma was not their ideal plaintiff, Weddington and Coffee decided it was best to proceed.

Roe was argued first at the state level but within the federal court system using a forum that was gaining popularity in similar types of cases: a three-judge panel.

Typical of any legal hearing, the opening discussions in *Roe* were technical in nature and concerned whether, from a legal standpoint, the plaintiff actually had a case worthy of a hearing by the court. The attorneys for the state of Texas argued that she did not, but the court disagreed.

This would be Weddington's first time presenting oral arguments in a contested case. In spite of some nervousness, she rose to the challenge. As luck would have it, Coffee had clerked for Sarah Hughes, a dominant personality among the federal judges on the panel and something of a legend in the state of Texas.* As Weddington cautiously began to speak for the first time as an attorney in court, Hughes, noticing how nervous the young attorney was, gave her a quick and reassuring wink. From that point forward, Weddington did not look back.

Later describing her strategy in her book *A Question of Choice,* she writes:

> My plan was to pound the point that law had never treated the fetus as a person, but I started with a more subtle message: "I would like to draw to the court's attention the fact that life is an ongoing process. It is almost impossible to define a point at which life begins or perhaps even at which life ends...." I went on to quote from former Supreme Court justice Tom Clark, a Texan, who had written, "To say that life is present at conception is to give recognition to the potential rather than the actual." (Weddington, 64)

Fresh out of law school and in her first contested case, the odds were stacked against Weddington. She and Coffee were up against an experienced and well-staffed Texas District Attorney's Office, which, although burdened with other cases, still had formidable manpower, resources, and case knowledge. In addition, Weddington and Coffee were attacking a law that had been on the books in Texas for over one hundred years. And while some of the restrictive laws in other states had been greatly liberalized, abortion was still illegal throughout the majority of states. Public opinion and even the majority of women opposed the legalization of abortion. It was no small challenge.

Despite the odds, the three-judge panel agreed with Weddington and Coffee that the Texas law was unconstitutional, but for unclear reasons it failed to issue injunctive relief. In the absence of an injunction, District Attorney Henry Wade announced that he would continue to prosecute doctors who performed abortions. This allowed Weddington to appeal to the United States Supreme Court.

Footnote:

*Hughes is probably most famous for swearing in Lyndon Johnson aboard Air Force One following the Kennedy assassination.

CHAPTER 2

The Woman as Victim?

Abortion is legal because babies can't vote.
—Joseph Bonkowski, "Quote Me"

O n the morning of December 13, 1971, oral arguments at the Supreme Court began in Washington, DC. By that time, of course, McCorvey's pregnancy had long since culminated in the birth of another baby who, like her second child, was also given up for adoption.

While the Texas attorneys attempted to render the case moot because McCorvey was no longer pregnant, the Court disagreed, noting that the lawsuit had been filed as a "class" action in which McCorvey's case would be considered a model for a class of people—in this case, all of the pregnant women in Texas seeking abortions.

After all the technicalities were out of the way, the merits of the case began to emerge. Justice Potter Stewart asked:

> JUSTICE STEWART: What is the asserted state interest? Does the—is there any legislative history on this statute?
>
> MS. WEDDINGTON: No, sir, Your Honor. No, sir, there is not. The only legislative history, of course, is that which is found in other states—which has been pointed out to the court before—and, Professor Means points out again, that these statutes were adopted for the health of the mother. Certainly, the Texas courts have referred to the woman as being the victim, and they have never referred to

anyone else as being the victim. Times have-have certainly changed. I think it's important to realize that in Texas self-abortion is no crime. The woman is guilty of no crime, even though she seeks out the doctor; even though she consents; even though she participates; even though she pays for the procedure. She, again, is guilty of no crime whatsoever.

It's also interesting that [in] our statute, the penalty for the offense of abortion depends on whether or not the consent of the woman was obtained prior to the procedure. It's double if you don't get her consent. (Note: Transcripts of the *Roe* oral arguments were produced from an audio recording obtained by the National Archives.)

One of Weddington's key arguments rested on the idea that the framers of the anti-abortion laws in Texas and across the country in the mid-1800s had created their laws only out of a concern for the pregnant woman, since an abortion was an extremely dangerous procedure in the nineteenth century, and not out of any concern to protect unborn human life. The implication is that if they were alive today, they would agree with Weddington and the pro-choice movement that since abortions performed by qualified doctors had become much safer in the twentieth century, the law had become obsolete. As would become a pattern, her opposition—in this case Texas attorney Jay Floyd—did little to challenge this allegation when Justice Stewart asked him to clarify the original purpose of the Texas law.

JUSTICE STEWART: In answer to my brother Marshall's question as to what is the interest of the state in this legislation; or, even, what is its purpose, its societal purpose—your answer was, I think, relying on your opinion, the most recent opinion of the Court of Criminal Appeals in Texas, that it was the protection of fetal life. And I think you also said that that was not, perhaps, its original purpose.

MR. FLOYD: Well, I'm not sure of that. I . . .

JUSTICE STEWART: Well, it may be rather important. In a constitutional—in a constitutional case of this kind, it becomes quite vital, sometimes, to rather precisely identify what the asserted interest of the state is.

MR. FLOYD: I think that original purpose, Mr. Justice, and the—a present prevailing purpose, may be the same in this respect: There have been statistics furnished to this court in various briefs from various groups, and from medical societies of different groups of physicians and gynecologists, or whatever it may be. These statistics have not shown me, for instance—for example, that abortion is safer than normal childbirth. They have not shown me that there are not emotional problems that are very important, resulting from an abortion. The protection of the mother, at one time, may still be the primary—but the policy considerations, Mr. Justice, would seem to me to be for the state legislature to make a decision.

JUSTICE STEWART: Certainly that's true. Policy questions are for legislative and executive bodies, both in the state and federal governments. But we have here a constitutional question. And, in deciding it, in assessing it, it's important to know what the asserted interest of the state is in the enactment of this legislation.

MR. FLOYD: I am ... and this is just from my—I speak personally, if I may ... I would think that even when this statute was first passed, there was some concern for the unborn fetus.

JUSTICE STEWART: When was it enacted?

MR. FLOYD: I believe it was 1859 [sic–1854] was the original statute. This [the amended version], I believe, was around 1900, 1907. Somewhere in there ...

JUSTICE STEWART: It goes back ...

MR. FLOYD: It goes back fifty ...

JUSTICE STEWART: ... to the middle of the nineteenth century?

MR. FLOYD: Yes, sir.

JUSTICE STEWART: Before that there were no criminal abortion laws in Texas, were there?

MR. FLOYD: As far as I know there were not, I don't know. I think this is, maybe, set out in some of the briefs. I ...

JUSTICE BLACKMUN: Well, in any event, Mr. Floyd, apart from

your personal attitude, your court has spoken on the intent of the statute, has it not?

MR. FLOYD: Yes. Yes.

JUSTICE STEWART: Well, I can't quite square that most recent pronouncement with the earlier decisions of the Texas court that refer to the mother as the victim. Can you?

MR. FLOYD: Well, uh as I say, Your Honor ... see, I don't think the courts have come to the conclusion that the unborn has full juristic rights—not ... not ... yet. Maybe they will. I don't know. I just don't feel like they have, at the present time.

Some observations can be made from this exchange. First, it is clear that while Jay Floyd may have had the best of intentions, he was woefully ill-prepared to defend unborn humans at a Supreme Court level. In this particular instance, Floyd was forced to acknowledge that he had no idea why nineteenth-century anti-abortion laws came on the books. As a direct consequence of this shortfall, he had no other option but to agree that protection of the woman must have been the primary reason for the law's existence. After speculating about possible reasons for the existence of the laws, he could only guess that "some concern for the unborn fetus" must have at least been a factor.

Needless to say, offering personal hunches is not an effective way of responding to a well-prepared opposing argument in a disputed court case at the Supreme Court level. While Floyd could only offer his best guess, Weddington, by contrast, seemed to have evidence on her side. Despite the fact that the law explicitly made it a crime to "procure" an abortion, she shrewdly pointed out that women in Texas had not been treated as criminals for seeking abortions. Rather, it was typically the pregnant woman who had been referred to as the "victim" in abortion-related court cases, whereas "doctors" were the ones who had been punished for the crime of abortion. This made it seem as though the nineteenth-century creators of the laws against abortion were concerned only with protection of the pregnant woman.

It was certainly fortunate for those advocating for the easing of abortion laws that the pivotal case eventually making it to the Supreme Court had originated in Texas. The "protection of women" aspect of Weddington's logic would have never gelled had the test case originated in, for example, Connecticut, which was one of several states that classified the woman convicted of procuring an abortion as a felon and sent her to prison. Although not punishing her as severely as the abortionist, the originators of the Connecticut law clearly had more than protection of pregnant women in mind.

Contrary to popular myth, abortions were rare in the first half of the nineteenth century, and abortion prosecutions rarer still. The Texas law had been enacted in 1854. While not the earliest U.S. abortion-related statute, it did, in fact, predate what would later become known as the nationwide "burst" of anti-abortion legislation that would begin in the 1870s as a result of what historian James Mohr calls the "physicians' crusade against abortion" (James Mohr, *Abortion in America*, Oxford University Press, Inc., 147).

The likely reason Weddington was able to find only cases in which the woman was referred to as "the victim" is because legal cases dealing with abortion which were rare to begin with almost always involved maternal deaths. This is so because, in addition to being largely ineffective, abortion techniques in the nineteenth century were extremely dangerous to the pregnant mother. Given that the vast majority of abortion attempts were made in private and rarely discussed, it was often difficult to prove that a woman had actually been pregnant, especially when most did not survive the abortion attempt. Many such cases were not even classified as abortion cases but poisoning. Given the difficulty of prosecution combined with a high mortality rate for mothers attempting abortion, it's not surprising that the cases Weddington found refer to the mother as the victim. The case could not address a fetus as "victim" if there was no evidence that a fetus had actually existed. As we shall see, this does not mean that nineteenth-century doctors, lawyers and judges—the movers and shakers behind anti-abortion laws—were as pro-abortion as Sarah Weddington would have us believe.

> MS. WEDDINGTON: Again, this is a very special type [of] case for the women because of the very nature of the injury involved. It is an irreparable injury. Once pregnancy has started, certainly this is not the kind of injury that can be later adjudicated. It is not the kind of injury that can later be compensated by some sort of monetary reward. These women who have now gone through pregnancy and the women who continue to be forced to go through pregnancy

have certainly gone through something that is irreparable; that can never be changed for them. It is certainly "great"; and it is certainly "immediate."

There is no other forum available to them. As we talked last time, they are not subject in Texas to any kind of criminal prosecution— whether the woman performs self-abortion, whether she goes to a doctor, finds someone who will perform it on her, she is guilty of no crime whatsoever.

And yet, the state tries to allege that its purpose in this statute was to protect the fetus. If that's true, the fact [that] the woman is guilty of no crime is not a reasonable kind of ... it does not reasonably follow.

Again Weddington argued that since the Texas law viewed the woman as the victim rather than a perpetrator, the fetus, therefore, cannot be the victim.

While Texas legislators and prosecutors may have looked with compassion on a woman who was desperate enough to attempt an abortion, the law did in fact prosecute "doctors" who, in the lawmakers' view, should know better than to provide illegal abortions.

But there was also another more practical reason why the Texas law, and indeed most laws in other states, did not hold the woman to be an accomplice but instead tended to view her as a victim. It was nearly impossible to convict someone accused of performing an illegal surgical abortion or administering a drug or potion that was intended to procure an abortion, without the supporting testimony of the woman who survived. If the woman were legally viewed as an accomplice rather than a victim, her testimony could not legally be used to prosecute the alleged abortionist. Therefore, any prosecutor who hoped to gain a conviction was often left with no alternative but to view the woman as a victim rather than an accomplice. If she were an accomplice, a conviction could only be obtained by securing additional eyewitness testimony from a third party. In most cases no third party witness existed, and even in the rare cases where one did, such a witness would often be reluctant to testify.

When this factor is considered, it certainly *does follow* that the woman who sought an abortion could be "guilty of no crime" while the primary objective of the law was protection of fetal life.

Here again, had Weddington's opposition been more knowledgeable on the nuances of anti-abortion law and case history, they might have effectively challenged her. Unfortunately, this was yet another de facto concession.

JUSTICE MARSHALL: What is Texas's interest? What is Texas's interest in this statute?

MR. FLOYD: Mr. Justice, the Thompson case, which has been cited to the court—*Thompson v. State*—the Court of Criminal Appeals did not decide the issue of privacy. It was not before the court; or, the right of choice issue. The state—the State Court, Court of Criminal Appeals, held that the state had a compelling interest because of the protection of fetal life—of fetal life, protection. They recognized the humanness of the embryo, or the fetus, and they said we have an interest in protecting fetal life. Whether or not that was the original intent of the statute, I have no idea.

JUSTICE STEWART: Yet, Texas does not attempt to punish a woman who herself performs an abortion on herself.

MR. FLOYD: That is correct, Your Honor. And the matter has been brought to my attention: Why not punish for murder, since you are destroying what you—or what has been said to be a human being? I don't know, except that I will say this. As medical science progresses, maybe the law will progress along with it. Maybe at one time it could be possible, I suppose, a statute could be passed. Whether or not that would be constitutional or not, I don't know.

JUSTICE STEWART: But we're dealing with the statute as it is. There's no state, is there, that equates abortion with murder? Or is there?

MR. FLOYD: There is none, Your Honor, except one of our statutes that if the mother dies, that the doctor shall be guilty of murder.

JUSTICE STEWART: Well, that's ordinary...

MR. FLOYD: Yes.

JUSTICE STEWART: ... felony murder.

MR. FLOYD: I would say so, Mr. Justice, yes.

Although Texas attorney Jay Floyd seems to have failed to do his homework, Sarah Weddington herself offers examples of what Floyd could not—albeit well after oral arguments for *Roe* were in the history books. While it is true that no state technically held abortion to be "murder," on page 250 of her book, *A Question of Choice*, Weddington writes about other states that did, in fact, prosecute women who consented to illegal abortions:

> It is claimed by some that women were not prosecuted before *Roe v. Wade*. But as Ellen Goodman pointed out in her October 1, 1988, *Washington Post* column, in 1958, before the reform movement, eighteen states had penalties for any woman who survived an illegal abortion. As late as 1972, it was illegal in fifteen states to aid or counsel a woman to have an abortion. A good many states considered the woman who had an abortion a criminal. Back then, a doctor who did an abortion in Connecticut was subject to as many as five years in prison; the woman as many as two.

Any state that would enact an anti-abortion law with the exclusive goal of protection of women from unsafe abortion procedures, then turn around and prosecute them after having a successful abortion is operating on a double standard. Obviously, the inconsistency rested not in a double standard in nineteenth-century laws but in Weddington's interpretation that the original intent had nothing to do with the protection of fetal life.

Like any skillful attorney, Weddington uses a lack of case history in which women (as opposed to the abortion provider) were successfully prosecuted under the Texas anti-abortion statute to suggest that nineteenth-century legislators agreed with her belief that a fetus is not worthy of legal protection. Yet, she acknowledges in her book that *other* states *did* prosecute women (even considering them criminals) when making the case for the difficulties women faced prior to *Roe*.

Regardless, whether the Texas law punished the mother was irrelevant. The law did in fact make procuring an abortion a crime in Texas. Under Weddington's logic, the woman was the only victim of the crime while the fetus had no rights—including even a right to continue living—and therefore could not also be a victim. In addition to simply denying rights to the unborn by fiat, this logic also falsely presupposes that there can only be one victim when the crime is abortion.

> MS. WEDDINGTON: The state has alleged and its only alleged interest in this statute is the interest in protecting the life of the unborn. However, the state has not been able to point to any authority,

of any nature whatsoever, that would demonstrate that this statute was, in fact, adopted for that purpose.

We have some indication that other state statutes were adopted for the purpose of protecting the health of the woman. We have an 1880 case in Texas—shortly after the 1854 statute was adopted—that states that the woman is the victim of the crime, and is the only victim that the court talks about.

We have all the contradictions in the statute, and the way so many things that just don't make sense. If the statute was adopted for that purpose, for example, why is the woman guilty of no crime? If the statute was adopted for that purpose, why is it that the penalty for abortion is determined by whether or not you have the woman's consent?

It has already been shown that the woman was often "guilty of no crime" in order to ensure conviction of the abortionist, who, without the mother's testimony (which would not be admissible as an accomplice), might avoid prosecution. With regard to the "penalty for abortion" being determined "by whether or not you have the woman's consent," the law simply recognized that the pregnant woman may not have been the primary driving force behind the "procuring" of an abortion. Given both the stigma and danger of abortion in the nineteenth century, it was often a legitimate question whether the woman had sought the abortion of her own free will or was pressured into an abortion by someone else—whether her lover, husband, father, or even the abortionist. Such a recognition is clearly not inconsistent with a primary objective of protecting fetal life.

Once again, however, with no challenge from the state of Texas, the court was free simply to adopt Weddington's logic and proceed unchallenged. It is therefore no great surprise that the cases mentioned by Weddington and Justice Stewart referred to the woman as a victim.

CHAPTER 3

The Fetus as Victim?

Blacks didn't choose slavery. Jews didn't choose the ovens.
Women don't choose rape. And babies don't choose abortion.
—RANDY ALCORN

R ather than challenge Weddington on the intent of the original law she was attacking, Jay Floyd conceded defeat on the question. But was Weddington correct? Was the Texas law originally enacted *only* to protect the woman or was there concern for the unborn child?

In her book *A Question of Choice,* Weddington states that:

> There was no evidence that [anti-abortion laws] were passed to protect the fetus or maintain a principle about "when life begins." The laws were intended, simply, to protect women. (Weddington, 40)

The legal structure of this assertion by Weddington is striking. Note that she does not definitely claim that fetal protection *was not a factor* in the passage of anti-abortion laws, she simply asserts that *there was no evidence* that the laws "were passed to protect the fetus or maintain a principle about when life begins." Of course, in reality, the fact that her opposition had failed to present such evidence did not mean it did not exist. In fact, there was plenty of evidence. It was simply not in Weddington's interest either to look for or accurately report on such evidence. Lack of information could certainly serve as an effective appeal should her logic meet with a serious challenge.

From a practical perspective, Weddington's tactic was brilliant. As any good lawyer understands, it is impossible for any person to know everything there is to know. Therefore her inability to locate evidence could be excused should her opposition happen upon the elusive pro-fetal intent behind nineteenth-century abortion laws. But if her opposition was weak, or lazy, or simply unable to locate such evidence (as proved to be the case) the notion that protection of the fetus was never a factor in the creation of anti-abortion laws would likely stick. The payoff was therefore worth the risk. And as it turned out, the payoff was greater than even Weddington had hoped.

On the flip side, for the Texas attorneys opposing Weddington, ignorance was a serious disadvantage, and it was clear that they were not well prepared for either of the two hearings.

Roe & Doe were first argued on December 13, 1971, but because of the vacancy resulting from the deaths of Justices Hugo Black and John Harlan, the Supreme Court consisted of only seven justices at that time. *Roe & Doe* were among several cases that were held over for reargument after newly appointed Justices William Rehnquist and Lewis Powell were seated. The date for the second hearing came nearly a year later on October 11, 1972. While Weddington argued against the Texas anti-abortion law in both hearings, her opposition changed. Assistant District Attorney Jay Floyd had argued for Texas in the first hearing, while his immediate supervisor, Robert Flowers, argued for Texas in the second hearing.

By the time the second hearing rolled around, Justice Blackmun—who would eventually write the majority opinion—knew that U.S. anti-abortion laws had begun to be enacted during the latter half of the nineteenth century. He questioned Flowers regarding *why* they were enacted, but Flowers's was at a loss. Intervening on Flowers's behalf, Justice Stewart, in obvious reference to the pro-abortion *amici curiae* briefs filed by Roy Lucas, Cyril Means Jr., and other pro-abortion proponents, voiced the reason that had been given there: protection of pregnant women from dangerous abortion techniques. Having no idea why the laws originally came on the books, Flowers could do little but agree that abortion must have been a common-law liberty until the mid-nineteenth century and even then had only become illegal due to the dangers abortion posed to the mother.

As it turned out, since Flowers had no answer, Justice Blackmun was then free to assert that prior to the advent of late nineteenth-century anti-abortion laws, according to Flowers's theory: "destruction of a person in the form of a fetus was legal?" Flowers had no alternative but to agree given his unfamiliarity with the history of abortion laws.

Whether he was aware of it at that point or not, Blackmun's history and logic were seriously flawed. Destruction of a "person" in the form of a fetus was never legal in Texas nor in any state prior to 1973. The specific question of "personhood" was not addressed in abortion laws.

While "personhood" would indeed become the touchstone of the *Roe* doctrine, the concept of *quickening,* with its implication of "ensoulment" or "animation," was the all-important consideration in common law as well as some of the early U.S. laws up until the mid-nineteenth century. *Quickening* is the moment in pregnancy when the mother first feels the movement of her unborn child. Of course the time of quickening varies but generally occurs between 16–18 weeks at a point when the fetus becomes large enough to move the uterine wall. Prior to quickening, the unborn human was generally (and mistakenly) believed not to be "ensouled," "alive," or "animated." If there was no life, there could be no "person."

Contrary to Blackmun's assertion, however (which had primarily originated with Prof. Cyril Means Jr., see chapter 5), with exceptions to save the life of the mother, the intentional destruction of a "person" in the form of a *quickened* fetus was indeed quite illegal in the United States under common law from its founding onward. And at various times there were even penalties, though not as severe, for the intentional destruction of a fetus prior to quickening.

Had Flowers been aware of this, he could have responded accordingly. Such information might have altered the course of subsequent events. As it turned out, this was yet another example of an unnecessary concession to Weddington's pro-abortion logic that was rapidly becoming the Court's maxim as well.

The specific paradox of legally permitting the destruction of "persons" in the form of fetuses was avoided after 1973 only due to the Court's own semantic safeguard. In language eerily reminiscent of *Dred Scott* (the 1857 case declaring slavery legal), the Court would declare that unborn humans were not "persons in the whole sense," thereby exempting itself (by its own decree) from creating a similar legal conundrum to the one erroneously theorized by Justice Blackmun.

Having ascertained that the Texas attorneys could provide no information on the enactment of U.S. anti-abortion laws, Justice Blackmun eventually embraced the Means-inspired Weddington doctrine. Speaking for the majority in the final opinion, Blackmun asserted that:

> Parties challenging state abortion laws [i.e. Weddington and the pro-abortion lobby] have sharply disputed in some courts the contention that a purpose of these laws, when enacted, was to protect prenatal life. Pointing to the absence of legislative history to support the contention, they claim that most state laws were designed solely to protect the woman. Because medical advances have lessened this concern, at least with respect to abortion in early pregnancy, they argue that with respect to such abortions the laws can no longer be justified by any state interest. There is some scholarly support for this view of original purpose. (Majority Opinion, *Roe v. Wade*, 410 U.S. 113, [1973] 151, hereafter "*RvW*")

By "some scholarly support" Blackmun was undoubtedly referring primarily to two articles written by New York Law School Professor, Cyril Means Jr., which essentially rewrote abortion history. As General Counsel for NARAL (then the "National Association for the Repeal of Abortion Laws," now "National Abortion Rights Action League"), Means's research had a decidedly pro-abortion slant. Law professor and abortion history researcher Joseph Dellapenna notes that, "The *Roe* majority opinion cites Means' two articles seven times while citing no other legal historian" (Joseph W. Dellapenna, *Dispelling the Myths of Abortion History*, Carolina Academic Press, 2006, 31, hereafter "Dellapenna").

The eventual outcome of the case is not surprising given the heavy and uncritical reliance on Prof. Means's material. For Justice Blackmun to label Means's briefs as "scholarly support" is something on the level of classifying an infomercial as objective reporting. Without a doubt, Professor Means had a well-maintained pro-abortion agenda.

CHAPTER 4

Doctors on Crusade

To forbid birth is only quicker murder. . . .
He is a man, who is to be a man; the fruit is always present in the seed.
—TERTULLIAN, *APOLOGETICUS*, 197

While protection of the pregnant woman may have been a factor in the enactment of restrictive abortion laws, there is no doubt that protection of the fetus was the primary concern.

Justice Blackmun himself had clearly stumbled upon this inconvenient truth at some point during his research on the majority opinion. While discussing the Means-inspired version of the history of abortion laws in the *Roe* majority opinion, he seems to contradict his earlier assertions by acknowledging the following:

> The attitude of the [medical] profession may have played a significant role in the enactment of stringent criminal abortion legislation during that period. An A.M.A. [American Medical Association] Committee on Criminal Abortion was appointed in May 1857. It presented its report . . . to the twelfth annual meeting. That report observed that the committee had been appointed to investigate criminal abortion "with a view to its general suppression." It deplored abortion and its frequency and it listed three causes of "this general demoralization":
>
> The first of these causes is a widespread popular ignorance of the true character of the crime—a belief, even among mothers themselves, that the foetus is not alive till after the period of quickening.

The second of the agents alluded to is the fact that the profession themselves are frequently supposed careless of foetal life....

The third reason of the frightful extent of this crime is found in the grave defects of our laws, both common and statute, as regards the independent and actual existence of the child before birth, as a living being. These errors, which are sufficient in most instances to prevent conviction, are based, and only based, upon mistaken and exploded medical dogmas. With strange inconsistency, the law fully acknowledges the foetus in utero and its inherent rights, for civil purposes; while personally and as criminally affected, it fails to recognize it, and to its life as yet denies all protection. (*RvW*, 141–2)

While this acknowledgment seems completely out of harmony with the rest of the *Roe* majority opinion, it stands as a glaring testament to the fact that protection of the fetus was every bit as important a factor (if not more so) in the creation of anti-abortion laws as was protection of the mother.

This stands in stark contrast to the claims of Weddington, Means, and the court majority. It leaves no doubt that protection of unborn human life was paramount in the creation of the very anti-abortion laws that were then under attack. And when one delves deeper into the "attitude" of the A.M.A., here casually referred to by Justice Blackmun, any lingering doubts vanish. Reading the 1857 Annual A.M.A. Report we find this:

As a profession we are unanimous in our condemnation of the crime [of abortion]. Mere resolutions to this effect, and nothing more, are therefore useless, evasive, and cruel.

If to want of knowledge on a medical point, the slaughter of countless children now steadily perpetrated in our midst, is to be attributed, it is our duty, as physicians, and as good and true men, both publicly and privately, and by every means in our power, to enlighten this ignorance.

If we have ever been thought negligent of the sanctity of foetal life, the means of correcting the error are before us. If we have ever been so in deed, there are materials, and there is good occasion for the establishment of an obstetric code; which, rigorously kept to the standard of our attainments in knowledge, and generally accepted by the profession, would tend to prevent such unnecessary and unjustifiable destruction of human life.

If the tenets of the law, here unscientific, unjust, inhuman, can be bettered—as citizens, and to the best of our ability we should seek this end. If the evidence upon this point is especially of a medical character, it is our duty to proffer our aid, and in so important a matter to urge it. But if, as is also true, these great fundamental, and fatal faults of the law are owing to doctrinal errors of the profession in a former age, it devolves upon us, by every bond we hold sacred, by our reverence for the fathers in medicine, by our love for our race, and by our responsibility as accountable beings, to see these errors removed and their grievous results abated. (*12 Transactions of the American Medical Association, Report on Criminal Abortion*, 1859, 73–8, The American Medical Association)

Clearly, protection of fetal life was the primary factor moving these nineteenth-century medical doctors to push for legislative action.

Surprisingly, Blackmun openly acknowledges this intent in the *Roe* majority opinion. After quoting the A.M.A report, he writes:

The committee then offered, and the association adopted, resolutions protesting "against such unwarrantable destruction of human life," calling upon state legislatures to revise their abortion laws, and requesting the cooperation of state medical societies "in pressing the subject."

In 1871 a long and vivid report was submitted by the committee on criminal abortion. It ended with the observation, "we had to deal with human life. In a matter of less importance we could entertain no compromise. An honest judge on the bench would call things by their proper names. We could do no less."

It proffered resolutions, adopted by the association, recommending, among other things, that it "be unlawful and unprofessional for any physician to induce abortion or premature labor, without the concurrent opinion of at least one respectable consulting physician, and then always with a view to the safety of the child—if that be possible," and calling "the attention of the clergy of all denominations to the perverted views of morality entertained by a large class of females— aye, and men also, on this important question." (*RvW*, 142)

This committee made up of medical professionals had no problem using words such as "child before birth," "living being," and "human life" to describe a human fetus and used the terms interchangeably—something Weddington would never do. And it was this same committee that effectively pressured state legislatures on a national level to enact strict anti-abortion laws.

In light of this, Weddington's attempts to present the intent of the architects of nineteenth-century anti-abortion laws as being similar to her own reasons for attacking them fall flat. The facts are simply at odds with Weddington's assertion that the laws were designed only with the protection of the woman in mind.

In a 2005 interview in preparation for the audio production of this book, St. Louis University sociology professor Dr. William Brennan pointed out the following:

> They [members of the American Medical Association in the mid-1800s] had such an impact on the state legislatures that James Mohr in his book *Abortion In America* called this the "physician's crusade against abortion" from the 1860s until the 1880s.
>
> They were very clear. They said that human life begins at conception. It doesn't begin at quickening. It doesn't begin at viability. It begins at conception. And they reiterated this several times in both 1859 and in 1871. "Thou shall not kill." They talked about "the innocent and helpless unborn children." They kept identifying the unborn child as the victim of abortion and not the woman. They repeat that time and time again. It's just amazing. They call abortion in 1871 a "murder" a "foul, unprovoked murder" and "its blood like the blood of Abel will cry from earth to heaven for vengeance." I've never read anything more direct and graphic and strong; anti-abortion statements, even today, than what the AMA indicated in 1859 and 1871. All you have to do is read through this account.

Given this fact, the question is raised: What provided the impetus for the "physicians' crusade" in the latter half of the nineteenth century? Or to put it more colloquially, what got the doctors all riled up in the first place?

In 2006, I conducted another interview with medical doctor, cofounder, and former president of the National Right to Life Committee, Dr. Carolyn Gerster. During our discussion Dr. Gerster explained how abortion came to be viewed by physicians in the latter half of the nineteenth century as being morally wrong.

It was several people observing it, but microscopes had developed to the point where they could see fertilization or at least they could see the ovum during this time—and it was a rabbit not a human ovum of course. But the proof of this was that this discovery changed all the laws in the territories of the United States. Before that it was felt that because they didn't have any conception of watching the process of fertilization, the young human being was felt to be in a sort of vegetative state and not animated until the woman felt the baby move within her womb. They used the antiquated basis for their law that beyond quickening this was a serious crime punishable by law.

I've had six full-term pregnancies and deliveries; we lost a little boy in infancy of pneumonia, but when you first feel that movement in your uterus it's about 17 to 18 weeks, and it feels sort of like a trout is in there, taking two flips. But that's when they believed, in the darker ages, that life began—when the mother felt the movement. But of course the baby was well-developed by that time. So with the knowledge that life began at conception/fertilization, medical science moved out of the Dark Ages into the Age of Enlightenment.

Dr. William Brennan concurs:

When does human life begin? This was a big question up until the 1850s and this is what the A.M.A. policy statement on abortion said in 1871: "No other doctrine appears to be consonant with reason and physiology but that which admits the embryo to possess vitality from the very moment of conception."

In fact, advances in medical science with regard to the observation of fertilization in mammals as well as human gestation were occurring throughout the early phases of the nineteenth century. Laws responded accordingly.

The English law regarding abortion responded to this new scientific consensus without awaiting the reeducation of the public. *Lord Ellenborough's Act* (1803) had, after all, treated abortion of a quickened child as a capital felony, but abortion before quickening as merely a serious misdemeanor. The English abortion laws were promptly amended to remove all distinctions based on quickening [in 1837]. English judges were just as responsive. (Dellapenna, 260)

English laws removed the antiquated quickening doctrine in favor of conception in 1837, and American laws soon followed suit. The Texas law under attack in *Roe*, enacted in 1854, made abortion a crime with no distinction before or after quickening.

Much of the push toward tough abortion laws in the latter half of the nineteenth century is attributed to the American Medical Association and in particular to one of its prominent members: Dr. Horatio Robinson Storer.

Dr. Storer was a pioneer gynecologist, naturalist, and anti-abortion crusader. In 1857 he started a medical practice in Boston and, in 1862, undertook a specialization in gynecology. He published widely in medical journals and wrote several popular pamphlets against abortion, including *Why Not? A Book for Every Woman*, which was an essay on the dangers and evils of abortion.

Dr. Storer's writings make it clear that the agitation among the medical community of the 1850s that precipitated the sweeping anti-abortion legislation across the nation focused not only on concern for the woman but also on a deep concern for fetal life. Like many of his peers, Storer was opposed to the widespread yet unscientific distinction of quickening. Storer called for legislation to stop what he called such "unwarrantable destruction of human life."

Typical of Storer's writings is this passage from his prize-winning essay, *Why Not?*

> Physicians have now arrived at the unanimous opinion, that the foetus in utero is alive from the very moment of conception. "To extinguish the first spark of life is a crime of the same nature, both against our Maker and society, as to destroy an infant, a child, or a man."
>
> ... By that higher than human law, which, though scoffed at by many a tongue, is yet acknowledged by every conscience, "the willful killing of a human being, at any stage of its existence, is murder." (Dr. Horatio Robinson Storer, *Why Not? A Book for Every Woman*,

American Medical Association, 1868, 15, http://www.abortionessay
.com/files/storer.html, see also *The Physicians' Crusade Against
Abortion*, Frederick N. Dyer)

Horatio Storer's father, David Humphreys Storer, was Professor of Obstetrics
and Medical Jurisprudence at the Harvard Medical School. In November 1855,
he gave a lecture at the medical school whose final section dealt with criminal
abortion. In 1859, Horatio cited his father's lecture as a major stimulus for his
anti-abortion "undertaking." In that lecture, David Storer said:

> To save the life of the mother we may be called upon to destroy
> the foetus in utero, but here alone can it be justifiable. The generally
> prevailing opinion that although it may be wrong to procure
> an abortion after the child has presented unmistakable signs of
> life, it is excusable previous to that period, is unintelligible to the
> conscientious physician. The moment an embryo enters the uterus
> a microscopic speck, it is the germ of a human being, and it is as
> morally wrong to endeavor to destroy that germ as to be guilty of the
> crime of infanticide. (Dr. David Storer, "Duties, Trials and Rewards
> of the Student of Midwifery," Dr. David H. Storer, Nov. 7, 1855,
> http://www.abortionessay.com/files/humphreys.html)

One of the earliest physicians to address what he considered to be an
epidemic of criminal abortion was Hugh Lenox Hodge, Professor of Obstetrics
at the University of Pennsylvania. Hodge spoke the following words to his
medical students in 1839 and again in 1854, and the address was published
on both occasions:

> So low, gentlemen, is the moral sense of the community on this
> subject—so ignorant are the greater number of individuals—that
> even mothers, in many instances, shrink not from the commission of
> this crime, but will voluntarily destroy their own progeny, in violation
> of every natural sentiment, and in opposition to the laws of God and
> man. (Dr. Hugh Lenox Hodge, "Foeticide, or Criminal Abortion: A
> Lecture Introductory to the Course on Obstetrics and Disease of
> Women and Children," University of Pennsylvania, 1869, http://www
> .abortionessay.com/files/hodge.html)

In January 1851, the Rhode Island physician John Preston Leonard published in the *Boston Medical and Surgical Journal* a long letter that included this passage:

> Besides these bills of mortality, the records of criminal courts will furnish sufficient proof that this crime is every day becoming more prevalent. It is humiliating to admit that there are a class of physicians who, Herod-like, have waged a war of destruction upon the innocent. (Dr. John Preston Leonard, "Quackery & Abortion," *Boston Medical and Surgical Journal*, 43, January 15, 1851, 447–81)

In his letter, Leonard recommended that the American Medical Association deal with the problem of criminal abortion and that the states pass strong laws against it. Leonard's letter was a key catalyst for the anti-abortion crusade Storer launched six years later which culminated in the passage of sweeping anti-abortion laws across the country.

Hundreds of physicians published articles, letters, and editorials in medical journals that defended the unborn from earliest conception and condemned the seekers and providers of unnecessary abortions. While many of these doctors also opposed abortion out of a concern for the pregnant woman, for most, this concern was subordinate to that of the unborn child.

While Sarah Weddington insisted that abortion laws were intended only to protect women from unsafe abortion procedures, simple common sense reveals a different story. As John Noonan Jr. points out in his book *A Private Choice:*

> ... the harshest laws against abortion were enacted as antiseptic practices became prevalent in hospitals, so that if the legislators' intent was primarily to guard the health of the gravida [pregnant woman], they were passing the *antithesis* of sensible legislation, forcing the woman bent on abortion to resort to abortion in unsanitary non-hospital conditions. By the standards of modern courts, the nineteenth century American legislators who had comprehensively banned abortion acted irrationally if they intended to prevent maternal deaths. (John T. Noonan Jr., *A Private Choice*, The Free Press, 1979, 52, hereafter "Noonan")

In fact this was exactly the rationale used by Weddington to *oppose* the restrictive Texas law, arguing that it forced women into the back alleys.

Yet despite Blackmun's acknowledgment of the AMA's push for anti-abortion laws to protect *both* the woman and the unborn child, and despite the inaccuracy of Weddington's claims, her distorted version of the Texas law's original purpose was adopted uncritically by the majority in *Roe v. Wade* and, consequently, has prevailed in the popular mind-set.

CHAPTER 5

Backstage Influences

"Constitutional Right" means "Whatever Liberals Want."
—ANN COULTER

While Weddington was certainly the public face of abortion advocacy, many of the ideas she expressed in court were not original. In fact, ironically, several of the key propositions that made their way to the Supreme Court via Weddington originated with men. In particular, law articles pushing for the legalization of abortion authored by New York Law School Professor, Cyril Means Jr., and recent law school graduate, Roy Lucas, had a major impact on Weddington's logic and ultimately that of the Supreme Court. Neither of these men were objective legal scholars. Both were heavily invested in the pro-abortion cause.

Like Sarah Weddington, Roy Lucas did not originally intend to become involved in a national debate about abortion but fully embraced his role in it when opportunity arose. Lucas recalls that "the word 'abortion' did not enter my vocabulary or mind" until December 1964 during his second year in law school, when his girlfriend informed him she was pregnant (David J. Garrow, *Liberty & Sexuality: The Right to Privacy and the Making of Roe v. Wade*, Macmillan Publishing Company, 1994, 336, hereafter "Garrow"). Much like Weddington's unwanted pregnancy, the resulting crisis for Lucas was eventually "resolved" after he was referred to Alan Guttmacher of Planned Parenthood who, in turn, discretely referred Lucas and his girlfriend to an abortionist in Puerto Rico. The "degrading" ordeal made such an impact on

Lucas that, in 1966–67 he wrote an essay on what he had concluded to be a woman's constitutional right to choose abortion. From that point on, Lucas was catapulted to the front lines of the war on the then-prevalent anti-abortion laws. The widespread attention his law article received came as a pleasant surprise to Lucas.

Professor Cyril Means Jr. was General Counsel for the National Association for the Repeal of Abortion Laws when he wrote the first of his two influential articles: "The Law of New York Concerning Abortion and the Status of the Foetus, 1664–1968: A Case of Cessation of Constitutionality" (*New York Law Forum*, Vol. 19, Num. 3, 1968, hereafter "Means I") and was still devoted to the movement when he wrote his second: "The Phoenix of Abortional Freedom: Is a Penumbral or Ninth-Amendment Right About to Arise From the Nineteenth-Century Legislative Ashes of a Fourteenth-Century Common-Law Liberty?" (*New York Law Forum*, Vol. 17, Num. 2, 1971, hereafter "Means II"). Means's research was funded by another pro-abortion group: the Association for the Study of Abortion (Dellapenna, 14).

Both of these men presented inaccurate histories of abortion law which, ironically, also disagreed with one another on key points. Means erroneously maintained that protection of pregnant women from dangerous abortion procedures was the only reason legislators began formally and specifically prohibiting abortion in the mid-nineteenth century. Lucas, on the other hand, erroneously suggested the laws resulted from a legal clamp-down on sexual activity based on repressive sexual mores in a prudish Victorian era. Despite their competing theories, both men insisted abortion laws had become obsolete.

Because both Means and Lucas were opposed to restrictive abortion laws, Weddington and ultimately Harry Blackmun relied heavily on their logic to create a new abortion orthodoxy whose tenets have now become commonplace.

Weddington had become a close friend of Means during the months leading up to *Roe*. Consequently, she relied heavily on Means's dubious conclusions and even cited his work by name several times during oral arguments. In fact, every justice had Weddington-supplied copies of Means's articles on the bench during oral arguments.

Consequently, Means's theory with respect to the purpose of American abortion laws was preferred by both Blackmun and Weddington as illustrated in Blackmun's majority opinion:

A second reason [for the law's existence] is concerned with abortion as a medical procedure. When most criminal abortion laws were first enacted, the procedure was a hazardous one for the woman. This was particularly true prior to the development of antisepsis. Antiseptic techniques, of course, were based on discoveries by Lister, Pasteur, and others first announced in 1867, but were not generally accepted and employed until about the turn of the century.

Abortion mortality was high. Even after 1900, and perhaps until as late as the development of antibiotics in the 1940s, standard modern techniques such as dilation and curettage were not nearly so safe as they are today. Thus, it has been argued that a state's real concern in enacting a criminal abortion law was to protect the pregnant woman, that is, to restrain her from submitting to a procedure that placed her life in serious jeopardy. (*RvW*, 148–9)

Although Means's contributions formed a key basis for the *Roe* version of the history of abortion, especially in the United States, both of his articles have been scathingly criticized by law experts on both sides of the abortion debate. For example, historian and Villanova law professor Joseph W. Dellapenna has characterized both articles as "neither objective nor accurate" (Dellapenna, 14), while David Tundermann, a pro-choice Yale law student in 1971 who worked with Lucas, described Means's conclusions as sometimes straining credibility:

[I]n the presence of manifest public outcry over fetal deaths just prior to the passage of New York's 1872 abortion law, Means disclaims any impact upon the legislature of this popular pressure (even though the statute itself copies the language of a pro-fetal group).

Tundermann prophetically added that:

Where the important thing is to win the case no matter how, however, I suppose I agree with Means's technique: begin with a scholarly attempt at historical research; if it doesn't work, fudge it as necessary; write a piece so long that others will read only your introduction and conclusion; then keep citing it until courts begin picking it up. This preserves the guise of impartial scholarship while advancing the proper ideological goals. (Memo from David

Tundermann to Roy Lucas, Legislative Purpose et al., 5 August, 1971,
as quoted in Garrow, pp. 853–54, note 41)

Tundermann's remarkable candor was not intended for public consumption
as the comments appear in a personal memo between himself and his boss at
the time, Roy Lucas. Tundermann's skepticism of Professor Means's research
had the effect of deterring the very pro-abortion Lucas from citing Means's
work in the briefs he was then preparing for abortion-related cases.

As it turned out, from a pro-choice perspective, the timing of Lucas's essay:
"Federal Constitutional Limitations on the Enforcement and Administration
of the State Abortion Statutes," which appeared in the June 1968 edition of
the *North Carolina Law Review* (vol. 46, hereafter "Lucas"), couldn't have been
better. In the years leading up to 1968, there had been a growing sentiment
across the country among liberal thinkers that existing abortion laws were long
past their expiration date. Most pro-abortion advocates realized, however, that
public sentiment was decidedly against total repeal. As a result, a movement
began to coalesce around the idea of abortion law *reform* rather than total
repeal. Many of those who are now recognized as influential early pro-choice
proponents, such as Allan Guttmacher, were then still publicly advocating
reform of the existing laws in lieu of total repeal. However, by boldly asserting
a woman's Constitutional right to choose abortion *on demand*, Lucas's article
dramatically challenged that method.

Lucas began his article by citing a figure of 10,000 as a reasonable
estimate of the number of U.S. maternal deaths resulting from "mishandled
criminal abortions" each year. Although he cites a law professor at the
University of Alabama as the authority behind this figure (Lucas, 28, note
1), former abortionist and early repeal advocate Dr. Bernard Nathanson
has subsequently stated that the 10,000 figure was essentially pulled out
of thin air since it sounded plausible and made the desired point (Resler
conversations with Nathanson, 2006). Regardless, the point Lucas wishes
to press is that even in spite of restrictive abortion laws in virtually all fifty
states, a large number of women were choosing to break the laws by seeking
abortions. Certainly if the 10,000 figure was even close to reality, common
sense would suggest that a much larger number of women must be obtaining
abortions illegally, since one would not expect every illegal abortion to result
in a maternal death. Whether the number was 10,000, 1,000 or 100, the point

was that women were dying, not because they willfully chose to put their lives in jeopardy, but because restrictive abortion laws forced them to seek abortions from unscrupulous and incompetent quacks.

Over the course of more than 1,200 pages, legal scholar and historian Joseph W. Dellapenna more than adequately challenges this notion (and refutes several others) in his book, *Dispelling the Myths of Abortion History.*

While undoubtedly some women intent on abortion attempted them, Dellapenna points out that at least until the late nineteenth century abortion techniques were, in fact, so dangerous they were rarely attempted. Women who were desperate enough to risk their lives through attempted abortion, however, were often unrewarded given the inefficacy of pre-twentieth-century abortion techniques. Prior to the twentieth century, abortion was attempted primarily through oral ingestion of various concoctions (many of which were poisonous) or through physical stress including violent beatings, or by invasive and rather primitive (and consequently nearly always fatal) surgical techniques.

While the main thesis of Means, Lucas, Weddington, and ultimately Blackmun was that abortion was a widely practiced common-law liberty prior to the advent of late nineteenth century anti-abortion laws, Dellapenna points out that the "common-law liberty" idea was a myth and that abortion was rarely attempted and even more rarely successful. Prior to the late nineteenth century, pregnant women who were determined to avoid motherhood more often practiced infanticide than abortion.

With regard to the idea that abortion was not criminal in England or America before the nineteenth century and that abortion was criminalized during the nineteenth century only to protect the life or health of mothers without regard for their unborn children, Dellapenna asserts that "regardless of how many times these claims are repeated, however, they are not facts; they are myths" (Dellapenna, 13). Dellapenna goes on to point out that abortion before quickening certainly was a crime with varying degrees of punishments under both English and American common law over the centuries leading up to the nineteenth when radical legal changes began to be implemented. While abortion of an unquickened fetus was seldom considered a felony, it was nearly always considered a "great misprision" (misdemeanor) if the woman survived and murder if she died.

Dellapenna observes that:

> The politicization of the history of abortion law reached its
> peak when the majority opinion in the landmark abortion decision

of *Roe v. Wade* was given over to a history of abortion. The Supreme Court used that history to inform its view of the values at stake in the controversy. Unfortunately, the Court largely got the history wrong, basing its views upon and contributing to a new orthodoxy on abortion history that forms a set of myths that are coherent with each other but are utterly false to the historical record as it has come down to us. (Dellapenna, 125–6)

Dellapenna then encapsulates the crux of his 1,200 page thesis by noting that the fallacies underlying the now-prevalent abortion orthodoxy were based on two "simple presumptions" both of which are false:

. . . that abortion was common throughout history; and that, despite routine denunciations by most or all members of contemporary ruling elites, abortion was in fact seldom punished. At the time *Roe* was decided only six cases widely scattered in time were known to have dealt with abortion in England before 1800, and several of those arguably appeared uncertain regarding whether a crime had actually been charged. Indeed, historian Shelley Gavigan, writing as recently as 1984, described the common law sources on abortion "very close to non-existent." Yet the history embraced in *Roe* could not withstand careful examination even when *Roe* was written. (Dellapenna, 126)

The dubious conclusion that abortion was a "seldom punished" crime no doubt stems from the reality that abortion was a seldom *prosecuted* crime, given the inherent difficulties involved in making such a prosecution stick. But if charges were brought and parties convicted, punishment was certain. Dellapenna further notes that research since *Roe* was decided also "demonstrates that both presumptions (frequency and non-punishment) are false" (Dellapenna, 126).

While the radical ideas presented in the Lucas article were making an impact on the mind-set of key pro-abortion proponents in 1968, a real-life drama had already played itself out for the American public six years earlier that highlighted what seemed to be significant deficiencies in American abortion law.

Sherri Finkbine, a Phoenix children's T.V. personality and mother of four, had once again become pregnant. Unlike Weddington or Norma McCorvey, however, Finkbine wanted another baby. But a problem developed when Finkbine heard that taking products which included the drug thalidomide while pregnant could result in severe birth defects. Sherri had taken a considerable amount of headache medications early in her pregnancy and was shocked to learn that some of those medications contained thalidomide. After confirming with her obstetrician that the drug would likely result in a severely deformed child, she began to seek a therapeutic abortion.

Under normal circumstances in Arizona, a legal abortion would likely have been granted in a difficult case like Finkbine's, but her local celebrity status as a hostess on the children's program *Romper Room* added a newsworthy element to the situation, eventually creating a scenario in which hospital officials found themselves reluctant to grant permission for an abortion due to the growing public attention (Garrow, 286-7).

After her story became front-page news across the country, Finkbine eventually decided to travel to Sweden to obtain a legal abortion there, after which it was determined that Sherri's unborn child had indeed been severely damaged by the effects of the drug.

The upshot of the Finkbine case was that an American public that had for decades considered abortion a taboo topic was now confronted with—up close and personal—a case in which, at least for some, induced abortion could be justified. The fact that Sherri could not receive a legal abortion in Arizona while carrying a severely deformed fetus served to highlight what many were presenting as serious deficiencies in existing abortion laws. This was a key boost to the struggling abortion reform movement which, in turn, generated the development of interest groups in several states that began visibly pushing for abortion law reform.

While all the laws allowed abortion to save the life of the mother, most drew the line at that point, not allowing the option of abortion in other hard cases, namely rape, incest, or severe fetal deformities. The public had tolerated the "rigidity" of the laws as written for a century, and when necessary, "therapeutic" exceptions were granted, usually by hospital committees. By the mid-1960s, however, several well-publicized cases including Finkbine's converged with loosening societal sexual mores as well as the burgeoning women's rights movement to modify the public consciousness with regard to abortion with surprising speed.

By 1968, abortion laws had been liberalized in three states: Colorado, California, and South Carolina, with ongoing challenges in several other states. Roy Lucas's radical ideas of a *Constitutional right* to abortion on demand entered the discussion against this backdrop. It wasn't long before Lucas's arguments began to alter the overall pro-abortion strategy from one of reform to out-and-out repeal.* In fact by the early 1970s, even many of the original reform advocates who had successfully liberalized abortion laws in a few states had begun to attack their own recently enacted reform laws as not going far enough. In under five years popular sentiment among leading pro-abortion advocates had dramatically switched from reform to repeal.

Footnote:

*Lucas actually attempted to push Weddington aside and argue Roe himself. Lucas also attempted to take control of the Georgia case (see for example: Faux, 219–34) arguing that the inexperience of both Weddington and Hames would surely result in losses and do damage to the pro-abortion cause they were all advancing. Lucas's heavy-handed tactics strained these and other relationships. His attempts to take over both cases failed, however, as both Weddington and Hames eventually asserted dominion over their respective cases and ultimately proved they could win despite the dire predictions of Lucas. Nevertheless, many of the arguments they used originated with Lucas.

CHAPTER 6

Should Privacy Include Abortion?

The care of human life and happiness and not their destruction
is the first and only legitimate object of good government.
—THOMAS JEFFERSON, SPEECH TO MARYLAND REPUBLICANS, 1809

The Lucas article created a buzz among leaders and influential people who were already active in the abortion reform and repeal movements. In it Lucas systematically attacked the interest a state might have in regulating or prohibiting abortion. While the pro-abortion logic Lucas employed was certainly not unique in and of itself, what was radical was Lucas's insistence that a liberty to choose abortion on demand (as opposed to a therapeutic abortion in response to a serious health risk) was guaranteed by a Constitutional right to privacy. This right to privacy had only recently been created (or recognized depending on one's perspective) by the Supreme Court in the 1965 *Griswold v. Connecticut* decision.

Once again, Cyril Means and Roy Lucas butted heads. Means believed it utter foolishness to think that a right to abortion could be established on a newly recognized penumbral right to privacy. With the exception of cases involving rape or fetal deformities, Means believed that any Constitutional challenge to abortion laws on that basis would necessarily be bound by the "fundamental notion of law and morals that one can be held responsible for the natural consequences of one's acts" (Garrow, 319). As a result, Means believed—at least in 1968—that any test case challenging abortion laws without the additional complicating factors of rape or fetal deformity was doomed to failure. Means could "perceive none in which there is the faintest chance that any court would sustain a contention of unconstitutionality" (Garrow, 319). This was not welcome news to other proponents of abortion on demand who preferred to see things as Lucas did.

In hindsight, one can easily see the error in Means's judgment, but in the late 1960s it remained a remote dream that any court, much less the Supreme Court of the United States, would discover a nearly unqualified right to abort hidden in the penumbral rights of the Constitution.

Ultimately, however, the Lucas-born idea prevailed while Means's thesis that both English and American women enjoyed "a common-law liberty to undergo abortion at any stage of pregnancy, whether fatal or not to themselves" (Means II, 374) also gained acceptance by the Supreme Court.

Like Means, Lucas suggested that, "in the Anglo-American legal sphere, abortion before 'quickening' was no crime under the common law of England," and that, "abortion apparently raised no legal or moral controversy in this country until the post–Civil War period" (Lucas, 1). These claims from both Lucas and Means would be picked up and repeated by virtually every pre-*Roe* pro-abortion advocate, argued as facts by Weddington in *Roe,* uncontested by opposing counsel, noted as facts by Harry Blackmun in the *Roe* majority opinion, and widely accepted thereafter. But the claims were patently false.

This right to privacy, Weddington and other pro-abortion advocates surmised, could also extend to a woman faced with an unwanted pregnancy. A decision to terminate a pregnancy, they believed, should rest with the woman, not with the government. Weddington's research led her to the 1965 *Griswold v. Connecticut* case in which the court held that certain aspects of family life were areas where the government should not intrude. At stake in *Griswold* was the question of birth control for married couples. The court ruled against the Connecticut law outlawing birth control, indicating that a married couple has a fundamental right to be "let alone."

The privacy right brought out in *Griswold* and carried over to *Roe,* though not specifically addressed in the Constitution, emanated from its Amendments and, according to Justice Blackmun, especially from the Fourteenth Amendment which states:

> All persons born or naturalized in the United States and subject to the jurisdiction thereof, are citizens of the United States and of the State wherein they reside. No State shall make or enforce any law which shall abridge the privileges or immunities of citizens of the

United States; nor shall any State deprive any person of life, liberty, or property, without due process of law; nor deny to any person within its jurisdiction the equal protection of the laws.

The Fourteenth Amendment was created in 1866 and adopted in 1868, which places it directly in the time frame when the most important burst of anti-abortion legislation in American history was occurring.

It is noteworthy that the same congressmen who had voted for the Fourteenth Amendment had also created, voted for, and enacted laws in the Federal Territories of Arizona, Colorado, Idaho, Montana, and Nevada that made the performance of an abortion on "a woman then being with child" a crime. To argue that the creators of the Fourteenth Amendment would have approved of their amendment as the basis of a fundamental right to privacy that included a woman's decision to have an abortion, is to argue in blatant contradiction to historical facts. These were the same legislators who had created tough anti-abortion laws.

It is more reasonable to conclude that the concept of a "person" was so basic to the framers of the Fourteenth Amendment that it was simply taken for granted to include a person in the womb. There is no indication that legislators in the latter half of the nineteenth century viewed the concept of a "person" to be separable from the concept of a living human being. And yet such a distinction is imperative if we are to accept Weddington's and ultimately the Court's logic.

Weddington characterizes the absence of any specific mention of the unborn in the Fourteenth Amendment or the Constitution as a sign that the framers of those documents were as pro-choice as she is. Yet as we have seen, with regard to their views on abortion, they were her polar opposite.

The cases referred to by Weddington had prompted the legislators to clarify the crime of abortion in 1856. Clearly the Texas court could justifiably portray the woman as a victim if she had died, in which case there would have been no way to determine whether the fetus had been "alive" at the time of the abortion by early nineteenth-century standards.

It is certainly true that for the most part women were viewed as victims when desperate enough to seek an abortion. Even those states that enacted punishments for women found guilty of procuring an illegal abortion still punished the abortionist more severely. But their willingness to punish the woman as well as the abortionist is a clear indication that protection of the woman was not the primary reason for the existence of the laws in the first place. Moreover, a majority of the abortions performed before 1860 in the U.S. were sought because a typically unmarried, pregnant woman desired to avoid the social stigma of illegitimate children. Women in such predicaments who were willing to undergo the dangers of abortion were often viewed sympathetically as the victims of men's seduction and lust. This, coupled with the fact that most abortion cases that were serious enough to end up in court usually involved serious injury or even death to the woman (clearly rendering her a victim), more than explains what Justice Stewart perceived to be an inconsistency.

With regard to the notion of using a "right to privacy" to cover a woman's choice for abortion, pastor, speaker and best-selling author Randy Alcorn had this to say in a 2006 interview:

> Some people talk about the constitutional right to privacy and of course the U.S. Constitution says nothing about a right to privacy. Now is privacy a good thing? Sure. But it's amazing what things we think are in the Constitution that aren't. Furthermore, privacy is never an absolute right. It is always governed by other rights. So if some guy is defending wife beating or child abuse that he does in his home on the basis of, "what I do privately is nobody's business but mine," we recognize that it doesn't matter whether you do that privately; whether you do that secretly. The point is that you're beating your wife. You're abusing a child. You can't justify it based upon privacy.

CHAPTER 7

Playing with Personhood

*If the legal order is a universe which can be developed
without reference to the natural order, only the will of the makers
of the legal order controls the recognition of legal existence.*
—JOHN T. NOONAN JR.

While Weddington and Coffee made great efforts to keep the focus of the hearing on the hardship placed upon pregnant women because of restrictive abortion laws, the undertone of all the *Roe* arguments, the key issue that was always lingering beneath the surface, making occasional appearances, was the moral basis for killing a human fetus.

JUSTICE STEWART: Regardless of the purpose for which the statute was originally enacted, or the purpose which keeps it on the books in Texas today, you would agree, I suppose, that one of the important factors that has to be considered in this case is what rights, if any, does the unborn fetus have?

MS. WEDDINGTON: That's correct. There have been two cases decided since the December 13th argument that expressly hold that a fetus has no constitutional rights—one being *Byrn v. New York* and the other being the *Magee-Womens Hospital* cases. In those situations, persons sought to bring that very question to the Court: does a fetus . . . in the one instance, *Byrn* was a challenge to the New York Revised Statute. The other was a situation where a person sought to prevent

Magee-Womens Hospital from allowing further abortions to be done in that hospital. And, in both cases, it was held that the fetus had no constitutional rights.

Several of the briefs before this Court would also argue that this Court, in deciding the *Vuitch* case, which has allowed abortions to continue in the District of Columbia certainly the Court would not have made that kind of decision if it felt there were any ingrained rights of the fetus within the Constitution.

Having successfully argued that the laws were intended only to protect the woman but were now out of date, and that the woman was guilty of no crime, and that a right to privacy should be broad enough to encompass a woman's decision to "terminate her pregnancy," Weddington then concluded that before the state could intervene in a woman's private decision to terminate a pregnancy, it had to have a *compelling interest*—something that was worthy of its intervention. Because the unborn were not persons according to Weddington, there was no compelling interest.

JUSTICE BYRON R. WHITE: Well, is it critical to your case that the fetus not be a person under the due process clause?

MS. WEDDINGTON: It seems to me that it is critical, first, that we prove this is a fundamental interest on behalf of the woman, that it is a constitutional right. And, second . . .

JUSTICE WHITE: Well, yes. But what about the fetus?

MS. WEDDINGTON: Okay. And, second, that the state has no compelling state interest. Okay, and the state is alleging a compelling state interest.

JUSTICE WHITE: Well yes, but I'm just asking you, under the Federal Constitution, is the fetus a person, for the purpose of protection under the due process clause?

MS. WEDDINGTON: All of the cases—the prior history of this statute—the common-law history would indicate that it is not. The state has shown no, uh . . .

JUSTICE WHITE: Well, what if—would you lose your case if the fetus was a person?

MS. WEDDINGTON: Then you would have a balancing of interest.

JUSTICE WHITE: Well, you say you have anyway, don't you?

MS. WEDDINGTON: Excuse me?

JUSTICE WHITE: You have anyway, don't you? You're going to be balancing the rights of the mother against the rights of the fetus.

MS. WEDDINGTON: It seems to me that you do not balance constitutional rights of one person against mere statutory rights of another.

JUSTICE WHITE: You think a state, a state interest, if it's only a statutory interest, or a constitutional interest under the state law, can never outweigh a federal constitutional right? Is that it?

MS. WEDDINGTON: I think—it would seem to me that . . .

JUSTICE WHITE: So all the talk of compelling state interest is beside the point. It can never be compelling enough.

Weddington conceded, albeit reluctantly, that if the fetus was considered to be a "person" then, with regard to the question of abortion, the competing interests of two persons would have to be weighed against one another. Her primary argument, of course, was that a fetus was not a person and therefore there was no need to "balance" competing interests. Justice White seems to have caught Weddington off guard by suggesting that the rights of the mother and those of the fetus should be balanced regardless of whether the fetus is labeled a "person." Considering the abstract nature of the term "person," White certainly had a valid point.

Beyond this, White further exposed a deeper underlying problem. Weddington was attempting to stack the deck in her favor by arguing that a state needed a "compelling interest" in order to intervene in a woman's decision of whether or not to terminate her pregnancy. Weddington was essentially asserting that no state interest could actually be compelling enough to overrule a federal constitutional right to privacy. In short, Weddington's logic seemed to indicate that even if the fetus were deemed a "person" the woman's constitutional right to privacy should still overrule a state's interest in protecting it.

When the absurdity of this extreme position was brought to light (ironically not by the opposing attorneys but by the justices themselves), Weddington was forced to backpedal:

> MS. WEDDINGTON: If the state could show that the fetus was a person under the Fourteenth Amendment, or under some other amendment, or part of the Constitution, then you would have the situation of trying—uh—you would have a state compelling interest which in some instances can outweigh a fundamental right. This is not the case in this particular situation.

One is hard pressed to imagine a viable scenario in which an "unborn child" (common legal terminology prior to *Roe*) is not also a "person." Even if Weddington were correct in asserting that unborn humans had never been specifically addressed as "persons" in American or British law, neither had they ever been addressed as nonpersons, something no one picked up on. But they certainly had been addressed as unborn "children" on many occasions—a fact Weddington and the Court chose to ignore while Flowers and Floyd took it for granted but never explicitly pointed it out for the record. The technical point Weddington was driving at was trivial at best, deceptive at worst.

But Weddington made a much more significant concession in this exchange:

> JUSTICE BLACKMUN: Well, do I get from this, then, that your case depends primarily on the proposition that the fetus has no constitutional rights?

> MS. WEDDINGTON: It depends on saying that the woman has a fundamental constitutional right, and that the state has not proved any compelling interest for regulation in the area. Even, even if the Court, at some point, determined the fetus to be entitled to constitutional protection, you would still get back into the weighing of one life against another.

> JUSTICE WHITE: That's what's involved in this case? Weighing one life against another?

> MS. WEDDINGTON: No, Your Honor. I said that would be what would be involved if the facts were different and the state could prove that there was a "person" for the constitutional right.

JUSTICE STEWART: Well, if—if it were established that an unborn fetus is a person, within the protection of the Fourteenth Amendment, you would have almost an impossible case here, would you not?

MS. WEDDINGTON: I would have a very difficult case.

JUSTICE STEWART: You certainly would. You'd have the same kind of thing— you'd have to say that this would be the equivalent—after a child was born, if the mother thought it bothered her health any having the child around, she could have it killed. Isn't that correct?

MS. WEDDINGTON: That's correct.

Here it becomes obvious, with even Sarah Weddington candidly conceding, that the absolute bottom line is *not* a fundamental right of the woman to make a private choice but rather how the fetus is defined by law.

Like most pro-abortion arguments, the right to privacy makes sense only within the context of reducing the fetus to a subhuman, nonperson level, otherwise the fetus's right to life—and the state's interest in protecting it— will certainly outweigh a woman's right to privacy.

Justice Stewart (who eventually sided with the pro-choice majority) here points out that if one were to legally hold the fetus to be a "person," then abortion is the moral equivalent to, "after the child was born, if the mother thought it bothered her health any having the child around, she could have it killed."

Given the context of Weddington's arguments, as well as those of her supporters and fellow pro-abortion advocates in the intervening years since 1973, her concession in the form of "That's correct" is noteworthy. Essentially her agreement amounts to an acknowledgment that the definition of the word "person" and whether it can or should appropriately be applied to the living, developing human in the womb *is the critical moral factor* underlying the entire debate. Never mind the "points" she had scored with regard to the law's original intent, the right to privacy, or whether the woman was a victim! None of that mattered if the term "person" could appropriately be applied to a human fetus! Fortunately for Weddington, the Court concluded it could not:

All this, together with our observation, supra, that throughout the major portion of the 19th century prevailing legal abortion practices were far freer than they are today, persuades us that the word "person," as used in the Fourteenth Amendment, does not include the unborn. (*RvW*, 158)

For Weddington, who was, of course, speaking on behalf of the entire pro-choice/pro-abortion movement, the state would have a compelling interest *only if* it could show that a fetus was a *person* within the context of the Fourteenth Amendment—a clear case of stacking the deck in her favor. Not surprisingly, it was her contention that the state had not done so. It didn't matter that the entity in the womb was alive or that it was human or that it had its own distinct blood type (often not compatible with the mother's) and unique genetic code. It didn't even matter that by the eighth week this living human entity resembled a baby. It didn't matter that an abortion could be successful only if this living human entity were killed in the process. All that mattered, apparently, was whether the state could establish that this "unborn fetus" is a "person"—an ambiguous, metaphysical term Weddington and the Court believed themselves at liberty to define and manipulate as necessary to achieve the desired effect.

Was Weddington correct in her assessment that the law had never recognized a fetus as a person? Technically perhaps, but prior to *Roe* certain areas of tort law allowed for recovery of damages for injury to what the law referred to specifically as an "unborn child" rather than a "fetus." When a will designated property to unborn descendents, it often referred to unborn "children." A future beneficiary of a trust was a "child" not a "fetus." (See for example: Noonan, 146–7.)

In the thirty years prior to *Roe v. Wade*, the Department of Health, Education and Welfare had interpreted the definition of the word *child* in the Social Security Act to include the unborn. Likewise, state courts had ruled that fathers had to support their children whether born or unborn. Directly confronting the property rights issue in the *Roe* majority opinion, while, ironically, using the term "children" in a prenatal context, Blackmun suggested that:

> . . . unborn children have been recognized as acquiring rights or interests by way of inheritance or other devolution of property, and have been represented by guardians *ad litem*. Perfection of the interests involved, again, has generally been contingent upon live birth. In short, the unborn have never been recognized in the law as persons in the whole sense. (*RvW*, 162)

In the months following *Roe*, the Supreme Court was eventually called upon to reinterpret the meaning of the word "child." Just as it had done in *Roe*, the Court determined that the word *child* as used in the Social Security Act no longer included the unborn (Noonan, 146, 151).

Despite Blackmun's conclusions, even today in an effort to protect unborn children, some states like Illinois and South Carolina prosecute pregnant women for endangering a minor by such things as illegal drug use during pregnancy. Yet the same mother is free to have the child killed through abortion.

About the inconsistency, pro-life author Randy Alcorn writes:

> Consider the bizarre implications of this double standard. If a woman is scheduled to get an abortion, but on her way to the abortion clinic, her baby is killed in-utero, the baby's killer will be prosecuted for murder. But if this murder doesn't occur, an hour later the doctor will be paid to perform a legal procedure killing exactly the same child. (Randy Alcorn, *Why Pro-life?*, Multnomah Publishers, 2004, 41, hereafter "Alcorn")

While attempting to make a compelling case for fetal personhood, as the following exchange between attorney Jay Floyd and Justice Thurgood Marshall illustrates, it hadn't always turned out as well as might be expected for the Texas attorneys:

> MR. FLOYD: We say there is life from the moment of impregnation.

> JUSTICE MARSHALL: And do you have any scientific data to support that?

> MR. FLOYD: Well we begin, Mr. Justice, in our brief, with the—the development of the human embryo, carrying it through to the development of the fetus from about seven to nine days after conception.

> JUSTICE MARSHALL: Well, what about six days?

> MR. FLOYD: We don't know.

> JUSTICE MARSHALL: But this statute goes all the way back to one hour?

MR. FLOYD: I don't . . . Mr. Justice, there are unanswerable questions in this field. I . . .

JUSTICE MARSHALL: I appreciate it.

MR. FLOYD: This is an artless statement on my part.

JUSTICE MARSHALL: I withdraw the question.

MR. FLOYD: Thank you. Or when does the soul come into the unborn—if a person believes in a soul—I don't know.

In their book, *Roe v. Wade: The Abortion Rights Controversy in American History*, N.E.H. Hull and Peter Charles Hoffer point out that: "Floyd, nervous at the start, had by the end of his thirty minutes at the podium done almost irreparable damage to the state's case" (N.E.H. Hull and Peter Charles Hoffer, *Roe v. Wade: The Abortion Rights Controversy in American History*, University Press of Kansas, 2001, 159).

Floyd's superior, Robert Flowers, argued for Texas when the case came up for reargument in October of 1972. Hoping to improve on their previous performance, Flowers, nevertheless, had an equally challenging time.

MR. FLOWERS: It is impossible for me to trace, within my allocated time, the development of the fetus from the date of conception to the date of its birth. But it is the position of the state of Texas that upon conception, we have a human being, a person, within the concept of the Constitution of the United States, and that of Texas, also.

JUSTICE STEWART: Now how should we—how should that question be decided? Is it a legal question? A constitutional question? A medical question? A philosophical question? Or, a religious question? Or what is it?

MR. FLOWERS: Your Honor, we feel that it could be best decided by a legislature, in view of the fact that they can bring before it the medical testimony—the actual people who do the research. But we do have . . .

JUSTICE STEWART: You think it's then—it's basically a medical question?

MR. FLOWERS: From a constitutional standpoint, no, sir. I think it's fairly and squarely before this Court. We don't envy the Court for having to make this decision.

Though likely unintentional, here was yet another serious blunder. If Flowers were correct that the Court had the power to decide the question of personhood, then the Court was free to decree unborn humans as "nonpersons." At issue is the fundamental question of whether human rights are intrinsically present in living humans from the beginning or if they are endowed at some point by the state. John Noonan adequately sums up the consequences of the latter point of view when he suggests that:

> If the legal order does not recognize any rights in a human being, such a human being is not a person. . . . To have no rights is to be a nonperson, and the legal order is to determine if you have rights and are or are not a person. (Noonan, 13–4)

As the saying goes, hindsight is 20/20. Certainly Flowers was on the spot and had little opportunity to think through the consequences of his responses. No doubt he answered to the best of his ability. But things were beginning to look bad for the unborn. The conversation continued:

> JUSTICE STEWART: Do you know of any case, anywhere, that's held that an unborn fetus is a person within the meaning of the Fourteenth Amendment?

> MR. FLOWERS: No, sir. We can only go back to what the framers of our Constitution had in mind.

At that point, Justice Stewart reminded Flowers that the framers of the Constitution did not write the Fourteenth Amendment, since the two documents were drafted nearly a hundred years apart from each other. Eventually, the conversation returned to the question of personhood when Justice William O. Douglas asserted:

> JUSTICE DOUGLAS: Well, if you're correct that the fetus is a person, then I don't suppose you'd have—the state would have great trouble permitting an abortion, wouldn't it?

> MR. FLOWERS: Yes, sir.

JUSTICE DOUGLAS: In any circumstance?

MR. FLOWERS: It would, yes, sir.

JUSTICE DOUGLAS: To save the life of the mother, or her health, or anything else?

MR. FLOWERS: Well, there would be the balancing of the two lives, and I think that uh . . .

JUSTICE DOUGLAS: But, what would you choose? Would you choose to kill the innocent one, or what?

MR. FLOWERS: Well, in this—in our statute, the state did choose that way, Your Honor.

JUSTICE DOUGLAS: Well . . .

MR. FLOWERS: In protection of the mother.

Here we see a basic miscommunication of facts. Certainly the pressure is high when arguing in front of the highest court in the land and, under those circumstances, the right words do not come easily. Nevertheless, Robert Flowers misspoke when he said that the state of Texas "did choose that way," adding fuel to Weddington's fire.

In reality, the state of Texas *in no way* made the choice for the woman when it came to saving her life through abortion. The state in fact *did not* choose one life over another. In a situation where the woman was confronted with a pregnancy that posed a genuine threat to her own life (such as an ectopic pregnancy), the state in fact *adopted pro-choice logic* making an exception to the prohibition of abortion and allowing the pregnant woman *to choose* abortion or not. But the state certainly did not force women under those circumstances to obtain an abortion; it did not make the choice for the woman and it certainly did not choose "to kill the innocent one." It merely made the option of abortion legal in that narrow instance.

The phraseology of the question put to Robert Flowers was inaccurate from the start as *both* the pregnant woman and the unborn child in that unfortunate circumstance were innocent—something Flowers might have picked up on. But Flowers's unfortunate choice of words seemed to suggest that the Texas statute had somehow already decided to "kill the innocent one," which then prompted Justice Marshall to ask:

JUSTICE MARSHALL: Well, could the state of Texas say that if it's for the benefit of the health of the wife they can kill the husband?

MR. FLOWERS: I'm sorry, I didn't understand your question.

JUSTICE MARSHALL: Could Texas say, if it confronts the situation, for the benefit of the health of the wife, that the husband has to die, could they kill him?

MR. FLOWERS: I wouldn't think so, sir.

JUSTICE MARSHALL: That's right.

MR. FLOWERS: I wouldn't think so.

So, here we have an incorrect conclusion being drawn from incorrect assumptions based on bad communication. The result was an unwarranted, extremely negative view of the Texas law. The law did not "kill" anyone. The intent of the law was to save human life, not destroy it. Yet here it is characterized as an uncaring monstrosity that somehow *decides* to kill innocent human life!

On a more rational level, the court seemed to fear that if it held a fetus to be a person, the repercussions could be severe in regard to extraordinary situations—the difficult cases such as when the mother's life is threatened by pregnancy. If the fetus were a person, could the state then proscribe abortion across the board, thereby indirectly causing the death of women faced with life-threatening pregnancies? Or was the alternative to "kill the innocent one"? Every rule has an exception, and it was obvious that the Texas law made an allowance for this very rare and tragic situation.

On the one hand, Weddington and the court seemed to see a contradiction between making *any* exceptions to abortion while recognizing that the fetus is a person. To them—or at least to the benefit of Weddington's case—this would violate the Fourteenth Amendment. Yet, as already pointed out, no right is unconditional. A person who kills another in self-defense is not guilty of murder under the law.

Certainly no one wants to see a situation in which the mother's life is genuinely threatened by carrying her pregnancy to term. The truth is, advances of modern medicine have made such situations almost nonexistent. While he was the Surgeon General, Dr. C. Everett Koop stated that in 36 years as a pediatric surgeon, he personally was not aware of a single situation in which a pre-born child's life had to be taken in order to save the mother's life. To him this extremely common pro-choice argument was nothing more than a smoke screen (Shettles and Rorvick, *Rites of Life*, Zondervan, 1983, 129, as quoted in Alcorn, 76).

But the question of potential maternal death in relation to abortion was, for all intents and purposes, a red herring. Life-threatening cases are nearly non-existent. Certainly, very rare cases exist where the mother's life is genuinely threatened, but, of course, even the Texas law allowed for abortion in those cases.

CHAPTER 8

Texas Fumbles

A single death is a tragedy; a million deaths is a statistic.
—Joseph Stalin

B y the time *Roe v. Wade* reached the Supreme Court, the state of Texas began to realize it had been hit with a broadside. But by then it was already too late to slow the juggernaut. Attorney Robert Flowers admitted later that he had prepared little in writing for oral arguments. (See for example: Marian Faux, *Roe v. Wade: The Untold Story of the Landmark Supreme Court Decision That Made Abortion Legal*, First Cooper Square Press, 2001, 280.) By contrast, long before the advent of laptop computers, Weddington had prepared detailed notes in a special notebook that provided almost instant answers to any question she believed the court would ask. She had participated in several moot court sessions prior to both hearings and had prepared in advance for difficult questions.

As for Texas, not only had it been caught off guard, it had also clearly underestimated the tenacity and skill of its opponent. When Jay Floyd began his oral arguments in the first hearing (1971) his opening remarks included a lame joke about debating a woman, who would surely get the last word. Floyd's joke came across as condescending and no one laughed. In the end, Weddington certainly did have the last word, or at least the last laugh.

But an attack on the Texas abortion law couldn't have come at a worse time for the Texas attorneys. By the time of the second hearing, Attorney General Crawford Martin had unexpectedly lost reelection so Flowers, Floyd, and the rest of the senior staff at Martin's office were looking for jobs in their spare time. Clearly, even overlooking their serious underestimation of Weddington, the Texas attorneys were not fully engaged from the start.

The low morale made it difficult to answer questions like this one from Justice Thurgood Marshall:

> JUSTICE MARSHALL: Well I understood you to say the state of Texas says it extends from the date of inception until the child is born.
>
> MR. FLOWERS: The date of conception until the day of … yes sir.
>
> JUSTICE MARSHALL: And that's it.
>
> MR. FLOWERS: Yes sir.
>
> JUSTICE MARSHALL: Now, you're now quoting a judge. I want you to give me a medical, recognizable medical writing of any kind that says that at the time of conception that the fetus is a person.
>
> MR. FLOWERS: I do not believe that I could give that to you, without researching through the briefs that have been filed in this case, Your Honor.

During our 2005 interview, St. Louis University Professor Dr. William Brennan commented on this.

> I recall in the [Roe] oral arguments one of the justices asked the pro-life attorney: "Can you give me any medical evidence which indicates that the fetus is a person at conception?" He kept asking him that question, and the attorney didn't have an answer. But it's a very inappropriate question in the first place because whether the fetus is a person at conception or later on, or whether the newborn child is a person, or whether the elderly person in a coma is a person, is not a medical question; it's a question of ethics and philosophy, not medicine. But the pro-life attorney did not pick up on that. And also I think the pro-life attorney could have said to the justice, "Well okay, I recognize that there is nothing that says, according to the Fourteenth Amendment, that the fetus is a person at conception, but before that the laws in this country also did not recognize black people as persons under the law, they did not recognize Native Americans as persons under the law, and many countries did not recognize

women as persons under the law. This means that the law is flawed and we should change the law rather than defining people out of the protection of the law."

As Dr. Brennan points out, law is appropriately subjective to morality. Laws are designed to protect human rights. The most basic of human rights is the right to life. As Dr. Brennan alludes, there were clear cases in American history where the law had been glaringly at odds with the basic rights of minority groups of humans. In these cases, the law had promoted the welfare of one group (mainly white males) at the expense of a minority group of humans: blacks, Native Americans, and women. These laws were invalid precisely because they failed to protect the most basic of human rights.

While this disparity could have been pointed out, Flowers instead allowed the conversation to get hung up on a semantic twist. In reality there was no doubt that the growing, developing human fetus was a "living human being." Justice Marshall, who sided with the *Roe* majority, chose not to attack the case Flowers was making on the grounds that the fetus was not a "living human being" but instead by challenging the notion of whether that living human being could be classified as a "person."

No doubt the pro-life attorneys realized how serious the situation was in terms of the potential danger to unborn humans that hung in the balance, but they failed to grasp the ease with which the Court could redefine human life. Had they foreseen the twisted logic that would soon be employed to legalize induced abortion in most cases, they could have reminded the Court that it would be held morally liable for rendering a decision with such ominous consequences on the basis that *it can't decide whether* an actual human life is killed by abortion, much less 50 million and counting. But the Texas attorneys had no crystal ball. They could not have known at the time how nuanced and evasive pro-choice arguments would become.

Still, they could easily have respectfully reminded the court of the severe consequences of being incorrect. Instead, Texas again conceded defeat.

CHAPTER 9

An Emotional Response: Do Legal Rights Attach at Birth?

We really need to get over this love affair with the fetus
and start worrying about children.
— JOYCELYN ELDERS, *NEW YORK TIMES*, JANUARY 30, 1994

While Texas licked its wounds, Weddington, on the other hand, continued to chip away at the idea that the state had any compelling interest or that a fetus was a person. It's only after birth, she asserted, that constitutional rights, and therefore "personhood" begins.

JUSTICE WHITE: Well, do you or don't you say that the constitutional...

MS. WEDDINGTON: I would say the constitutional...

JUSTICE WHITE: ... right you insist on reaches up to the time of birth, or...

MS. WEDDINGTON: The Constitution, as I read it, and as interpreted and as documented by Professor Means, attaches protection to the person at the time of birth. Those persons born are citizens. Uh, the enumeration clause, we count those people who are born. The Constitution, as I see it, gives protection to people after birth.

Although the Court would eventually bring *viability* into the equation,

Weddington's arguments in *Roe* focused on birth as the key point at which human rights should attach to the developing human. *Viability* is the time frame in pregnancy at which a human fetus has a reasonable chance of surviving outside the womb based on the success rate of infants who are born prematurely. Currently, viability occurs at around 22 to 25 weeks, but as technology progresses, viability moves closer to conception.

Because of *Roe*'s eventual emphasis on viability, it has become popular belief among the public that abortion is no longer legal after a fetus becomes viable. While the percentage of abortions does drop after 24 weeks, late-term abortions are still legal when the woman's health is said to be at stake. When "health" is defined broadly, things such as "emotional distress" can qualify. But Weddington made no mention of viability in her oral arguments. While she recognized a growing weakness in her arguments favoring abortion the further a pregnancy progressed, she couldn't get away from the legal convenience of birth as the pivotal point.

> MS. WEDDINGTON: It is our position that the freedom involved is that of a woman to determine whether or not to continue a pregnancy. Obviously I have a much more difficult time saying that the state has no interest in late pregnancy.

> JUSTICE WHITE: Why? Why is that?

> MS. WEDDINGTON: I think that's more the emotional response to a late pregnancy, rather than it is any constitutional . . .

> JUSTICE WHITE: Emotional response by whom?

> MS. WEDDINGTON: I guess by persons considering the issue outside the legal context.

Acknowledging that it is certainly possible—perhaps even likely—that people outside the legal arena might respond emotionally to the intentional destruction of a human fetus would seem to indicate an awareness on Weddington's part that there is at least a possibility that killing an unborn child—especially late in pregnancy—might be morally wrong. Yet, from a legal standpoint, she could offer no logical reason why birth made such a difference. Contrary even to her own misgivings, she makes it clear that the freedom to obtain an abortion right up to the moment of birth was exactly what she was seeking on behalf of all women.

Offering a glimpse into what had occurred during a strategy session while preparing for the second hearing in *Roe v. Wade*, Weddington writes:

> The Court seemed uncomfortable with my prior argument that birth was the peg at which legal rights should attach, and that "when life begins" is an individual leap of faith that no one can prove; people tend to say "I believe." But we could find no substantial legal peg for maintaining that rights began prior to birth. Although we were not entirely satisfied with our conclusion, most at the session felt it was best for me to stick to the point as I had been making it: Legal rights attach at birth. (Weddington, 136–7)

What stands out here is Weddington's acknowledgment that "we were not entirely satisfied with our conclusion." Keep in mind that the "we" she is referring to is the pro-abortion lobby. These were leaders in the pro-abortion movement, all of whom were dedicated to the idea that a woman has an unlimited fundamental right to choose abortion. Yet Weddington candidly acknowledges that even among this "hard-core" group, there was something unsettling about the notion of advocating abortion up until the moment of birth. Still, she couldn't articulate, or chose not to, exactly what it was that created the feeling of uneasiness. The closest she came to expressing any compassion for a fetus about to be killed by abortion was her acknowledgment that everyday people, as contrasted with lawyers and judges, might feel some emotions when considering the termination of a late pregnancy outside the sacrosanct setting of a courtroom.

Regardless, in order for legal rights to attach at birth, there must be a moral basis for *excluding* those rights prior to birth. What was that moral basis?

Arguing for Texas in the second hearing, attorney Robert Flowers could see no reason to deny the right to life prior to birth:

> MR. FLOWERS: What would keep a legislature, under this grounds, from deciding who else might or might not be a human being or might not be a person?

> JUSTICE STEWART: Well generally speaking I think you would agree that up until now the test has been whether or not somebody has been born or not. And that's the word used in the Fourteenth Amendment.

> MR FLOWERS: Yes sir.

JUSTICE STEWART: That's what would keep a legislature, I suppose, from classifying people who have been born as not persons.

MR. FLOWERS: Your Honor, it seems to me that the physical act of being born—I'm not playing it down. I know it's—a very momentous incident. But what changes? Is it a non-human, and changing by the act of birth into a human? Or would...

JUSTICE STEWART: Well, that's been the theory up until now in the law.

MR. FLOWERS: Well, in other words, it has been the theory that we have—deriving from non-human material—a human being after conception. Well, Your Honor...

JUSTICE STEWART: You see, that's the reason I asked you at the beginning, within what framework should this question be decided? Should it be a theological one...

MR. FLOWERS: Yes.

JUSTICE STEWART: ...a philosophical one, or a medical one. Or, are we confined here to dealing with—

MR. FLOWERS: I think, Your Honor, that the Court—

JUSTICE STEWART: —the constitutional meaning of it.

MR. FLOWERS: I wish I could answer that. I believe that the Court must take these—the medical research—and apply it to our Constitution the best it can. I said I'm without envy of the burden that the Court has. I think that possibly we have an opportunity to make one of the worst mistakes here that we've ever made.

That a human being could exist without being considered a person was so farfetched to the Texas attorneys it apparently wasn't ever given serious consideration. Neither were the implications of such an idea. That Justice Stewart would state that birth had been the test of personhood up to that point in legal history is, at best, misleading. It's difficult to determine exactly what Justice Stewart had in mind, but unborn children had clearly been viewed as living humans with a right to life at least from quickening onward for hundreds of years. As even some abortion advocates of the day were willing to acknowledge, abortion after quickening was a serious crime.

Certainly the text of the Fourteenth Amendment spoke of "persons born" but the Amendment was not speaking to the issue of abortion nor to the rights or alleged lack thereof of unborn children. It was, instead, correcting a problem the Supreme Court had created in *Dred Scott v. Sandford* that allowed slavery to continue on the basis that black humans were not "citizens" of the United States, nor could they ever be, and therefore were not entitled to the rights that accompany citizenship. Abortion was illegal in the United States at the time of the ratification of the Fourteenth Amendment. The Texas anti-abortion law, for example, had been passed fourteen years earlier. Moreover, the legal idea expressed in the amendment as "persons born" logically implies the concept of "persons unborn." The designation of "persons born or naturalized in the United States" was intended to distinguish between *citizens* of the United States verses "persons born" elsewhere, not between persons and human nonpersons. There was no such concept as a "human nonperson" in the womb at the time.

Justice Stewart seemed to be reading much more into the text of the Fourteenth Amendment than was actually there. Remarkably, in the heat of the moment, Flowers agreed with Justice Stewart's questionable logic. Nonetheless, as the conversation continued, it became clear that the question of personhood from both a legal and philosophical standpoint had the potential either to retain anti-abortion laws or pave the way for abortion rights:

> MR. FLOWERS: Gentlemen, we feel that the concept of a fetus being within the concept of a person, within the framework of the United States Constitution and the Texas Constitution, is an extremely fundamental thing.
>
> JUSTICE STEWART: Of course, if you're right about that, you can sit down, you've won your case.
>
> MR. FLOWERS: Your Honor—
>
> JUSTICE STEWART: Except insofar as, maybe, the Texas abortion law presently goes too far in allowing abortions.

MR. FLOWERS: Yes, sir. That's exactly right. We feel that this is the only question, really, that this Court has to answer.

Whether Flowers fully grasped the significance of personhood or not, Justice Stewart certainly did.

MR. FLOWERS: But I find no way that I know that any court or any legislature or any doctor anywhere can say that here is the dividing line. Here is not a life and here is a life, after conception. Perhaps it would be better left to our legislators. There they have the facilities to have some type of medical testimony brought before them, and the opinion of the people who are being governed by this.

JUSTICE STEWART: Well, if you're right that an unborn fetus is a person, then you can't leave it to the legislature to play fast and loose with that—in dealing with that person. In other words, if you're correct, in your basic submission that an unborn fetus is a person, then abortion laws such as that which New York has are grossly unconstitutional, isn't it?

MR. FLOWERS: That's right, yes.

JUSTICE STEWART: Allowing the killing of people.

MR. FLOWERS: Yes, sir.

JUSTICE STEWART: Of persons.

MR. FLOWERS: Your Honor, in Massachusetts, I might point out—

JUSTICE STEWART: So you can't leave this up to the legislature. It's a constitutional problem, isn't it?

MR. FLOWERS: Well, if there would be any exceptions within this . . .

JUSTICE STEWART: And the basic constitutional question, initially, is whether or not an unborn fetus is a person, isn't it?

MR. FLOWERS: Yes, sir, and entitled to the constitutional protection.

JUSTICE STEWART: And that's critical to this case, is it not?

MR. FLOWERS: Yes, sir, it is. And we feel that the treatment that the courts have given unborn children in descent, in distribution of property rights, tort laws, have all pointed out that they have, in the past, have given credence to this concept.

CHAPTER 10

"Texas, Turn Out the Lights"

*America needs no words from me to see how your decision
in Roe v. Wade has deformed a great nation.*

MOTHER TERESA

O f course Flowers was right in that areas of tort law had viewed the unborn child as a legal entity entitled to certain rights upon birth. But rather than cite specific cases or even present detailed biological information on fetal development (which had been done in the supporting amicus briefs), for the most part Flowers simply argued that a fetus was a person because the state of Texas held it to be so.

Like his predecessor, Jay Floyd, Robert Flowers may well have had the best of intentions, but he simply did not articulate the pro-life case very well and, at times, appears to have done more harm than good:

> JUSTICE BLACKMUN: Well, I think—I'm just wondering if there isn't basic inconsistency there. And let me go back to something else that you said. Is it not true—or is it true, that the medical profession itself is not in agreement as to when life begins?

> MR. FLOWERS: I think that's true, sir. But, from a layman's standpoint, medically speaking, we would say that at the moment of conception from the chromosomes, every potential that anybody in this room has is present from the moment of conception.

> JUSTICE BLACKMUN: But then you're speaking of potential of life.

> MR. FLOWERS: Yes, sir.

JUSTICE BLACKMUN: With which everyone can agree perhaps.

One wonders if Weddington was duly appreciative of the assistance given to her case by the opposing attorneys. Remarkably, Flowers not only openly agreed with the pro-abortion notion that "the medical profession itself is not in agreement as to when life begins" but then further weakened his own case by agreeing that at the moment of conception we're only speaking about "potential of life . . . with which everyone can agree"—which was about as close as Blackmun could get to blatantly informing Flowers that he was aiding and abetting the opposition. These agreements by Flowers were fatal to the pro-life cause as the concept of "potential life" at conception was seized upon by Justice Blackmun as a starting point on which "everyone can agree."

Flowers lost even more ground in this exchange with Justice Rehnquist:

> JUSTICE REHNQUIST: Mr. Flowers, doesn't the fact that so many of the state abortion statutes do provide for exceptional situations in which an abortion may be performed—and presumably these do date back a great number of years, following Mr. Justice Stewart's comment—suggest that the absolute proposition that a fetus from the time of conception is a person, just is at least against the weight of historical legal approach to the question?

> MR. FLOWERS: Yes, sir. I would think, possibly, that that would indicate that. However, Your Honor, in this whole field of abortion here, we have on the one hand a great clamoring for this liberalization of it. Perhaps this is good. Population explosion. We have these so many things that are arriving on the scene in the past few years that might have some effect on producing this type of legislation, rather than facing the facts squarely. I don't think anyone has faced the fact, in making a decision, whether this is a life in a person concept.

This further fed into Weddington's strategy. Was Texas actually conceding that abortion might be a good thing after all as a means of controlling the exploding population? In hindsight, it would appear not. But Flowers's terminology was so hopelessly flawed that one can only speculate what his true intentions might have been. It seems as though Flowers was attempting to make the case that what was then perceived to be a burgeoning population would likely provide the necessary impetus to prompt state legislatures to take up consideration of abortion legislation, which, in turn, would, presumably, provide a "good" result such that the question of "whether this is a life in a person concept" would be dealt with.

Regardless of what Flowers meant to say, his actual words likely did more harm than good for the pro-life cause. And if the state could not back up its claim that a fetus is a person, as they say in Texas, you might as well turn out the lights, the party's over.

MS. WEDDINGTON: I think Mr. Flowers well made the point when he said that no one can say "here is the dividing line; here is where life begins; here is—life is here; and life is not over here." In a situation where no one can prove where life begins, where no one can show that the Constitution was adopted—that it was meant to protect fetal life, in those situations where it is shown that that kind of decision is so fundamentally a part of individual life of the family, of such fundamental impact on the person . . .

JUSTICE WHITE: Well, I gather your argument is that a state may not protect the life of the fetus or prevent an abortion even at any time during pregnancy?

MS. WEDDINGTON: At this—

JUSTICE WHITE: Right up until the moment of birth?

MS. WEDDINGTON: At this time my point is that this particular statute is unconstitutional.

CHAPTER 11

Ignorance Is Bliss

*[W]e eschew moral analysis at the risk of failing to understand what it is
we are actually doing through political choices and social policies.*
—Beverly Wildung Harrison

What may not have been clear at the time is that Justice White was zeroing in on a glaring weakness in Weddingon's "logic." Although she maintained a hard-line stance during both sets of oral arguments in *Roe* with regard to birth as the pivotal point, even Weddington herself acknowledges discomfort at the thought of abortion late in pregnancy:

> I knew that everyone, me included, was uncomfortable with the idea of abortion in the later stages of pregnancy. But I had been looking for a legal "peg" on which to hang an answer. There simply was not such a peg until birth. (Weddington, 117)

Despite this unexplained uneasiness, Weddington passionately argued that birth was the logical point at which human rights should attach to the developing human. Convenient as it was in the form of a "legal peg," birth was, nevertheless, obviously not the beginning of human life. For centuries even the common law had recognized that as an obvious fact. The unavoidable implication for Weddington was that simply being alive and human was not reason enough to guarantee a basic right to continue with one's life so long as that life was located inside the womb of a pregnant woman. While Weddington did her best to avoid discussion of this radical, new outlook on preborn human life, the court recognized that it must, at least for posterity's sake, address the issue.

In the end, the court provided a simple, though completely unsatisfactory, solution to Weddington's dilemma by asserting that:

> Texas urges that, apart from the Fourteenth Amendment, life begins at conception and is present throughout pregnancy, and that, therefore, the state has a compelling interest in protecting that life from and after conception.
>
> We need not resolve the difficult question of when life begins. When those trained in the respective disciplines of medicine, philosophy, and theology are unable to arrive at any consensus, the judiciary, at this point in the development of man's knowledge, is not in a position to speculate as to the answer. It should be sufficient to note briefly the wide divergence of thinking on this most sensitive and difficult question. (*RvW*, 159)

To elaborate on Dr. Brennan's point, a hypothetical analogy might be helpful. Let us consider a general in the United States military who has been commissioned by the government to test the effectiveness of a new bomb. In response, the general locates an island in the Pacific Ocean that is believed to be uninhabited. Without first sending teams to the island to determine whether human beings are present, he simply orders the experimental bomb to be dropped on the island. When teams are later sent to the island to measure the bomb's destruction, it is then discovered that a castaway had indeed been living on the island for several months (along with his volleyball friend, Wilson).

While the general certainly did not intentionally kill the castaway, since he was operating under the assumption that human life was not present on the island, his order to proceed with the bombing certainly did result in the death of an innocent human being. Should the general be charged with a crime? Most of us, I think, would answer that he should at least be charged with something on the level of manslaughter, wrongful death, or negligent homicide. Although murder was clearly not his intent, his actions were certainly negligent and resulted in the death of a living human being.

While no analogy is perfect, this one is particularly relevant when considering the conclusion the *Roe* court eventually came to, in which the court acknowledged that it was rendering its decision *despite its inability to answer the question* of "when [human] life begins" (*RvW*, 159).

In the case of our hypothetical general, it may well have turned out that no living humans were present on the island. For all anyone knew, the island was in a remote location where the presence of human life had not been expected. Still, we would expect that the general should have made an effort to determine *for sure* whether the island was actually devoid of human life before ordering an action that clearly would result in death for any potential humans on the island.

In the case of abortion, there is no question that human life is present. Unlike our analogy, the growing, developing, human being is itself, in fact, *the direct target* of abortion. If that living human remains alive and developing in the womb after the abortion, then the procedure was not successful. In this case, one could argue that the analogy is flawed and should be adjusted to the point where the general had to have been informed that a human being was reported to be living on the island, but determining the truth of that report would have been inconvenient and the general chose to ignore it. With that added factor, how many of us would conclude that the general should be held responsible for the death of the castaway? Most, I think, would agree that he should.

But one could still make a reasonable case that the analogy continues to be flawed when it comes to the action of the U.S. Supreme Court. In order to further bring the analogy closer to reality with regard to the legalizing of abortion on demand, one might add that not only did the general ignore the report of one human living on the island, but he also ignored a report suggesting that there was a thriving city with over 50 million inhabitants living on the island. Disregarding this information—not on the basis that it was false, but simply arguing that people disagree on whether it is true—the general proceeds to bomb the island, destroying its 50 million inhabitants. In such a case, how would one go about describing the guilt of the general? Would a charge of negligent homicide be sufficient?

The undeniable reality is that what "Texas" was urging—that human life begins at conception—is *the consensus* from a biological standpoint. Flowers and Floyd simply did not do a good job of either articulating or substantiating this fact and instead made matters worse by agreeing with Weddington on her "lack of consensus" assertion.

Despite this weakness, Texas could (and did) point to conception as the most rational, logical starting point for human life. Remarkably, though in hindsight not surprisingly, the court ultimately preferred Weddington's appeal to ignorance over Texas's observable biology.

In her book, *A Question of Choice*, Weddington twice notes that scientists believe "life began once billions of years ago and has been a continuum ever since, marked by important moments such as conception, implantation, quickening, viability and birth" (Weddington, 136, 248). If Weddington makes this assertion in an effort to lend scientific credibility to her case, the tactic fails upon even a cursory examination. If bolstering her case with an air of scientific respectability was not the intent, then the assertion is irrelevant.

As is often the case with pro-abortion arguments, this one employs a linguistic sleight-of-hand trick to produce the desired effect. The idea that "life began once billions of years ago and has been a continuum ever since"— whether true or not—says nothing about the morality of intentionally killing *individual* human lives. Surely Weddington would never argue that killing a two-day-old baby is justified because "life began once billions of years ago and has been a continuum ever since." Such "logic" is clearly unacceptable. The intentional taking of each individual human life is the relevant factor to the question of abortion, not the generic notion of "life" in its broadest context. Moreover, the life of each individual human clearly did not begin billions of years ago as, no doubt, Weddington fully understands, and indeed candidly admits when she argues that:

> I would like to draw to the court's attention the fact that life is an ongoing process. It is almost impossible to define *a point at which life begins* or perhaps even at which life ends. (Weddington, 64, emphasis added)

Here, again, the sleight-of-hand tactic is employed. What is truly remarkable is that seven out of nine Supreme Court justices uncritically fell under the spell of the trick. Regardless, Weddington's language is ambiguous. The fallacy is easily exposed by simply inserting the relevant qualifiers needed to clarify the assertion. To be clear, Weddington's statement *should* read as follows:

> The *broad phenomenon* of "life" is an ongoing process. It is almost impossible to define a point at which *each individual human* life begins or perhaps even at which *each individual human life* ends.

Eliminating the ambiguity, however, does not eliminate the fallacy. Not only is the broad phenomenon of "life" as a continuum irrelevant to the morality of taking an individual human life, but Weddington's appeal to the alleged uncertainty of pinpointing its beginning is also fatally flawed—especially given the context here of her desire to recruit science in support of her pro-abortion ideas.

When speaking in purely biological terms, there is no question as to when human life begins. In fact, the phenomenon can be scientifically observed. While it is certainly true that fertilization is itself a process with a beginning, middle, and end rather than a specific point in time, there is no question that at the completion of the process a new, unique, individual human life, as characterized by the fusion of 23 paternal and 23 maternal chromosomes, begins to exist. From a biological standpoint, that individual human life *simply did not exist* prior to the unique joining of those chromosomes.

Whether the resulting new individual human life represents the fusing of two previously existing human lives on a broader "continuum" into one new, unique, human life, or whether the new human simply arose from living material donated by two living humans on the same "continuum," or whether an omnipotent being infuses a life-giving apparently immaterial soul is altogether irrelevant. The important and indisputable fact is that the new, individual human life clearly had *a beginning* prior to which he or she simply did not exist and after which life continues until death occurs naturally or is induced.

Therefore, the scientifically observable point at the completion of fertilization is indeed a precise, convenient, and more importantly *accurate* beginning for each individual human life. There is no question that a self-contained, growing, developing, and by any account, *living* human organism exists after fertilization and that that same individual human did not exist prior to the process. The existence of a "continuum" which is made up of the accumulation of billions of *other* individual human lives is irrelevant when considering the starting point of each individual human life. In short, biology is simply at odds with Weddington's nebulous conclusions.

Though Weddington's logic in this regard is rather easily dismantled, in the years since *Roe*, slightly more cogent biologically based arguments have developed, some of which, when packaged with authoritative-sounding terminology, give the illusion of respectability. Despite the slick packaging, at their core these still amount to radical and unsupported ideas that attempt to make the case that a developing embryo and fetus is not an individual life because that entity allegedly draws "life" from the host organism (mother) through the umbilical cord. Such arguments generally assert that until the fetus is capable of sustaining its life without physical dependence on the mother* it cannot be considered an individual human life.

Nevertheless, biology contradicts this notion since the fetus is certainly a distinct, living, human organism as is clearly demonstrated by the facts that the fetus has his or her own unique blood type (which in some cases is incompatible with the mother's), fingerprints, DNA, and roughly 50 percent of the time is a different gender than the mother. While the fetus certainly *attaches* to the mother's body through the umbilical cord and thereby temporarily draws nutrients and oxygen from her, there is no question that pregnancy involves a dependent relationship between two separate individuals: namely, mother and, as yet, her unborn child.

While attempting to use science to her advantage as expressed in the "continuum" argument on the one hand, Weddington was simultaneously attempting to forge a rational argument based almost entirely on ignorance by asserting that since no one—or more precisely, no group of experts—could agree on "when life begins," it should therefore be up to the pregnant woman to make that determination.

The first problem with this tactic is that two distinct concepts are competing to be the subject of Weddington's (and by extension the Court's) use of the word "life." Again, from a biological standpoint there is no question that each individual human life begins at conception. Uncertainty only enters the picture when one ponders the beginning of the legal concept known as "personhood." It is on this abstract concept that experts are unable to agree— as might be expected—since personhood itself is a mutable concept. It is, in fact, the pliable nature of the legal notion of "personhood" that allowed Weddington's arguments, flawed though they were, to be adopted by the court.

A second problem lies in the fact that the language of the *Roe* opinion is often sufficiently ambiguous to allow reasonable speculation about the exact meaning the Court had in mind. The earlier Blackmun citation ("We need not resolve the difficult question of when life begins.") is perhaps the classic example. From a biological standpoint, the court "need not resolve" the question of when *each individual human* life begins since the question had already been resolved a century earlier by scientific observation. What the court was apparently suggesting—however stealthily—is that consensus was not extant with regard to the proper attachment of *the philosophical concept of personhood* to the developing human in utero. Given that pronouncement—however dubiously stated—as a context on which to build, the Court then felt at liberty to attach its own *legal pronouncement* of "personhood" wherever it deemed appropriate. While rhetorically the court emphasized a "compelling point" at viability, practically it ended up effectively applying "personhood" exactly where Weddington wanted it: at birth. Putting aside emotional distractions that might interfere with one's decision-making ability when considering abortion in the later stages of pregnancy, Weddington calmly asserted that birth offered the most convenient legal peg on which to hang personhood. The Court itself acknowledged that the very concept of personhood (and therefore where to place it, assuming one was going to hold that it was *not* present at the beginning) was paramount:

> The appellee (the attorneys for the state of Texas) and certain amici argue that the fetus is a "person" within the language and meaning of the Fourteenth Amendment. In support of this, they outline at length and in detail the well-known facts of fetal development. If this suggestion of personhood is established, the appellant's case [Weddington's case], of course, collapses, for the fetus' right to life would then be guaranteed specifically by the amendment. The appellant conceded as much on reargument. On the other hand, the appellee conceded on reargument that no case could be cited that holds that a fetus is a person within the meaning of the Fourteenth Amendment. (*RvW,* 157)

That no case could be cited specifically holding a fetus to be a "person" within the meaning of the Fourteenth Amendment is hardly surprising. Prior to *Roe,* abortion was against the law according to statutes that *had no need* of employing the word "person" in reference to a fetus. In fact, the term "person" was also not generally used in reference to the mother. Instead, as Joseph Dellapenna exhaustively points out in his 1,200+ page exposé of popular abortion myths, the term "child" or "unborn child" was the preferred method of legally referencing a human fetus as is demonstrated in the very language of the Texas statute Weddington was attacking.**

In fact, the term "unborn child" was so common to legal language prior to *Roe v. Wade* that even pro-choice Justice Stewart unwittingly referenced "unborn children" during oral arguments!

JUSTICE STEWART: Does the Texas law in other areas of the law give rights to unborn children—in the areas of trusts, estates and wills, or any of the other . . .

In its rush to grant Weddington's wishes, the Court failed to explain how the creators of laws designed to prohibit destruction of "unborn children" could have simultaneously viewed those same "unborn children as "nonpersons" and that, on that basis, would have approved of the Court's making the term "personhood" pivotal to the point where life or death for tens of millions of human fetuses hung in the balance. Nevertheless, pivotal was exactly what the term "person" became with Blackmun fully conceding that if the state could somehow establish the notion that a fetus was indeed a "person" then Weddington's case collapses, with even Weddington herself conceding as much during the second round of oral arguments.

Footnotes:
*The term "mother" is never used by pro-abortion proponents—except by oversight—when describing a pregnant woman. The terms "woman" or "pregnant woman" are always preferred since they psychologically free the woman of any obligation to her unborn child. Nevertheless, the term "mother" is appropriate since the new human life inside her womb is indeed already dependent on her for survival. In a classic case of wanting to have one's cake and eat it too, pro-abortion advocates readily exploit the idea that the fetus is dependent on the mother when that dependence can be used as a justification for abortion prior to viability, but they are unwilling to acknowledge that the same dependence produces an obligation for the mother to care for her unborn child.

**Texas Penal Code—Article 1195—Destroying Unborn Child: Whoever shall during parturition of the mother destroy the vitality or life in a child in a state of being born and before actual birth, which child would otherwise have been born alive, shall be confined in the penitentiary for life or for not less than five years.

(Note the use of the word "mother.")

CHAPTER 12

Who Defines Personhood?

Human rights are not a privilege conferred by government.
They are every human being's entitlement by virtue of his humanity.
—MOTHER TERESA

The fact that neither side of this hotly contested debate can adequately substantiate its respective claims with regard to personhood to the satisfaction of the opposing side becomes a highly relevant—though nearly always neglected—part of the discussion. While the philosophy of Weddington maintains that since the question of personhood (as opposed to the beginning of human life) has no scientific answer, it should be left up to each individual woman to decide the matter for herself. The philosophy of life maintains that those who wish to keep the unrestrained liberty to kill a living human fetus must first prove that abortion does not kill persons. Failure to provide a conclusive demonstration, as illustrated in our hypothetical analogy to the irresponsible, bomb-testing general (chapter 11), amounts to moral negligence. Since pro-choice proponents cannot prove that it is even possible to have a living human body without that body simultaneously possessing "personhood," the very real possibility exists that abortion kills persons. Yet, the pro-choice community is very seldom challenged in this respect.

If personhood represents nothing more than the definitional whim of powerful Supreme Court justices who are free to arbitrarily set and move it about as they please, then the pro-choice logic of *Roe* and subsequent Supreme Court rulings is revealed to be little more than a rigged semantic game. When personhood is a matter exclusively defined by judges or pro-choice philosophers, then no one is beyond reclassification as a nonperson. If personhood is the essential (but intentionally abstract) quality one must possess before one's life can be guaranteed by the Constitution, then judges hold the power of life and death in their hands—a situation I doubt the framers of the Constitution would approve of. In that case, judges no longer interpret the Constitution but actively redefine it according to their own preference with serious consequences for the humans under its jurisdiction. This is a glaring problem with *Roe v. Wade.* Remarkably, in the *Roe* majority opinion, seven of nine Supreme Court justices have rather cavalierly asserted the authority to define personhood and then subsequently held it to be the critical factor on which Constitutional protection of human life hinges.

> The appellee (i.e. the state of Texas) and certain amici argue that the fetus is a "person" within the language and meaning of the Fourteenth Amendment. In support of this, they outline at length and in detail the well-known facts of fetal development. If this suggestion of personhood is established, the Appellant's case (i.e. Sarah Weddington's case), of course, collapses, for the fetus' right to life would then be guaranteed specifically by the amendment. The appellant conceded as much on reargument. On the other hand, the appellee conceded on reargument that no case could be cited that holds that a fetus is a person within the meaning of the fourteenth amendment. (*RvW*, 156)

Note the specific language in the above quote. Justice Blackmun reminds us that the pro-life attorneys suggested that a fetus is a "person" with direct application to the Fourteenth Amendment, which states that no state shall "deprive any person of life, liberty, or property, without due process of law; nor deny to any person within its jurisdiction the equal protection of the laws." Blackmun concedes that "if this suggestion of personhood is established" for unborn humans, then Sarah Weddington's case collapses. Why? Because the fetus would then be guaranteed a right to life directly from the Constitution simply by virtue of being a "person."

In support of the pro-life attorneys' claim to fetal personhood, Blackmun informs us that they "outline at length and in detail the well-known facts of fetal development." While attorneys Floyd and Flowers only made vague references to fetal development during oral arguments, the amicus briefs submitted on their behalf went into detail on the subject, as Blackmun acknowledges. Blackmun goes so far as to concede that if personhood is to be established on the basis of the "well-known facts of fetal development," then Weddington has no case. In other words, if one is a person by virtue of being alive and human, then abortion cannot be a Constitutional right. Obviously, if Weddington's argument was to prevail, personhood cannot be defined as having any correlation to the "well-known facts of fetal development." And that is precisely what happened.

The constitution does not define "person" in so many words. Section 1 of the Fourteenth Amendment contains three references to "person." The first, in defining "citizens," speaks of "persons born or naturalized in the United States." The word also appears both in the due process clause and in the equal protection clause. "Person" is used in other places in the Constitution. . . . But in nearly all these instances, the use of the word is such that it has application only postnatally. None indicates, with any assurance, that it has any possible pre-natal application.

All this, together with our observation, supra, that throughout the major portion of the 19th century prevailing legal abortion practices were far freer than they are today, *persuades us that the word "person," as used in the Fourteenth Amendment, does not include the unborn.* (*RvW*, 157, emphasis added)

And there we have it. With a few strokes of the pen, an entire class of living human beings is arbitrarily defined as nonpersons. If the unborn were not persons, then the unborn were no longer under Constitutional protection.

CHAPTER 13

When Does Human Life Begin?

We are all alike on the inside.

—MARK TWAIN

The late Dr. Mildred Jefferson was a general surgeon, longtime public policy activist, cofounder and past president of the National Right to Life Committee. In 2005 I interviewed her as part of the audio production for this work. Her insight into the question of abortion and achievements on behalf of unborn human beings is significant. In addition to these accomplishments, Dr. Jefferson was also the first black, female graduate of Harvard Medical School. With regard to the *Roe* majority opinion, Dr. Jefferson had this to say:

> I know that Mr. Justice Blackmun used an outdated textbook when he wrote the majority opinion sitting in the library of Johns Hopkins medical school. And at that point there was still information that could have given him a better understanding of prenatal development. And if you look at the notes that are supposed to be a record of what they were actually doing and saying as they were deliberating, you don't see deliberations of great legal scholars, you hear people who have a level of discussion which is not beyond just the ordinary propaganda discussion of Planned Parenthood tracts.

Carolyn Gerster is a (retired) medical doctor specializing in internal medicine. She's also a cofounder, former vice president and president of the National Right to Life Committee. Here is what she said in an interview we had in 2006:

Human life begins, scientifically, at the completion of the union of sperm and ovum which takes several hours. When the ovum is fertilized, the zona pellucida is penetrated then by the sperm and the first cell divisions start. And everything is decided at that minute; the color of your hair, how tall you are going to be, your general IQ. Certainly environment has an effect on the individual but the limits are set at that time. Whether you're going to develop rheumatoid arthritis, like I did recently, whether you're going to have cancer, all of that is decided during the first 24 hours. By the end of the first week there are about 7,500 cell divisions, and it's at that point that the young human being—which is called a blastocyst—and the blastocyst starts the long trail down into the uterus where it is implanted at about 10 to 14 days. But at that time the young human being is already two weeks old on average, and the woman doesn't even realize, of course, that she's pregnant.

Writing in the textbook *Introduction to Infant Development*, Queen's University of Belfast Professor Peter Hepper expands on Dr. Gerster's explanation of the beginning of human life:

During the next 5–7 days the blastocyst establishes a primitive placenta and circulation, thus ensuring the supply of nutrients and oxygen essential for continued development. Two weeks after fertilization, pregnancy is established. As well as developing a placenta the blastocyst must also ensure pregnancy continues, and it secretes hormones: first, to prevent menstruation and thus stop the shedding of the uterine lining and consequent loss of the pregnancy; and, second, to prevent the mother's immune system from attacking the embryo or fetus. (Peter Hepper, Alan Slater, and Michael Lewis, eds., *Introduction to Infant Development*, Oxford University Press, 2006, 41)

In *Essentials of Human Embryology*, Dr. Keith Moore states:

Human development begins after the union of male and female gametes or germ cells during a process known as *fertilization* (conception). Fertilization is a sequence of events that begins with the contact of a sperm (spermatozoon) with a *secondary oocyte* (ovum) and ends with the fusion of their *pronuclei* (the haploid nuclei of the sperm and ovum) and the mingling of their chromosomes to form a new cell. This fertilized ovum, known as a *zygote*, is a large diploid cell that is the beginning, or *primordium*, of a human being. (Keith L. Moore, *Essentials of Human Embryology*, Toronto: B. C. Decker, Inc., 1988, 2)

Writing five years later, Dr. Moore hadn't changed his mind:

Zygote. This cell, formed by the union of an ovum and a sperm (Gr. *zyg tos*, yoked together), represents the beginning of a human being. The common expression "fertilized ovum" refers to the zygote. (Keith L. Moore and T.V.N. Persaud, *Before We Are Born: Essentials of Embryology and Birth Defects*, 4th edition, Philadelphia: W. B. Saunders Company, 1993, 1)

Medical Embryology tells us that:

The development of a human being begins with fertilization, a process by which two highly specialized cells, the *spermatozoon* from the male and the oocyte from the female, unite to give rise to a new organism, the *zygote*. (Jan Langman, *Medical Embryology*, 3rd edition, Baltimore: Williams and Wilkins, 1975, 3)

According to Van Nostrand's *Scientific Encyclopedia*:

Embryo: The developing individual between the union of the germ cells and the completion of the organs which characterize its body when it becomes a separate organism. . . . At the moment the sperm cell of the human male meets the ovum of the female and the union results in a fertilized ovum (zygote), a new life has begun. . . . The term embryo covers the several stages of early development from conception to the ninth or tenth week of life. (Douglas Considine, ed., *Van Nostrand's Scientific Encyclopedia*, 5th edition, New York: Van Nostrand Reinhold Company, 1976, 943)

Human Embryology & Teratology tells us:

Although life is a continuous process, fertilization is a critical landmark because, under ordinary circumstances, a new, genetically distinct human organism is thereby formed. . . . The combination of 23 chromosomes present in each pronucleus results in 46 chromosomes in the *zygote*. Thus the diploid number is restored and the embryonic genome is formed. The embryo now exists as a genetic unity. (Ronan O'Rahilly and Fabiola Müller, *Human Embryology & Teratology*, 2nd edition, New York: Wiley-Liss, 1996, 8, 29)

(Note: Many of the previous quotes as well as additional information can be found at: http://www.princeton.edu/~prolife/articles/embryoquotes2.html.)

Dr. Gerard Magill is a bioethics professor at Duquesne University. In 2006 I had the privilege of interviewing Dr. Magill in conjunction with this project. Here is what he had to say about the beginning of human life:

> There is no doubt that from conception onward a form of human life with its own individual DNA begins. Nobody denies that. Even the strongest utilitarian "baby is only human after birth" argument still accepts that DNA initiates at fertilization. There is a human life begun at conception. That's undeniable.

Dr. Carolyn Gerster:

> In fact I was just looking at my old text of *Developmental Anatomy* by Arey, and actually it first came out in 1946, and on page 47 it says, ". . . the meeting of the male and female sex cells are all preliminary to their union, combination or zygote which definitely marks the beginning of a new individual." This new individual has never existed before and will never exist again. This has never been disputed; this is the big lie that the opposition has because they don't want it to be said that they're killing human beings.

Dr. William Brennan:

> They [pro-choice proponents] take a specific point of view which is really a secular humanist point of view. A "quality of life" point of view is what they really take. And again, they're lying besides. Human life, according to science, begins at conception. They say just because people disagree when human life begins—that may be a philosophical kind of thing—but scientifically, beyond the philosophy, scientifically, factually, all of the embryonic textbooks are in agreement that human life begins with the union of sperm and egg. And we've known this since the mid-1800s.

Dr. Jefferson:

> At about six weeks we change the name from *embryo* to *fetus.*
> *Embryo,* in the Greek, meaning something that's growing or teeming
> within, and then we go to the Latin term *fetus,* "little one," and we
> use that name because that's the point at which the developing
> new member of the family begins to look like the rest of its family.
> Offspring. That's why we call it *fetus.*

While on the subject of the beginning of human life, Dr. Gerster related
the following story:

> Just looking back at history a little bit, in the early '80s I was
> waiting to testify before the Senate subcommittee on "When
> human life begins" and a representative from the American Medical
> Association preceded me, and I listened in absolute astonishment
> to hear that man say that there is no consensus on when human life
> begins. You could say there's no consensus that the earth is round;
> there's still flat-earth societies out there someplace, but there's
> never been any serious doubt [about when human life begins] since
> approximately 1869.
>
> I don't know whatever possessed me to do it, but we had a Great
> Dane at that time by the name of Elsa, and the boys were very
> interested in seeing Elsa raise a family. And with a Great Dane
> pregnancy is very difficult because of the way they're built—very
> high with a tilted pelvis. So we weren't very successful. And so I went
> to my veterinarian for advice and he gave me a book called: *This Is
> Your Great Dane.* And there in chapter two it shows a diagram of the
> dog reproductive system, and I still have it somewhere, but I took it
> with me to the hearing. And it says: "Assuming your dog is fertile and
> you've selected the right day of the reproductive cycle, the sperm of
> the male penetrates the ovum of the female and the life of the puppy
> begins." So I turned around and faced my colleague over there in the
> back row and I said, "How come the veterinarians know all about
> that and the AMA does not?" And it brought down the house! It was
> the only jolly moment in the hearings. So it's true that it's intellectual
> dishonesty. Actually, I think they would do better if they would just
> say "We know this is a living human being and we agree with you on

that, but we think that this living human being has different rights at different stages," but not to say that it's not a living human being.

There is no confusion among biologists about "when human life begins." We don't find textbook authors battling one another over competing theories regarding the starting point of a new human life. Embryology students are required to know the facts, and so the facts are matter-of-factly presented. "Debates" over the beginning of human life are essentially philosophical and political in nature and do not center on the biological beginning of human life but on the beginning of "personhood" or "ensoulment." Stating the obvious about as succinctly as possible, Bruce M. Carlson writes:

> Almost all higher animals start their lives from a single cell, the fertilized ovum (zygote). . . . The time of fertilization represents the starting point in the life history, or ontogeny, of the individual. (Bruce M. Carlson, *Patten's Foundations of Embryology*, 6th edition, New York: McGraw-Hill, 1996, 3)

PART 2.

How Has Language Affected the Abortion Debate?

CHAPTER 14

A Few Choice Words

Words have no power to impress the mind
without the exquisite horror of their reality.
—Edgar Allan Poe

P ro-life writer Randy Alcorn writes: "The only way pro-choice logic can prevail is if people believe the unborn are less than fully human" (Alcorn, 26).

Since most people do not attend or perform abortions and have little knowledge of the actual facts surrounding abortion, the public's perception is not formed through firsthand experience but rather through information communicated to it through words and pictures.

During the course of the oral arguments in *Roe*, while listing her reasons for legalizing abortion, Sarah Weddington had made this comment:

> MS. WEDDINGTON: Even though the state, in its brief, points out the development of the fetus in an eight-week period, the same state, does not require any death certificate, or any formalities of birth. The product of such a conception would be handled merely as a pathological specimen.

Weddington here refers to an unborn human as "the products of conception" and as a "pathological specimen." Weddington's choice of words was no accident. She had prepared very carefully for oral arguments and knew exactly what she was saying. From the very beginning of the legal battles which culminated in *Roe*, language was carefully manipulated to de-emphasize the impact of abortion on the unborn and focus attention on the difficulties presented to women by unwanted pregnancies.

While the goal in the courtroom should be objectivity, Weddington was well aware that politically correct speech could play a critical role in key legal battles like *Roe*.

If Weddington's argument here is accurate and the fetus is really nothing more than a pathological specimen, then abortion is little different from any other surgical procedure. Tumors, for example, are removed by doctors on a routine basis while no one argues that the doctor has killed a human being in the process! Certainly one could not argue that an unwanted tumor had any fundamental right that would supersede the woman's rights. If a human fetus were really nothing more than a pathological specimen, there would be no controversy over abortion.

Dr. William Brennan:

> Weddington defining the unborn as "a pathological specimen" is really just another way of dehumanizing the unborn. And the unborn have been defined as "nondescript cells" as "pathological specimens" as "waste products" as "medical waste"—all these terms are used to degrade the unborn, and she's just following in that tradition.

Yet despite her assertions, even Weddington admits to being "uncomfortable with the idea of abortion in the later states of pregnancy" (Weddington, 117). If one is to accept Weddington's previous logic at face value, her concern over late-term abortions seems to have no merit. Legal rights did not attach until birth. So why fret over late-term abortions? Though not directly stated, it would seem that even the champion of abortion herself subtly admits that abortion is obviously something more than the simple removal of tumors, pathological specimens, or products of conception.

During our interview, Randy Alcorn stated:

> And you also don't find recovery groups and support groups for people who have had root canals and appendectomies. You know, there's no National Association of Appendectomy Survivors that gets together and have their own conferences and they work through their particular issues. No. Because those things are not traumatic, they don't involve the loss of a human being's life as abortion does.

Deep down, even the most hard-core, pro-choice advocates seem to understand that abortion kills a developing human being. As Dr. Mildred Jefferson points out, if it doesn't, it's not a successful abortion.

The doctor has to deal with the physical reality and that involves the practical science of the development. Because essentially, the mother who has gone to the doctor has made a contract for a procedure which is expected to guarantee that she ends up with a dead baby.

Dr. Gerard Magill:

When you and I are elderly people we are elderly people; we are old human life. When we are middle-aged, we're middle-aged human life. And when we are young and babies, we are baby human life. You have embryonic human life; you have zygote human life. Human life from the very beginning is human life; it just goes through different stages. It doesn't qualify the fact that it's human life.

If you remove as an elderly patient one of your lungs or your kidney, you're deprived of that organ; it doesn't take anything away from your quality of claiming to be human life. And so with a[n unborn] baby, because it's not yet developed those organs—or an embryo—it doesn't mean to say that the quality of its status as a human person is diminished, it's just that it's at an early stage. In other words, the concept of human life by very definition is chronologically determined from beginning to the end.

When we die we no longer claim that we are human life other than the fact that we are dead. When a fertilized egg starts into the formation of embryonic status it's just going through an inherent self-controlled pathway towards growth that requires some external facilitation such as a womb. A[n unborn] baby doesn't require oxygen in the way we do when we're born so there's—you know, it requires a different support mechanism from pre- and post-birth, the way elderly people require different support mechanisms as they are strong or weak or sick. Just as a born person, to have homeostasis, requires a support mechanism; it's called oxygen and food and nutrition and hydration. The fact that there's a support mechanism that makes it indispensable for its growth, doesn't take away from the fact that the entirety of it is self-contained. So the essence of what human life is, the fact that it's growing from the very beginning from a tiny function, that is, a fertilized egg with its own DNA, the mystery is the fact that the inherent package is already built in towards growth. Anything that contradicts that is just simply being unscientific.

Yet Weddington denies humanity to a human fetus in her book:

We stated further that the unborn fetus was not legally a "human being" and that therefore killing a fetus was not murder or any other form of homicide. Homicide in Texas applied only to one who had been born. A fetus was not considered by the law equal to a "human being." (Weddington, 97)

CHAPTER 15

"Dredful" Rulings

A book might be written on the injustice of the just.
—PAULINE KAEL

While Weddington perhaps unwittingly admits that abortion does indeed involve killing of *something*, she matter-of-factly states that because the law applied subhuman status to the unborn, it is therefore not murder to kill a fetus. The parallels between this type of reasoning and the Nazis' philosophy about Jews or slaveholders' views regarding blacks are striking.

In his book *The Abortion Holocaust,* author and professor Dr. William Brennan writes:

> The assumption underlying "legal nonpersonhood" is that some individuals and groups are considered so far below the level of humanity they do not even deserve the rights which any ordinary citizen enjoys. In essence, the "legal nonperson" designation serves as a device for defining the victims out of the human race and beyond the protection of the law where they can be manipulated, exploited, and annihilated with impunity. (William Brennan, *The Abortion Holocaust,* St. Louis: Landmark Press, 95)

Dr. Brennan:

> The terminology changes. If the child is wanted, the child is a human being. If the child is not wanted, the child is a fetus, protoplasm, what have you. Now again, the same thing happened in

the Third Reich. Why were they killed? Because they were unwanted. And what did they call them? Subhumans; waste products; what have you. And the same principle holds today. The terminology is twisted to justify and cover up the harsh realities of what happens to the victims. The euphemisms are medicalized. Here's a prime example: Joseph Fletcher, a prominent bioethicist who's no longer with us said, "Pregnancy when unwanted is a disease; a venereal disease." Of course this is what the Nazis said about the Jews. They refer to them as "syphilis," "venereal diseases," and what we are doing is—when we kill Jews— we are performing a public health service. Again, medical treatment—the medicalization of killing. If you can put it within the context of medicine it gets all kinds of legitimacy.

Dr. Mildred Jefferson:

Separating the physical reality of human personhood from the legal concept of personhood enables the thing that developed in the Soviet Union, so that you could declare any person living outside the womb as a nonperson to deprive them of their lives. And at least in the previous circumstance in the United States when Dred Scott was declared property and not a legal person, not entitled to the protections of citizenship, the court didn't forfeit the slave's life.

Dr. Brennan:

I think language plays a leading role here. And the key semantic device to define those deemed expendable, both in the past and in the present, is through the word: nonperson. And I would say that of all the terms used, nonperson is the most devastating of all because nonperson, the concept "nonperson," is the only one which has been enshrined into law. And a legal nonperson is an entity without rights including the right to life itself.

While abortion proponents often cry foul when either the Nazis or slavery are mentioned in context with abortion, the similarities are conspicuous.
William Brennan:

The Jews were defined as not human. And what was done to the Jews was called something other than killing. They never said they were killing Jews, they said they were simply "evacuating Jews" to the east for purposes of "special treatment in the rehabilitation and concentration camps" of the Third Reich. Today the abortionists say "we're not killing humans, we're just evacuating products from the womb in the antiseptic settings of reproductive health services and clinics." The same terminology.

The push for legalized sanction of slavery in the United States culminated in the now infamous *Dred Scott v. Sandford* [60 U.S.] Supreme Court decision of 1857, which held, among other now mind-boggling conclusions, that the framers of the Constitution regarded blacks as "so far inferior that they had no rights which the white man was bound to respect" (*Scott v. Sandford*, 60 U.S., p. 407, hereafter "*SvS*"). In a parallel to *Roe v. Wade* impossible to miss, the proslavery Court ruled that neither slaves nor their descendants could ever become citizens, and therefore blacks in the United States would not find protection under the Constitution as persons in the whole sense of the term.

Dr. Brennan:

> The *Dred Scott* decision of 1857 relied on such person denying constructs as "noncitizens" and "not part of the people" (*SvS*, 411) to reaffirm the denial of fundamental rights to African Americans. In the words of the court, I quote: "Members of the Negro race have never been regarded as part of the people or citizens of the state. Negroes are not included and were not intended to be included under the word 'citizens' in the Constitution." [*Dred Scott v. Sandford*, 60, U.S.] Just as *Roe* did not recognize the unborn in the law as persons, *Dred Scott* failed to regard black people as part of the people or citizens of the state.

Writing a mock dissenting opinion in his book, *What Roe v. Wade Should Have Said*, Michael Paulsen fittingly notes that Dred Scott "cast a long shadow of illegitimacy over the judiciary" (Jack M. Balkin, *What Roe v. Wade Should Have Said*, New York University Press, 2005, 200, hereafter "Balkin"). As unbelievable as *Dred Scott* logic is to contemporary society, its similarity to the conclusions found in *Roe v. Wade* is inescapable. In his book *A Private Choice*, John Noonan Jr. writes:

> Invoking the right of private property, the apologist of slavery defended the choice of owning slaves, free of legal restraint and moral

criticism. Invoking the right to dispose of one's body, the apologist of the liberty [of abortion] defended the choice of taking fetal life, free of legal restraint and moral criticism." (Noonan, 88)

Dr. William Brennan:

> A year after *Dred Scott,* the nonperson expression itself began appearing in slavery cases. A prime example is the Virginia Supreme Court decision *Bailey v. Poindexter, esq.,* 1858. This ruled and I quote: "In the eye of the law a slave is not a person but a thing." So the *Roe* contention that the unborn have never been recognized in the law as persons echoes the *Bailey* ruling that in the eye of the law the slave is not a person.

Ironically, it was precisely in response to *Dred Scott* that the Fourteenth Amendment was passed which corrected the Supreme Court's error by stating that all persons born or naturalized in the U.S. were indeed citizens. However, the same Amendment failed to specifically protect the unborn. But, according to the *Roe* Court, incredibly, it nevertheless *did* grant the abortion liberty to pregnant women through an unwritten concept called privacy.

As Noonan points out:

> It is a propensity of professionals in the legal process to dehumanize by legal concepts those whom the law affects harshly. No more attention need then be paid to them. On a grand scale the masking of humanity by legal concepts went on for more than two hundred years when English and American judges, legislators, and lawyers created and sustained the legal system of human slavery. They eliminated embarrassment for themselves, and made the system work, by never letting themselves, as judges or lawyers, consider the human beings they were affecting. These human beings became "property." (Noonan, 153)

Dr. Brennan:

> Numerous state laws classified slaves as quote: "personal property along with furniture, utensils, land, and domestic animals." In the *Dred Scott* decision the Court reassuringly noted a piece of slavery history, that, quote (I'm quoting from *Dred Scott*): "A negro of the African race was regarded as an article of property and held and bought and sold

as such in every one of the 13 colonies." (*SvS*, 408) From this, Justice Roger Brooke Tawny and his judicial brethren concluded, and I quote *Dred Scott* again: "The right of property in a slave is distinctly and expressly affirmed in the Constitution." (*SvS*, 451)

Besides black people in this country being downgraded to the level of nonpersons, for much of their history the original inhabitants of North America were treated as less than persons under the law. It was on this basis that state governments and federal agencies disregarded over 371 treaties promulgated with various Indian tribes and nations. A prime example: In 1879 the Pancas, a friendly band of Indians known for their agricultural productivity led by their chief, Standing Bear, left a government reservation and began an arduous journey to their ancestral home in the territory of South Dakota. When they stopped off in Nebraska they were taken into legal custody by General George Crook and treated as runaways. Standing Bear brought a suit against General Crook for illegal detention. In the proceedings that followed known as *Standing Bear v. Crook* the district attorney argued that Standing Bear could not live wherever he chose because Indians were not persons under the law. The exact same status that black slaves had in the antebellum American South and the exact same status that unborn children have today: nonpersons. History repeats itself.

And one other group that we should at least allude to: women have also been defined as nonpersons. Several court decisions have even indicated this. [Cases] rendered in England define women as nonpersons. This is part of the terminology used in these cases. [In] a case: *Nairn v. The University of St. Andrews* the court ruled that female graduates of St. Andrews were not entitled to vote because, quote: "The statutory word 'person' did not include women in those circumstances." This was 1909. In 1931 in this country after the Nineteenth Amendment was passed, I think in 1919 or 1920 to give women the right to vote, this was a Supreme Court case, *Welasky v. Massachusetts,* [in which] this state declared that women could not serve on juries since, quote: "The intent of the Legislature must have been, in using the word 'person' in statutes concerning jurors and jury lists, to confine its meaning to men." So again women have also been the victims of nonpersonhood. But it's the same kind of mentality that you take away their rights by defining them as nonpersons before the law. Now the next step is, look, if they're not persons what are they? They are property. Okay, they're not persons they're property.

CHAPTER 16

Nonhuman Human Research

Hypocrisy is the homage that vice pays to virtue.
—François de La Rochefoucauld

L egally defining a group out of the human race does not render that group subhuman in reality. Randy Alcorn writes: "Something non-human doesn't become human by getting older and bigger; whatever is human is human from the beginning" (Alcorn, 33).

In an interview, Randy Alcorn pointed out that:

> A fetus is a young baby so is there a difference in terms of level of development? Yes. Is there a difference between a teenager and an adult? Sure. Are they both human beings? Yes. Is there a difference between a young child and a teenager? Of course. Does that difference constitute a difference in humanity and a difference in value as people? Absolutely not.

Dr. Gerster:

> As they slide down the birth canal there is no elixir of life that lubricates the baby as it goes through, and there's no ensoulment or whatever you want to call it that comes in with the first breath of air. That's an asinine argument because if it's a human being in the light of day it's a human being in the darkness of the womb 30 minutes before.

Dr. Magill:

The homeostasis of the growing fertilized egg responds to multiple different environments, and it responds to them at the appropriate time in the appropriate manner in its growth cycle. And its response to them is an interactive response based on the actual demands of the growing embryo. So a growing embryo at the point of fertilization could not possibly implant. It has to go through a developmental stage before it is capable of implanting. And that's how the human body works. And to claim that the relationality or the interactivity of a fertilized egg through those first two weeks as it implants compromises its status as human life is like saying, well the baby all the way through until death is not really human because it goes through very different interactivity with its environment.

Like the Jewish question of Nazi Germany and the slave question in nineteenth-century America, downgrading the unborn to a subhuman level in *Roe v. Wade* opened the door to various types of exploitation. Scientists who wanted to conduct research on fetuses who were scheduled to be killed anyway packaged and presented their requests as beneficial for the rest of society. The logic behind the desire to conduct research on unborn babies is revealing as demonstrated in this 1974 statement by the Department of Health, Education and Welfare:

The opposition to research involvement of the fetus and the abortus appears to be based in part on the assumption that the needed research can be obtained through research with animal species or with adults. Unfortunately these assumptions are not valid. (HEW, "Protection of Human Subjects," Federal Register 39: 30649, "Fetuses, Abortuses, and Pregnant Women," as quoted in Noonan, 124–5)

The irony was that research on the unborn child was desirable *precisely* because scientists knew what the courts had denied . . . that the unborn fetus *is* a living human being.

Dr. Jefferson:

Human beings give rise to human beings. They cannot give rise to anything else. So when they come up with this argument [that the unborn are subhuman] it is just too absurd to even be considered.

While research on animals provided some beneficial data, nothing was so ideal to scientific exploration as a genuine *human* subject.

Dr. Brennan:

> In the *Yale Law Journal*, Nancy Field credits *Roe v. Wade* with conferring on the mother a *de facto* property interest in her fetus and argues this provides a basis for the use of the aborted fetus for research purposes.

Once the courts had legally relegated the unborn to a subhuman level, researchers sought permission to exploit the situation precisely because they knew otherwise.

But, just as in *Dred Scott* America and in Nazi Germany where reality presented a moral barrier, the power of language could be used to reduce harsh realities to mere technical procedures and fundamental rights.

CHAPTER 17

The People and Their Speech

*Free women must be strong women, too; and strong women, presumably,
do not seek to cloak their most important decisions in euphemism.*
—Naomi Wolf

Communication through language is such a basic and common part of our lives, we often overlook its relevance in shaping our opinions. In a battle over passionately held yet competing ideas such as abortion where public opinion is critical to both sides, language itself becomes a weapon on both a conscious and an unconscious level.

Consider some possible medical terms. A *zygote*, for example, is a biological term used to describe a fertilized egg prior to implantation in the uterus. After implantation (which typically occurs around one week to ten days after conception) we have an *embryo*, which is defined as an animal (in this case a human animal) in its earliest stages of development in the womb up to approximately eight weeks. Then the term *fetus* is typically applied. *Fetus* is simply Latin for unborn young. These are the generally accepted medical and scientific terms.

In layman's terms we have the following: unborn, unborn child, unborn baby, unborn human being, preborn, developing child, etc.

As can be plainly seen, in the simple vernacular of *common, everyday* English, the connotations slant noticeably in favor of the pro-life position while the medical terminology, though not specifically favoring, at least avoids denigrating, the pro-choice position. Yet, any of these terms can be used to describe the same entity that grows and develops inside a woman's uterus during pregnancy.

When *Roe* was first being argued, politically correct speech within the pro-choice community had not yet been perfected. After years of arguing in the public square, both sides of the debate have long since selected their own pet phrases and buzzwords to make the most impact on their arguments. The pro-life side, however, had no need of changing the common language. The pro-choice side did and it has, in large part, done so.

Ironically, Sarah Weddington claims the opposite in her book. Commenting on the use of politically correct speech, Weddington suggests that:

> Anti-abortion speakers and writers also used language masterfully. As they fine-tuned their rhetoric, they replaced the scientific terms "zygote," "embryo," and "fetus" with "baby". They encouraged frequent use of words such as "killing" and "murder." (Weddington, 178)

Remarkably, while making the case for the proper use of language in the abortion debate, Weddington completely turns the tables on the facts, ignoring that for virtually all of American history prior to 1973, scientific terms were *not* used by anyone other than the scientific community. There was no need for the public to use medical or scientific lingo in discussing the unborn child because no one was arguing that an unborn child was not a "person in the whole sense." Certainly some believed that the unborn child was not "animated" or infused with a soul until the mother first felt movement, but even that notion became outdated as the nineteenth century wore on. Nearly every law on the books that dealt with humans in the womb referred to them as "unborn children."

Weddington's assertion that it was the pro-life lobby that turned language use on its head, as opposed to the pro-choice side, is demonstrably false. Exactly the opposite is illustrated by pro-choice writer Marian Faux, in her book, *Roe v. Wade: The Untold Story of the Landmark Supreme Court Decision That Made Abortion Legal* (Cooper Square Press, 2001, hereafter "Faux"). On page 120, Faux candidly apologizes on behalf of Weddington's early pro-abortion peers' much-too-straightforward language use, noting that, in the early days of abortion reform efforts, unsophisticated but sincere pro-abortion advocates "had not yet become cautious about the language they used to describe abortion" (Faux, 120). Faux's acknowledgment of the need to adapt everyday language use to something more "cautious" is revealing in itself. But one can clearly understand her point when considering the language of the following early mailer created by some of Weddington's staunchest allies in Dallas and recorded in Faux's book. Advocating for repeal of then-existing anti-abortion laws, the Dallas group suggested that:

> The situation is analogous to the bootleg liquor traffic that flourished during Prohibition at great risk to the consumer and at great profit to the bootlegger. In the case of abortion, the damage is compounded because it is inflicted on two innocent victims, the woman and the unwanted child. If legal, reasonably priced abortions were available, there would be no need for law enforcers to blink at the criminal abortionists because an urgent, desperate need would be adequately and legitimately met by society. The hypocrisy and discrimination built into our present system would be ended. (Faux, 120)

Here then is indisputable evidence, freely cited by a pro-choice writer, that it was in fact the pro-choice side of the debate that engaged in a conscious effort to reshape common language usage in order to further its own political objectives. Referencing an "unwanted child" as being one of "two innocent victims" of abortion is a clear case of currently unacceptable terminology for modern pro-choice proponents. Yet this mailer was created by Weddington's pro-abortion peers in Dallas, most of whom—if not all of whom—she knew and worked with closely in a concerted effort to legalize abortion. Perhaps sensing the need for polemical rescue, Faux informs her readers that:

> Like most other reformers at this stage of the movement, the Dallas women interchanged the terms "fetus" and "child"; not for another year would they insist on using only the scientifically correct terms "embryo" and "fetus" to describe an unborn young from age one to eight weeks and after eight weeks until the moment of birth respectively. They had not yet begun to use the term "pro-choice" and still referred to themselves as "pro-abortion," a term they would later realize was inaccurate and even find repugnant. With a similar disregard for semantics, the Dallas Committee's earlier brochures also bore the bold title *Abortion by Choice*, which was later changed to *Motherhood by Choice*. (Faux, 120–1]

Contrary to the implications of Weddington, Faux reports that it eventually dawned on these early abortion advocates that their own language use was "inaccurate" and even "repugnant," necessitating a change in their usage from what had been common.

As Dr. Mildred Jefferson pointed out in our 2006 interview, contrary to Weddington's assertions, it is the pro-choice community that has attempted to replace over two hundred years of common speech in the U.S. with scientific terminology in a concerted and deliberate effort to dehumanize the unborn since *Roe v. Wade.*

Dr. Jefferson:

> Nobody in casual or ordinary conversation outside schoolrooms and campuses uses the term "embryo," "zygote," or "fetus." They [pro-abortion advocates] are the ones who try to put those terms into popular discussion to hide the fact that you're only dealing with stages in the development of the life of an unborn baby. So, they are the ones who are guilty of turning language use on its ear.

Randy Alcorn:

> The question is: Is this language accurate? That's the whole issue. In other words, what [Weddington] is not saying is that historically people used to say—I mean two hundred years ago, one hundred years ago—a woman is carrying what? A child. You know, when you're pregnant you have inside of you, what? A baby. I mean this is what everybody knew. *Then* came the terminology zygote, embryo, fetus. Fetus is a little bit older but even [with] that nobody would say: "Oh, you're carrying a fetus." No, you're carrying a child. You know, even thirty years ago it was very popular when my wife was pregnant with our daughters, for women to have those cute little T-shirts with an arrow pointing down and saying something like "baby on board" or, you know, something like that. And it was a reference to the fact that there was a child. And everybody knew. Nobody said something like, "Oh come on! That's not true! That's a zygote. That's a fetus. That's an embryo." No, everybody knows that a pregnant woman is carrying a child. So what Sarah Weddington doesn't state is that the return to "baby" and "child" as terminology that pro-lifers are advocating is indeed a return. That's the way it was. Pro-choice advocates picked up on dehumanized, scientific terminology that takes away the emphasis upon the humanity of the preborn. Now if we really understand

"zygote," "embryo" and "fetus," we would understand that that's just a human being at another stage of development.

In fact, the word "fetus" has been so overused by the pro-choice community that many Americans are now convinced that in some profound way a fetus and a baby are two completely different things. John Noonan writes:

> For the pro-abortion party, to expand the law was only to win a political victory. What was necessary to establish the liberty [of abortion] in its full dimensions was to change the language. Only then would the liberty be secure in the popular consciousness. (Noonan, 146)

A clear, yet subtle, example of language alteration comes from Weddington herself as she describes the Texas law she attacked in *Roe v. Wade*. Prior to *Roe* the term "mother" was commonly applied to a pregnant woman, even one who was seeking an abortion, as illustrated by the language of the Texas statute in which the term "mother" appears three times in reference to a pregnant woman seeking or undergoing an abortion.

Note that the term "mother" appears in article 1194, 1195, and 1196.* In her book, *A Question of Choice*, Weddington quotes Article 1196 as follows:

> It was legal to perform an abortion only if it was "procured or attempted by medical advice for the purpose of saving the life" of the woman. (Weddington, 39)

Pro-abortion proponents like Sarah Weddington cringe at the thought of labeling a woman seeking an abortion a "mother." I have participated in online discussions with pro-abortion advocates who greatly protest the use of the term "mother" to describe a woman seeking or undergoing an abortion. They prefer the term "woman" or "pregnant woman."

Nevertheless, as can clearly be seen from the statute itself, use of the term "mother" was commonly applied to a pregnant woman prior to *Roe v. Wade*.

And yet Weddington argues that anti-abortion speakers intentionally used words like *killing* and *murder* to describe abortion. Of course, from the legal perspective, Weddington knew she had the force of law on her side when referring specifically to murder, since abortion had generally (though not universally) not been considered equal to murder unless the mother died as a result of the abortion. However, as already noted, prior to *Roe*, abortion was unquestionably considered a serious crime with serious consequences. It is Weddington's coupling of the term "killing" with "murder" that reveals a motive of sheltering the generic concept of killing behind the legal concept of murder. While technically and legally not murder, abortion *is* most certainly the killing of a living human being.

Footnote:
*Texas Penal Code—Article 1191—Abortion: If any person shall designedly administer to a pregnant woman or knowingly procure to be administered with her consent any drug or medicine, or shall use towards her any violence or means whatever externally or internally applied, and thereby procure an abortion, he shall be confined in the penitentiary not less than two nor more than five years; if it be done without her consent, the punishment shall be doubled. By 'abortion' is meant that the life of the fetus or embryo shall be destroyed in the woman's womb or that a premature birth thereof be caused.

Texas Penal Code—Article 1192—Furnishing the Means: Whoever furnishes the means for procuring an abortion knowing the purpose intended is guilty as an accomplice.

Texas Penal Code—Article 1193—Attempt at Abortion: If the means used shall fail to produce an abortion, the offender is nevertheless guilty of an attempt to produce abortion, provided it be shown that such means were calculated to produce that result, and shall be fined not less than one hundred nor more than one thousand dollars.

Texas Penal Code—Article 1194—Murder in Producing Abortion: If the death of the mother is occasioned by an abortion so produced or by an attempt to effect the same it is murder.

Texas Penal Code—Article 1195—Destroying Unborn Child: Whoever shall during parturition of the mother destroy the vitality or life in a child in a state of being born and before actual birth, which child would otherwise have been born alive, shall be confined in the penitentiary for life or for not less than five years.

Texas Penal Code—Article 1196—By Medical Advice: Nothing in this chapter applies to an abortion procured or attempted by medical advice for the purpose of saving the life of the mother.

http://supreme.lp.findlaw.com/townhall/hot/abortion/abortion.html

CHAPTER 18

Semantic Gymnasts

How clever you are, my dear! You never mean a single word you say.
—Oscar Wilde

The pro-choice community realized early on that in order to make their cause socially acceptable, the killing aspect of abortion needed to be covered up.

In an unusually candid editorial written three years prior to *Roe v. Wade,* Dr. Malcolm Watts unveiled a strategy of what he called "semantic gymnastics" to bring about a change in the predominantly pro-life American national conscience. Writing for the prestigious California Medical Association, Dr. Watts emphasized the fact that though the Judeo-Christian ethic, which valued every human life, was still dominant in the culture, there was ample evidence to suggest that it was eroding. In order to bring about a new ethic:

> ... it has been necessary to separate the idea of abortion from the idea of killing, which continues to be socially abhorrent. The result has been a curious avoidance of the scientific fact, which everyone really knows, that human life begins at conception and is continuous whether intra- or extra-uterine until death. (Editorial: "A New Ethic For Medicine and Society," *California Medicine,* 1970, 68)

During our interview, Dr. Brennan commented on this:

> This is one of the most forthright statements I've ever seen in the literature. The California Medical Association said this: In order to get abortion incorporated in the law we have to do several things. First of

all, we have to erode the Judeo-Christian ethic of equal and intrinsic value for all human beings and replace it with a quality-of-life ethic where relative values are placed on human life. But they even went a step further and said the way that we do this is through a policy of "semantic gymnastics." And they even identified two principles under semantic gymnastics. Number one and I'm quoting: "separate the idea of abortion from the idea of killing, which continues to be socially abhorrent." In other words, call abortion something other than killing. Cover it up with euphemisms.

Secondly, we must avoid "the scientific fact, which everyone really knows, that human life begins at conception." In other words, deny the humanity of the unborn; say that what exists before birth is not human. You notice they say, what we have to do is avoid the *scientific fact*; not the philosophical speculation; the theological imposition; but the scientific fact that human life begins at conception. And they go on to say that, "this schizophrenic sort of subterfuge is necessary because, while a new ethic is being accepted [the quality-of-life ethic], the old ethic [the sanctity-of-life ethic] has not yet been rejected."

And they indicated that, and I'm quoting: "the very considerable semantic gymnastics used to justify taking human life would be ludicrous if it was not often put forth under socially impeccable auspices." That is as long as doctors say what exists before birth is not human and what they're doing to that entity is not killing, then it's accepted. It's transforming fiction into truth. They call this "a schizophrenic sort of subterfuge"! That these two principles—abortion is something other than killing and the unborn something other than human—they call it "a schizophrenic sort of subterfuge." They're saying these are lies. These are lies so severe that they qualify as a major mental disturbance: a schizophrenic sort of subterfuge. But they say that this is necessary in order to change the law and get the new ethic in.

Such candor is a rarity among pro-abortion proponents, but keep in mind that Dr. Watts was writing to a selective audience consisting of those in the medical profession, not the general public. In subsequent years pro-abortion semantic gymnasts have become quite skillful at separating the concept of abortion from the actual act of killing. One way to avoid the notion of killing, as John Noonan observes, was to avoid mentioning the one for whom the killing was intended:

> How was the being eliminated by an abortion to be referred to? Preferably, not at all, for any reference raised questions about the being's status. In the ideal reduction achieved by the *Journal of Marketing*, discussing the proper pricing of abortion for a profit, there were only "producers," "suppliers," and "consumers." Producers performed the abortion; suppliers provided the necessary equipment; consumers were the mothers of the unborn. Could abortion be described without mentioning its object? Yes, by referring only to the condition of the mother. For this reason, *termination of pregnancy* was a favored nounal phrase of the pro-abortion party, and *to terminate a pregnancy* a favored verbal locution. The object of the action became the mother's state. The other object was dropped from view. (Noonan, 147, emphasis in original)

On the other hand, if one were to grant the reality of "killing" and yet still advocate for "abortion rights," one might be successful if it could be established that while killing admittedly occurs, what is killed is either not human, not fully human, or not a "person in the whole sense." Terms used in the debate have evolved to some extent in that some pro-choice advocates are now willing to grant that the child in the womb is both alive and human from conception onward. And while some stop short of granting "personhood" to the unborn until birth, others are willing to concede that, even if the fetus is a person they still believe a woman should have the right to choose abortion since the person, in the form of a fetus, is still attached to the woman's body and is dependent on her for survival. The woman's bodily integrity then, according to the most radical abortion rights supporters, trumps the right to life of the fetus, *even if the fetus is a person.*

CHAPTER 19

Unreproductive Freedom

Controversy is only dreaded by the advocates of error.
—Dr. Benjamin Rush

This new argument is both shocking for its candor and dangerous for its implications because many pro-choice advocates have obviously arrived at the conclusion that the paradigm shift from a sanctity-of-life ethic to that of naturalism and moral relativism embodied in a quality-of-life ethic is so pronounced as to no longer justify the need to hide behind semantics.

In my interview with Randy Alcorn, he noted that:

> The logic that usually goes with that is that this child is just a part of the woman's body until the child is born. Scientifically that's utterly false. You have to recognize that this child has his or her own eyes and ears and mouth and nose and all of these parts of the body. You also have to realize that half the time this pre-born child is male. So in that case not only is every cell of this child's body different with a different DNA, but then every pregnant woman—if this child is really just a part of her body—has two noses, four legs, two sets of fingerprints, two brains, two circulatory systems, two skeletal systems and half the time she also has male genitals. Well that's silly! You know that the child's male genitals do not belong to the mother. Neither does the rest of that child's body.

> So, we now have a scenario in which we must recognize that these are two separate human beings. Now the question is: Is it reasonable

or unreasonable to expect someone to be inconvenienced temporarily in order to allow another human being to live?

And I've had this discussion on a radio program with a pro-choice person who was saying, how can you expect a woman who doesn't want to carry this child to do it? And I said, well, in a given case often women are going in, something like, the earliest abortions are at eight weeks along in development and often it's 10 weeks, 12 weeks, it's later in the first trimester. All right, they now have babies who are born, even down to 19 but frequently 20 to 22 and certainly 24 weeks; end of second trimester babies who do fine in these neonatal units. So we are not even talking about nine months of pregnancy before that child can be viable outside the womb, but often were actually talking three months from the time that a woman otherwise would get an abortion, she knows she's pregnant, she's decided on the abortion, so: Can you hold on for three months? Often it's two months. Can you hold on for two months? And of course if the woman is getting a second trimester abortion it may be even now if it's late second trimester. And I think that partial-birth abortion is the classic example of that; this child is viable. This child can be delivered and adopted into a family of the millions of Americans that are waiting to adopt. But then to think that being pregnant now means not just that I don't have to put up with the inconvenience but that even when the child is viable, it's like having the right to have a dead child as opposed to giving a child up.

It's important to remember that any abortion that does not kill the fetus is not a successful abortion. So pro-choice proponents have adopted a set of phrases acceptable to the general public when speaking on the subject. Rather than someone who takes a pre-born human life, abortionists have become health-care providers. They are promoted as heroes who provide the means for women to exercise a fundamental right. Abortion itself has become little more than pregnancy interruption, termination, or preferable still: "reproductive freedom."*

Footnote:
* (Comments from various pro-choice speakers at the Pro-Choice March on Washington, April 5, 1992):

"I'm convinced that all women should have access to the best reproductive health-care services available when they're faced with their own difficult and very trying decisions."

"But we're here to tell the world that there's nothing moderate about our response to the assault on our reproductive rights."

"The right to equal access to reproductive health and freedom is a fundamental liberty from which women's empowerment springs."

"I know that those who would deny women reproductive choice would deny women the right to decide when they will work, when they will have children, in short how they will live their lives."

"There must be equal access to reproductive rights and reproductive services."

"As women the right to make choices and to control our own lives is the essential issue of our humanity." (A refutation by former Illinois Congressman, Henry Hyde)

"We're not talking about women's health care; we're not talking about a choice. We're talking about the surgical procedure that dare not speak its name: abortion. They call it reproductive health care; they call it choice; they call it anything but what it is: the intentional killing of a defenseless unborn child."

CHAPTER 20

A Child or a Choice?

A person's a person, no matter how small.
—Dr. Seuss

In her book, *The War on Choice*, Planned Parenthood President Gloria Feldt reminds us that: "The corruption of language leads to a corrosion of thought" (Gloria Feldt, *The War on Choice: The Right Wing Attack on Women's Rights and How To Fight Back*, Bantam, 2004, 174, hereafter "Feldt").

While Feldt would surely not agree, the corruption of language actually goes back to *Roe* and continues on with a steady diet of pro-choice terminology that has indeed lead to the corrosion of a national ethic.

Consider the language in this question posed to Sarah Weddington by Justice Potter Stewart:

> JUSTICE STEWART: Does the Texas law in other areas of the law give rights to unborn children—in the areas of trusts, estates, and wills, or any of the other . . .
>
> MS. WEDDINGTON: No, Your Honor, only . . . only if they are born alive. We have—the Supreme Court of Texas recently has held in one case that there is an action for prenatal injuries at any stage prior to birth, but only upon the condition that it be born alive. The same is true of our property law. The child must be born alive. And I think there is a distinction between those children which are ultimately born; and I think it is appropriate to give them retroactive rights.

But I think that's a completely different question from whether or not they had rights at the time they were still in the womb.

Here, Justice Stewart, who sided with the pro-choice majority in *Roe*, refers to "unborn children."

Weddington writes specifically about this incident in her book noting on page 118 that she "should have picked up on that terminology." Interestingly enough, Weddington herself uses the key word "child" in her response. Obviously, Weddington is stating her belief that, once born, a child is a child, which she is then willing to grant retroactive rights to. However, Weddington's use of the pronoun "they" indicates the noun "children" are the same individuals prior to birth. Her only distinction between the two entities has to do with time and location rather than physiological development or the mysterious acquisition of "personhood." Obviously, the law could not grant retroactive rights to a "product of conception" or a "pathological specimen." Yet it could grant retroactive rights to unborn children, provided they emerge from the womb alive.

While Weddington certainly does her best to avoid the obvious difficulty, it seems the truth, in this case, is difficult to cover euphemistically.

The pronoun "they" in her statement obviously refers back to the earlier noun "children." But this logical connection is simply not acceptable when arguing from a pro-choice perspective. Use of the word *baby* or *child* can only apply after birth. Prior to birth, the mother is not a mother, she's merely a "pregnant woman;" a child is not a child, it is a "fetus."

But the fallacy of this approach is obvious in that pro-choice advocates break out of everyday common speech in favor of medical terminology *only when describing* the individual they're attempting to dehumanize. For example, pro-choice proponents do not insist on referring to the pregnant mother as a "gravida" or a newborn baby as a "neonate." Yet, they do avoid phrases like "unborn child," even though prior to *Roe* it was simply a matter of common speech.

Before he became president of Planned Parenthood and long before *Roe v. Wade,* pro-abortion icon Alan Guttmacher published a guide for expectant parents in which he used the terms "fetus," "human fetus," and "child" interchangeably. Interestingly enough, his book was about creating a baby, and he wrote that "the exact moment" in the creation of a baby occurred at fertilization (Noonan, 156).

CHAPTER 21

You Can't Have It Both Ways

Either life is always and in all circumstances sacred,
or intrinsically of no account;
it is inconceivable that it should be in some cases the one,
and in some the other.
—MALCOLM MUGGERIDGE, BRITISH JOURNALIST

Even while arguing on behalf of the unborn in *Roe v. Wade*, attorney Jay Floyd unwittingly aided the opposition through his choice of words. Floyd lost points for the state of Texas when *this* topic came up . . .

JUSTICE STEWART: Texas doesn't grant any exemption in the case of a rape, where the woman's pregnancy has resulted from rape—either statutory or otherwise—does it?

MR. FLOYD: There is nothing in our statute about that. Now, the procedure . . .

JUSTICE STEWART: And such a woman wouldn't have had a choice, would she?

MR. FLOYD: The procedure—and now I'm telling the Court something that's outside the record—as I understand, the procedure when a woman is brought in after a rape, is to try to stop whatever has occurred, immediately, by the proper procedure in the hospital. Immediately she's taken there, if she reports it immediately. But, no, there is nothing in the statute.

Floyd's unclear use of terminology here probably blurred the justices' understanding of what he was referring to. While arguing against abortion, was Floyd now using pro-choice terminology when considering the question of rape?

He refers to "whatever has occurred," as well as "the proper procedure." These terms actually seem to have been misinterpreted by at least one justice—Chief Justice Burger—who later expressed surprise that Texas doctors were circumventing the law and providing abortions to victims of rape.

But in all likelihood, Floyd was not referring to abortion at all, but rather emergency contraception. Since fertilization does not occur immediately following intercourse, if a victim of rape can quickly get to the hospital, she can have emergency contraception where conception can sometimes be prevented.

However, as with life-threatening situations, the percentage of abortions actually resulting from rape is very low—typically less than 1 percent of all abortions.

Taken together, the three main pro-choice arguments used to justify abortion, the safety of the mother, rape, incest, and fetal abnormalities amount to less than 5 percent of all abortions performed in the United States each year.

But even while arguing that abortion is justified in such cases, the pro-choice community contends that it does not promote abortion itself, rather *freedom of choice*. This approach has been particularly effective as Americans value freedom, and the freedom to choose is about as American sounding as anything can be.

So successful is the concept of "choice" that the favorite term of its advocates to describe their opposition is now "anti-choice." Gloria Feldt, for example, never ascribes the term "pro-life" to her opposition in her book but instead always uses the term "anti-choice." Of course the only possible options encompassed in the choice regarding an existing unwanted pregnancy boil down to either having an abortion or not. So, by definition, pro-choice advocates are necessarily pro-legal-abortion, since without it there is no choice. While the choice not to abort leads to other possible choices, the choice for an abortion is a dead-end choice.

But if, as they insist, the fetus is not a baby, and if, as Weddington claims, killing a fetus is not homicide, there is no controversy, so why not promote abortion itself as something worthy of defending, rather than choice?

The late Dr. Bernard Nathanson was one of the cofounders of NARAL, the National Association for the Repeal of Abortion Laws. Since all abortion laws were effectively repealed when *Roe* was announced, the acronym was reworked and now stands for the National Abortion Rights Action League. But those in the know at NARAL have apparently decided that even the term "Abortion Rights" is too offensive, so the official name is now NARAL Pro-Choice America, again emphasizing "choice" over abortion.

In the years prior to *Roe v. Wade*, Dr. Nathanson was considered a champion of abortion rights and a darling of pro-choice feminists. At one point in his career he operated the largest abortion clinic in the world. Years later, after having made a complete reversal in his thinking on abortion, Dr. Nathanson offered a rare, insider's view into the logic and strategies of the upper levels of pro-choice philosophy. Nathanson publicly admitted that "pro-choice" was something coined in the late 1960s by pro-abortion proponents like himself, Larry Lader, Betty Friedan, and others in response to the realization that they could not afford to call themselves "pro-abortion" because that term was "simply too offensive" (Resler, conversations with Bernard Nathanson, 2006). Nathanson further acknowledged that polls among the general public indicated that about 95 percent of the population were unalterably opposed to abortion. "So we certainly couldn't call ourselves 'pro-abortionists' and hope to persuade the public to our point of view," Nathanson candidly confessed. "We had to couch it in more euphemistic terms, and so we called ourselves 'pro-choice.' And after all, who could be against choice in the American system?"

Dr. Jefferson:

> They looked for years to find something with the emotional sale-ability of "right to life" which we didn't even invent; we borrowed that from Thomas Jefferson and that crew. So they tried many things and they finally came up with "pro-choice." And they tried to—for the first few years that they were trying it out—tried to focus on *who makes the choice,* and then they've done everything they could to distract attention away from *what* the choice is.

Who would deny a woman the freedom to choose whether or not to surgically remove her appendix if the appendix were causing distress? Who could argue that the appendix has a right to life? Or that the rights of the appendix should be balanced against the rights of its host? Removal of the appendix would be seen by society as a good and liberating procedure. So why not be in favor of it? Moreover, who could find any justifiable compelling state interest in the protection of unwanted appendices? Who could morally argue that a woman (or man for that matter) should be obligated to retain the offending tissue? Such a rigid stance is clearly absurd since there is an obvious moral distinction between the human tissue that makes up an appendix and the human being from whence it came.

Randy Alcorn:

People talk about: "Don't say I'm pro-abortion, just say that I'm pro-choice." Well, in every other area you can't say you're pro-choice. We have to talk about *what choice* is on the table. What choice are we discussing? Because if we're talking about whether you like Chinese food or Mexican food, everybody's pro-choice about that. What kind of car you drive, where you live, what kind of clothes you wear, you know, things like that; we're pro-choice about those things. But we're not pro-choice about child abuse, we're not pro choice about rape, kidnapping, theft. Everything we've got a law against means we're not pro-choice about that thing.

So, if I ask somebody, "Are you pro-choice about whether somebody breaks into your car and steals your stereo?" They are decidedly *not* pro-choice about that. So stop saying, "I'm pro-choice." Nobody's pro-choice in general.

You say you're pro-choice about abortion, okay, now let's talk about what abortion is. So are you actually pro-choice about taking children before they're born, small children, with beating hearts, with measurable brain waves; you are pro-choice about cutting them to pieces, while they're alive, taking their lives in this very hideous, inhumane way. And *that's* what you're pro-choice about. I mean, let's just define what we are actually talking about. And, see, that's when you get beyond the rhetoric. Because as long as you say "pro-choice," well, who wants to be anti-choice? But when it comes to killing little children, that's not something that I can be pro-choice about.

Dr. Jefferson:

They deal with unreality. There is no such thing as being pro-choice. It's language that I don't ever use because it is evasive and fraudulent. The public fight is not about choice; it's about what the choice is. And no pregnant woman has an unlimited range of choices.

She only has two choices. She can only get pregnant in one way. She has to have a baby in some way and that's then where her two choices lie; to try to do whatever she can to deliver a living baby or to hire a skillful enough abortionist that she is guaranteed to have a dead baby. And to even hold forth that such unlimited range of choices occur as in the open-ended "pro-choice" without defining what the choices are is totally deceptive; so that I don't ever use that terminology and always try to expose it as being fraudulent and deceptive. And as long as they fool themselves this way, you can expect that they will make irrational decisions.

Dr. Magill:

Well it's anti-choice of a very specific deed. It's basically saying that, yeah, you don't have the rightful freedom to choose that deed. And I think that's a perfectly legitimate constraint upon choice; that that's not a reasonable choice. You don't have the freedom to go out and choose to bop somebody over the head with an ax. That's a restraint on your choice. So in that sense, it's a restriction on your choice—a *legitimate* restriction on your choice. There are some things that are simply wrong, and you ought not to do them. Even though you may have the freedom to do them, you don't have the *moral freedom* to rightly choose them.

Dr. William Brennan:

The most common euphemism invoked today to conceal the horrors of killing inside the womb is the word "choice" and its derivatives: "pro-choice," "right to choose." The Nazi doctors constructed a similar code word to cover up their horrendous atrocities, the term "selection." The whole reason that Nazi Germany came to be is that some took it upon themselves to choose, to select, who would live and who would die. The language of choice has become so predominant in the pro-abortion world that even the word "abortion" has been expunged from the pro-abortion lexicon. The right to choose, the right to select, constitute deplorable slogans. Beneath these democratic-sounding phrases is an especially hideous form of oppression: the right to choose, the right to select, to kill other human beings. Just as the Nazi doctors had the right to select who would expire in gas chambers, today's doctors, in conjunction with others, have the right to choose to select who will perish in abortion clinics or hospitals.

Randy Alcorn:

When people talk about, "Well, okay, I'm not in favor of abortion but I believe in people's right to have an abortion. I'm pro-choice about abortion even if I think it's the wrong choice." Yes, but the only reason you should be against abortion is the exact same reason why you should be against somebody else having an abortion. Now if a child's life is not being taken here, why are you against it in the first place? But if a child's life is being taken here, then aren't you compelled to be against other people doing it also? You can't have it both ways.

PART 3.

Is a Fetus a Person?

CHAPTER 22

Potentially Meaningful Potentialities

[W]ith no hype at all the fetus can rightly be called a marvel of cognition, consciousness and sentience.
—Sharon Begley, *Newsweek*, May, 1991

Supreme Court Justice Harry Blackmun felt it necessary to employ euphemistic phrases when writing the *Roe* majority opinion choosing to use the term "potential life" to refer to what fellow pro-choice Justice Stewart had called "unborn children" during oral arguments. But "potential life" was an oxymoron. If the fetus were merely a "potential" life, there would be no need for induced abortion to kill anything. As John Noonan Jr. writes, "What is living is not potential, but actual life."

> A philosopher, as much as a person of common sense, understands that life in the human womb is partly promise, partly actuality, but the promise is contained in what is already actual.
> There is no reason to denominate the active new individual as pure "potential." (Noonan, 156)

While Noonan observes quite properly that "the promise is contained in what is already actual," the reason "to denominate the active new individual as pure 'potential'" is that such a denomination relieves those doing the denominating of any obligation to respect what would otherwise be actual human life. While actual life can certainly be killed, there is no such thing as destruction of potential life—only destruction of the ingredients necessary for actual life. If a man murders me, he also destroys any potential offspring that might have otherwise arisen from me, but he cannot be charged with the murder of my potential offspring as potential offspring do not yet exist and, indeed, may never exist. Clearly then, the redefining of actual human life in the womb as mere potentialities has serious and quite intentional ramifications.

In his typically biting eloquence, John Noonan explains that under Mr. Justice Blackmun's interpretation, the U.S. Constitution:

> ... did not appear to perceive the unborn's existence, except as that existence had to be conceded to make the performance of an operation destroying the unborn comprehensible. (Noonan, 11)

On the other hand, Justice Blackmun and the *Roe* majority were fully aware of the undesirable obligation that results from recognizing actual verses potential human life in the womb. The Court stated that:

> We repeat, however, that the State does have an important and legitimate interest in preserving and protecting the health of the pregnant woman, whether she be a resident of the State or a nonresident who seeks medical consultation and treatment there, and that it has still *another* important and legitimate interest in protecting the potentiality of human life. These interests are separate and distinct. Each grows in substantiality as the woman approaches term and, at a point during pregnancy, each becomes "compelling." (*RvW*, 162–3)

The Court failed to explain how a state's interest in protecting "the potentiality of human life" could grow to a compelling point sufficient enough to interfere with a woman's decision to abort while that life remained merely potential. What factors would cause the state's interest to grow in protecting what does not actually exist? In fact, what interest does a state have in protecting "the potentiality of human life" at all? With all due respect, such a line of reasoning seems ridiculous. Until actual life actually exists, why would the state have any interest in protecting its potentiality? Does a state, for example, have an interest in protecting unicorns? Until unicorns are shown to actually exist, what interest could a state possibly maintain in the legal protection of the *potentiality* of unicorns? And how would such a potentiality legally manifest?

Such an argument seems tantamount to the familiar pro-choice complaint that some right-to-life proponents are so extreme as to value the rights of sperm over those of an adult woman. In contrast to potential humans, sperm, at least, actually exist, making a policy to protect them comprehensible. "Potential humans" are as comprehensibly protected by the law as are unicorns. Clearly, the Court did not actually mean what it had actually stated. Either human life in the womb was *at some point actual* or the state's interest in protecting it could never be compelling enough to override *an actual* woman's decision to terminate her real pregnancy until birth—at which point the abortion question is moot.

The trouble, of course, was that the Court was plainly attempting to impose a graduated scale of *value* on an entity that was in fact either potential or actual human life under a framework in which the court's very language recognized "a point during pregnancy" in which potential theoretically became actual. Contrary to the desires of the Court and Sarah Weddington, however, there was no middle ground. Biology had accommodated neither the U.S. Supreme Court nor the pro-abortion agenda. Nonetheless, with virtually no prompting from Weddington, the Court came to the unexpected conclusion that *viability* offered an ideal solution:

> With respect to the state's important and legitimate interest in potential life, the "compelling" point is at viability. This is so because the fetus then presumably has the capability of meaningful life outside the mother's womb. (*RvW,* 163)

Looking past the pandering language, one is still at a loss to comprehend a state's "important and legitimate interest" in protecting "potential life." Regardless, Justice Blackmun further complicates matters by introducing viability into an already unnecessarily complicated equation as a point at which human life in the womb allegedly becomes worthy of legal protection but, apparently, *only because* it can now be *removed* from the womb with a reasonable chance of survival—which, again, renders the abortion question moot. For the Court, actual human life in the womb was apparently unmeaningful so long as it remained in the womb. Because the Court found human life in the womb to be unmeaningful, it then felt at liberty to redefine that life as mere "potential."

But by adding the qualifier "meaningful," the Court now seemed to be inadvertently conceding that what it had just labeled "potential" life might instead be actual life after all that was simply not meaningful enough to qualify for legal protection under the Supreme Court's radical new interpretation of the Constitution. *Meaningful*, of course, is subject to a wide variety of interpretations. Not surprisingly, the Court does not clarify matters by defining "meaningful" or explain why a fetus capable of sustaining its life while located inside the womb is less meaningful than a baby capable of sustaining its life outside the womb. Reason would suggest that neither the unborn child nor the baby are capable of independently sustaining their lives indefinitely. Both rely on others for their continued existence. Why then is the life of a baby allegedly more meaningful—to such an extent that it becomes worthy of legal protection—than when previously located inside the mother's womb? Is location the pivotal factor in determining the "meaningfulness" of human life?

Ethics professor at Duquesne University, Dr. Gerard Magill:

> Well, viability is very important from a scientific point of view. It means that if the baby, through difficulties of the mother, has to be born earlier than the nine-month period, that it can survive. That's what viability means, you can survive outside the womb with the assistance of science. We put that to approximately 23 weeks, just now. As I said, the earliest time would be 21 weeks; that's what viability means. If you're born before viability; if you're born through a miscarriage for example at 9 weeks or 10 weeks there's nothing science can do, or technology can do, to rescue you. You are destined to die. That's all viability means.

> The fact that we are growing human beings means that there's a point where we are early growing human beings and there's a point where we are so early that we are actually not independent.

> But the more important point about viability is that viability is just a function of development. And it's a function of when the developing entity, in this case a human being, is independent of its surroundings—more or less independent of its surroundings in terms of being able to survive outside the womb.

> It's certainly . . . some people use viability as an argument of "human life begins then" or "personhood begins then" or "we should protect babies from that point," and that's fine for people who want to make that argument in the pro-choice lobby. They're perfectly

entitled to use that, it's just arbitrary. It's not a plausible argument because viability, by definition, if you agree to viability as a standard of protecting human life, the inference is it got to that point because of its precedent condition and that precedent condition is the same human life that you're talking about protecting.

The *Roe* opinion does indicate that at the onset of "viability" (which is not really a specific point in time but rather a general frame of reference during which some premature babies have survived) the state could take an interest in protecting "potential life."

Dr. Mildred Jefferson points out that:

> Well viability is not really the problem of the unborn child; viability is determined by what we outside have created to mimic the environment that the unborn child was growing in before he was so rudely disturbed. And if they duplicated the exact environment, he would live happily along and develop. So, we shouldn't blame the unborn child. We should blame human beings outside the womb for not duplicating exactly what he had been growing in, because if you did that they would continue to live.

Dr. Carolyn Gerster agrees:

> Viability is a matter of environment. If I take a two-week-old baby and throw him in a swimming pool he would go down like a stone and drown. But my seven-year-old son at that time was an excellent swimmer. So this is development and environment. If you put a person on Mount Everest and take away his clothing, he becomes suddenly nonviable in that atmosphere. So what we're talking about is stage of development and environment.

The Constitution, according to Justice Harry Blackmun, began to recognize at the beginning of the third trimester of pregnancy, a type of being in the womb who, though still apparently not possessing a "meaningful" existence, nevertheless had *a potential* for meaningful life outside the womb. This was so, apparently, because other wanted babies had actually survived premature expulsion from the womb at around that general time frame. One wonders how exactly the same *potential* did not also exist in the same entity prior to viability. In fifth grade, my son had the potential to play a tuba correctly but did not yet have the ability to do so. As time progressed, he developed the potential into an actual ability. But the same potential was there in the same individual from the beginning of his life. Justice Blackmun seems to be confusing *the potential* for meaningful life outside the womb which exists in the unborn from conception onward, with *the actual ability* to sustain one's life outside the womb which occurs at a certain point in fetal development.

Dr. Jefferson:

> But even that is very dishonest. Here's the helpless unborn child who has to prove that it's capable of living outside the womb before it's given a chance to live outside the womb. He [Blackmun] said, "capable of living outside the womb, albeit with artificial means." Technology has already advanced beyond what the U.S. Supreme Court references.

The power of the state to protect unborn human life during the third trimester, much less before, was unacceptable to the purveyors of choice. Consequently, Blackmun was compelled to add a fine-print qualifier to the state's interest which virtually negated its capacity to protect fetal life at any point in pregnancy.

While the Constitution, according to Justice Blackmun, recognized a *potential* for meaningful life at the onset of viability, it also recognized in *Doe v. Bolton* the mother's *actual* and nearly unrestricted liberty to have an abortion if her health required it, which was defined as the mother's "state of well being" (Noonan, 12). In layman's terms, if the mother wanted a late-term abortion and could convince a doctor that her state of well being would be negatively affected by carrying the pregnancy to term, she could have the desired abortion at any time during pregnancy. And there are, of course, doctors who are willing to perform late-term abortions for virtually any reason. Again, quoting Noonan:

> . . . it would be a rare case where a doctor willing to perform an abortion would not be convinced that his patient's emotional well-being required the abortion she asked for. (Noonan, 12)

Weddington herself admitted candidly during oral arguments and even more explicitly later in her book that she grew somewhat uncomfortable with abortion the closer it took place to birth (Weddington, 117). But she found herself at a loss when it came to locating a legal "peg" worthy of protecting the unborn child's life until she could actually see a living child.

Many modern defenders of abortion insist that because of *Roe*'s post-viability limitation, abortion on demand does not exist in the United States and that late-term abortions are only done to save the life or health of the woman. Basing their argument on *Roe,* they fail to understand or simply fail to acknowledge that the liberal health provision in the *Doe v. Bolton* decision completely nullifies *Roe* in this respect. Again, with succinct clarity Noonan sums up the result from a fetal perspective by stating, in reference to the third trimester of pregnancy, that the Constitution "withdrew with one hand the protection it appeared to extend with the other" (Noonan, 12).

Weddington's agenda had been to push for unlimited access to abortion through all nine months of pregnancy. While *Roe* may have come up just shy of that goal, *Doe* achieved total victory.

CHAPTER 23

Minority Report

*If liberty means anything at all, it means the right to tell people
what they do not want to hear.*
—George Orwell

In response to *Roe v. Wade*, the state of Rhode Island passed a law that
recognized the unborn as persons within its borders. Of course the law
was immediately challenged in the federal courts by lawyers for Planned
Parenthood and the ACLU. As a result, the state of Rhode Island offered to
present witnesses willing testify to the humanity of the unborn. But, acting by
himself, Federal Judge Raymond Pettine refused to hear the state's witnesses
commenting that:

> The United States Supreme Court made it unmistakably clear that
> the question of when life begins needed no resolution by the judiciary
> as it was not a question of fact. (Federal Judge Raymond Pettine, *Doe
> v. Israel*, as quoted in Noonan, 17)

In this remarkably candid statement, Judge Pettine actually describes *Roe*
logic fairly accurately. Remarkable as it sounds, the question of when human
life begins was simply avoided. If the Court had been taking a "when does
human life begin" test, it would simply have left the question blank. In short,
there was no factual basis underlying the decision. The Court's judgment
would not rest on reality but on ignorance. Nevertheless, it declared that it
understood the gravity of the question that had been placed before it:

> We forthwith acknowledge our awareness of the sensitive
> and emotional nature of the abortion controversy, of the vigorous

opposing views, even among physicians, and of the deep and seemingly absolute convictions that the subject inspires. One's philosophy, one's experiences, one's exposure to the raw edges of human existence, one's religious training, one's attitudes toward life and family and their values, and the moral standards one establishes and seeks to observe, are all likely to influence and to color one's thinking and conclusions about Abortion. (*RvW*, 116)

The language used throughout the decision is noteworthy. Despite Weddington's attempt at least to give the appearance that science and factual observation must come down on the pro-choice side, nowhere in the opinion does the Court itself attempt to justify its decision based on factual knowledge of human development. Instead, we are assured that the Court realizes that one's emotional attitudes, philosophy, and personal experiences can "influence and color one's thinking and conclusions about abortion." One wonders whether the Court would feel comfortable using such "logic" with any morally dubious subject other than abortion? Would the Court be justified acknowledging that one's philosophy, religious training, and moral standards may influence and color one's thinking and conclusions about rape? Should a wide variety of opinion on that matter be tolerated? Or would the Court simply state that rape is unacceptable in a moral society regardless of how one's philosophy may color one's thinking?

That the Court recognized the can of worms it was opening was no consolation. Attempting to pacify the response through patronizing language did nothing to soften the blow. Instead it served to illuminate the lack of any factual basis underlying the decision.

Nevertheless, once the Court had reduced the unborn to the level of unmeaningful potentialities by sheer proclamation, no state, it would seem, was at liberty to challenge the Court's judgment. As John Noonan writes:

> Personhood was a question not of fact, but of fiat, and only the Court's fiat counted. (Noonan, 17)

At this point one might legitimately question whether the Supreme Court of the United States actually possesses the authority to consign any group of human beings to an unmeaningful subhuman, nonperson level. Did the Court actually hold the power to define who was or was not a person? Would the framers of either the Constitution or the Fourteenth Amendment have approved of such actions by a nonelected, elite group of privileged individuals?

Dr. Jefferson:

> They went to the U.S. Supreme Court to force their views on us because they couldn't win them in the bodies where the will of the people is manifest. That's why they had to go to the U.S. Supreme Court, that branch of the government that does not derive its just powers from the consent of the governed. That was the only way they could get it.

John Noonan sums up the implications of the *Roe* majority opinion as follows:

> In the matter of abortion the words of the Constitution did not change, but on January 22nd, 1973, its meaning did. On that date Justice Harry Blackmun found in the Ninth Amendment's reservation of power to the People or in the Fourteenth Amendment's reference to liberty—he was not entirely sure which—a liberty to consent to an abortion. On that date the Constitution came to mean that abortion was an American freedom. (Noonan, 9)

Even pro-choice writers like Connie Paige have conceded the point:

> [Blackmun] had spelled out conditions under which abortion was and was not legal—essentially drafting law rather than delivering an opinion on it. (Connie Paige, *The Right to Lifers, Who They Are, How They Operate, Where They Get Their Money*, New York: Summit Books, 1983, 46, hereafter "Paige")

Paige then quotes former Watergate prosecutor Archibald Cox as saying:

> The failure to confront the issue in principled terms leaves the opinion to read like a set of hospital rules and regulations. ... Neither historian, nor layman, nor lawyer will be persuaded that all the prescriptions of Justice Blackmun are part of the Constitution. (Archibald Cox, *The Role of The Supreme Court In American Government*, Oxford University Press, 1976, as quoted in Paige, 113–4)

Though the majority of the justices agreed with Blackmun, Weddington, and pro-choice ideology in general, Justices Rehnquist and White both dissented. Justice Rehnquist's dissent was fairly short and centered around the idea that the right of "privacy" did not extend to a woman's decision to terminate a pregnancy since a legal abortion was not a private event.

Justice White's dissenting opinion eloquently articulated the mounting opposition to legalized abortion. White cut through the secondary issues and focused on the heart of the matter, pointing out that, minus the exceptions often argued, *Roe* essentially dealt with pregnancies that pose no danger whatsoever to the life or health of the mother.

> With all due respect, I dissent. I find nothing in the language or history of the Constitution to support the Court's judgment. The Court simply fashions and announces a new constitutional right for pregnant mothers and, with scarcely any reason or authority for its action, invests that right with sufficient substance to override most existing state abortion statutes.
>
> ... The Court apparently values the convenience of the pregnant mother more than the continued existence and development of the life or potential life which she carries.
>
> ... In a sensitive area such as this, involving as it does, issues over which reasonable men may easily and heatedly differ, I cannot accept the Court's exercise of its clear power of choice by interposing a constitutional barrier to state efforts to protect human life and by investing mothers and doctors with the constitutionally protected right to exterminate it. (*RvW*, 410 U.S., Justice Byron White, Dissenting Opinion, 171–7)

White does an excellent job summing up the pro-life position on *Roe*. Even in 1973 many professionals in the medical and scientific communities held that human life, personhood included, begins at conception. But even if they were to concede to the pro-choice position that *personhood might not begin at conception*, White pointed out, the court was still morally irresponsible to say that abortion on demand is acceptable all the way through pregnancy since the Court fully acknowledged that it was not able to empirically determine at what point human life is present and when it isn't.

For the Supreme Court to present such a thesis based on complete ignorance, fully acknowledging the possibility, indeed even the likelihood that it could be wrong, and then fashion a constitutional right where none had existed before based solely on its own admitted ignorance, according to White, scientists, doctors, and millions in the general public, was a gross abuse of power. Nevertheless, *Roe* has managed to stand, and has even become the symbolic pillar of the feminist movement, despite many challenges, for four decades and counting.

Dr. Mildred Jefferson:

> Sarah Weddington is a very impressive looking gal and standing before the court those seven men who signed the majority opinion would have given her anything she asked for. And I think in a later discussion by Mr. Justice Blackmun he admitted as much. *Women were asking for it, so we just gave them what they wanted.* He had a different explanation at a different time, but I think that one came from his heart.
>
> The basic problem is that she set a line that enabled the court to follow and come up with what I have referred to before: they have not accepted the case where they addressed the matter of whether the unborn child was a full legal person in the meaning of the Fifth and Fourteenth Amendments. And just as they took her line of argument without addressing the key issue, they have bypassed it.
>
> But in subsequent cases and I think it was *Webster* July 3, 1989—in the *Webster* case where there is no majority opinion, I think that Chief Justice Rehnquist has pointed a direction for us to get *Roe* reversed. I do not believe *Roe* is going to be reversed on an abortion restriction case. I believe it will be reversed on an unborn child protection case. And Chief Justice Rehnquist's opinion—in his consensus opinion in that case—he holds that the state has a compelling interest in protecting the life of the unborn child.
>
> And this long after July 3rd, '89 we have not litigated the meaning or boundary of that Rehnquist opinion. And I think that is what is going to give us the key to getting the unborn child into consideration by the Court and to getting the unborn child defined as a full legal person in terms of protecting his life and his right to live long enough to be born.

CHAPTER 24

Photographs and Heartbeats

The pro-life slogan, "Abortion stops a beating heart," is incontrovertibly true.
—NAOMI WOLF

H uman development is not an unknown area of medical science studied in secret and shrouded in mystery. On the contrary, we know more about human development in the womb than ever before.

The use of ultrasound has revolutionized the study of fetal development even since *Roe*, giving us an open window to the womb. The "well-known facts of fetal development" are, of course, well known among scientists and doctors. Doctors can and do routinely treat the unborn child as a patient—a human patient—diagnosing potential developmental problems and even correcting them through surgery before birth.

The fact that surgeries are now performed on the fetus in the womb has brought a new moral dilemma to the defenders of the abortion liberty. The paradox lies in the fact that the supporters of choice insist that the human fetus in the womb is not a person, not a living human being and—in short—not an unborn baby. Fetal surgery is challenging that idea.

Dr. James Thorp is a specialist in the area of perinatology. A board-certified maternal-fetal medicine physician, Dr. Thorp has a special interest in high-risk obstetrics, prenatal diagnosis, and ultrasound. His enthusiasm for prenatal care and the accompanying insights into prenatal life quickly became apparent during our interview in 2006.

Dr. Thorp:

There's a lot of exciting work and investigation right now into the fetus and treatment of the fetus. Much of the closed procedures that

I've done are either fetal blood sampling, in other words inserting a needle into the fetus to obtain blood and then transfusing the fetus if necessary. That's the vast majority of procedures I've done inside the womb. Other procedures would be placing stents or shunts to relieve obstruction whether that's in the chest cavity—we used to do those in the brain cavities; we don't do those anymore. We still do them in the bladder to save kidneys inside the womb; so those are typically closed fetal surgeries.

These cases present a challenge to the pro-choice community since they are always performed on a *wanted* fetus whose mother most certainly views him or her as her baby. Furthermore, they emphasize the fact that the fetus is treated as a separate, individual patient. An appendectomy, for example, is a surgical procedure in which the patient's appendix is removed for the benefit of the patient. However, in fetal surgery, while the mother is certainly an important part of the operation, the goal of the surgery is to access and treat the body of the fetus for its own benefit as an individual person. What was science fiction in the early 1970s is now everyday fact.

Dr. Thorp:

There are a number of investigators around the world and in the United States that are doing some real exciting open surgeries. And there are physicians in the Boston area and also physicians in Florida in the St. Petersburg area and Tampa area that are actually operating on fetal hearts in the womb. And this is very, very exciting to me. There are some syndromes in which the aortic valve—and if you remember the heart, there's four chambers and there's two upper chambers, the atrium and the two lower chambers, the ventricles. The ventricles send their blood out to the major arteries, the right side: the pulmonary artery; the left side, the left ventricle: the aorta.

Those valves between the ventricles and the great arteries, we call them semi-lunar valves, and if those valves, for example, the aortic valve between the ascending aorta and the left ventricle; if that's obstructed that will cause the left side of the heart to not develop: the so-called "hypoplastic left heart." And if that can be repaired in the womb at 22 to 23 weeks it may cause the left ventricle to grow normally. And in fact this is now being done. And it has been done in other parts of the world but also here in the United States in Tampa, St. Petersburg, and also in Boston. There's several cases that have been done successfully. And that's just fascinating.

Dr. Ruben Quintero has done a lot of laser surgery inside the womb where he can actually take a very small caliber scope, put it in a bladder and actually fix the bladder outlet obstruction so that the baby can actually then urinate inside the womb, which is where all the amniotic fluid comes from, and save the kidneys, so the kidneys will develop. And certainly Dr. Quintero and others around the country have several cases where that's been done successfully.

Several doctors, two primarily, Dr. Julian Delia up north and Dr. Rubin Quintero have treated the complication called "twin-twin transfusion syndrome" with laser therapy inside the womb. In other words, this is a complication where twins will be connected at the level of the placenta by blood vessels, and if it's severe both fetuses will end up dying. If it's less severe both babies may be born premature and be very impaired. Well, Dr. Quintero and Dr. Delia can go in there with a laparoscope and a laser and actually block the vessels that are abnormally connected between the two fetuses and repair them *in utero* and have the pregnancy go on to near term and have two perfectly normal babies.

A current procedure performed for the benefit of the unborn child as a patient is corrective surgery for spina bifida. Spina bifida is a paralyzing birth defect that results when the spinal cord fails to fully close in the early stages of pregnancy. If the baby survives, spina bifida often leaves debilitating defects including accumulation of fluid in the brain and a number of other negative conditions.

Dr. Thorp:

> Some of the open surgeries that have been performed and are still investigational, probably the most significant is that of "open neural tube defect." Open neural tube defect is an embryologic maldevelopment of the spinal column, in the spinal cord, where the spinal canal is open and the spinal cord and spinal nerves are exposed to the noxious stimuli in the amniotic fluid which results in damage, nerve damage.
>
> And these groups of neural tube defects can range anywhere from

very mild to very severe. But what some investigators have performed is opening the womb up at 22 or 23 weeks, exposing the defect in the spine, and repairing it, closing it. And the alleged benefit of that is that, number one, if you close the spine up that that will protect the nerves from the damage that occurs with continued exposure to the amniotic fluid and allow better function after birth.

And there are currently—and much credit to the National Institute of Health in our government—that they have funded a huge, randomized, controlled, prospective trial called the MOMS trial. And they are randomizing *in utero* surgery versus surgery after birth, so if a mother is found to have a neural tube defect at 18 to 20 weeks and are interested in participating in this trial then they will be randomized by the trial center to either have their baby fixed in the womb or after birth.

Dr. Joseph Bruner of Vanderbilt University in Nashville, Tennessee, has performed several successful corrective surgeries for spina bifida babies while still in the mother's womb. Some of these surgeries have been captured on film.

One particular photo by freelance photojournalist Michael Clancy generated some controversy when it showed the baby, in this case 21-week-old Samuel Armas, grasping the finger of the physician, Dr. Joseph Bruner.

I interviewed Clancy in 2006, and he explained the incredible story behind the amazing photograph that completely changed his life.

Michael Clancy:

August the 16th, 1999, I got a call from *USA Today* to photograph the surgery of Samuel. And I had shot—I think one reporter figured it out to be a frame every 15 seconds—I shot nine rolls in an hour and 13 minutes. I kept thinking, *This is so graphic. What is USA Today going to use from this surgery?* And all of a sudden the uterus shook and the doctors had pretty much finished the procedure and nobody was near the uterus. And, you know, obviously something happened that wasn't supposed to. And this little fist came flying out! And I absolutely nailed the shot. I got four frames off. I had my camera set at 1/60th of a second; top-of-the-line Canon EOS camera, and it will fire eight frames per second. I fired three of those four frames in less than half a second. This happened so fast.

At the time, even Clancy did not realize just how much of a stir his photo would create. Michael Clancy continues:

> And the frame that everyone knows is the third in the motor drive sequence. But the wild thing was I was grabbed from behind in an attempt to stop me from getting a picture. A nurse who had been standing behind me the whole time carried me two or three steps and said, "You can get a better shot from over here," in a real strained voice because I'm a big guy.
>
> There were 15 people surrounding that surgery, and you know we were all crowded to get a spot and I was told I could not move for the entire procedure. You know, you cannot move in any direction. And Robert Davis was there, sent from *USA Today*. He flew in. I could hear him talking to a medical tech. And he had no idea what happened. The nurse next to me didn't see it. She said, "What happened?" I said, "The child reached out," and she said, "They do that all the time." Those words just haunt me.

Due to the rigid standards of *USA Today* who had hired Clancy, his photo has been accepted worldwide as authentic. But the controversy occurred when Dr. Bruner later made comments to the effect that the baby did not grasp his finger or even move the arm out of the womb on his own since he was under anesthesia at the time.

Michael Clancy:

> When Samuel reached out and I got those pictures, so much happened within the next, like, five minutes. The surgery was over. We all went into the hallway: John Howser, Dr. Bruner, and I. And we met with Alex Armas. He's the father. And he was just on pins and needles waiting to see what Dr. Bruner had to say. And Bruner looked at me as he said to Alex Armas, "I had a little fun with the photographer. I posed a picture for him." And I know that my face must've turned white and my jaw hit the floor, and I knew then that they were going to deny that it ever happened.

The photo clearly shows the baby's arm outside the mother's womb. Dr. Bruner acknowledges that he then instinctively offered his finger for the baby to hold. And that of course is when Clancy snapped a series of photos. So the controversy centers around whether the baby actually moved his arm out of the uterus under his own power, as the photographer claims, or whether the doctor actually pulled the baby's arm out, as the doctor claims.

Michael Clancy:

> You know, I mean, this is a career-ending situation for a journalist. It went to press saying that the child reached out on his own. And then, of course, the doctor had three months and then he was able to give a statement. But three months passed with my cutline. And the whole [staff of the] *Tennessean* was saying, "You're going to get a Pulitzer Prize. Something's wrong if you don't." Then the doctor got a chance and he told the *Tennessean* reporter all kinds of things. He said, "Depending upon your political point of view this is either a child reaching from his mother's womb and taking the hand of a human being, or it's me pulling the hand out and posing the picture." And that about ended my career. Every editor at the *Tennessean* came to me and said, "What's going on here, what's the story?"

While speculation as to what actually occurred is probably pointless, it is interesting to note that the photos definitively show the baby's hand in the position a baby takes while holding the finger of an adult. Clancy himself says he saw and captured on film the point where the baby "squeezed" the doctor's finger. And Clancy indeed offers a series of photos on his website that present a compelling case for a conscious unborn baby grasping a doctor's finger. Clancy adds, "*USA Today* has told the story three or four times, and they just leave it up to your interpretation. They don't say one way or another."

But there may be an additional factor driving the discrepancy between Clancy's version of events and the hospital's version. The fear of lawsuits is typically a powerful motivator. And in the medical profession, the question of proper medical practice is always a sensitive issue.

Michael Clancy:

> Obviously how much anesthesia you give an unborn child through his mother—Samuel got nothing extra. He was not anesthetized. They did not give him anything special; it was given to his mother. It came through the umbilical cord, and yeah, Samuel

wasn't thrashing around during most of the surgery, but he did wake up. He came out of it too soon. And these are questions that these doctors don't want to answer. How much do you give to keep these children right on the brink of, you know, being anesthetized?

And where the possibility of one lawsuit exists, the threat of others is often present. Michael Clancy continues:

> You know, I got an e-mail from the head of anesthesiology at Vanderbilt, Fetal Surgery Department, threatening me to change the story on my website to reflect that Samuel was under anesthesia and could not have reached out, or I would suffer the wrath of the Vanderbilt law team. I can't go through something like that. I don't have any money! (laughs) I'm poor! And I went to a bunch of attorneys because when—Dr. Bruner pretty much ended my career when he said different things than I said and all of my editors came to me. You know what? I applied for jobs all over the country. Photo editors knew all about the controversy behind the picture. "What really happened?" That's what they would say. "What really happened?" You know, so. . . . And it's a great story; it's just taken a long time for the truth to come out.

Complicating matters is the fact that *Life* magazine had wanted a similar set of photos from the same doctor for an upcoming edition, but the photos Clancy had shot for *USA Today* had the potential to scoop those plans. Michael Clancy:

> The real key to all this is the editors at *Life* magazine. I went through a four-day negotiation with them in buying all rights to the photo. And the second day they asked me what speed of film it was, and I told them 800. And that meant that they were actually considering using it. They wanted to know what the quality was. Well, it wasn't *Life* magazine quality. The picture that—the Max Hellwig shot—the quality is *Life* magazine quality. It's incredible but it's a posed photo.
>
> And, you know, I just thought they would react differently when I called them to tell them about my picture. But they got furious and they wanted to fight. And they tried—the first thing they said was, you know, "We want to buy all rights to the photo. We want to buy it to kill it." I said, "Bad choice of words."

And the *Life* magazine people do not agree with how I am allowing this photo to be used. And so it was old news by the time their issue came out. *Life* magazine was so upset with Vanderbilt for allowing this information to be leaked to me that they were, you know, that this was their upcoming cover, and I called *Life* magazine and kind of jumped right into a battle because I wanted them to use the real picture, not a posed one. This is real and theirs is posed. And I told them that I'd make it old news by the time you went to press with yours. That's exactly what I did when they said they wanted to buy it to kill it. I went to war against them. I found a New York picture agency to aggressively market this photograph overseas. And they went to *VSD* magazine in France, and it hit the October issue with a four-page layout.

After having scooped the cover of the millennium edition of *Life* magazine, the photo continued to generate controversy.

Michael Clancy:

But *Life* magazine pulled their stuff when Matt Drudge was pulled off of his show for trying to show the picture. I told my agent, I said, "No tabloids. I don't want this picture to be mocked and laughed at in a tabloid." And so one day he calls me and says the *National Enquirer* wants this picture. And I said, "Will they use it respectfully?" And he promised me they would. And the November '99 issue of the *National Enquirer* was held up by Matt Drudge on his Fox TV show and the censor said, "No, you can't show it." And he walked off the stage and that was the end of the show.

As for Clancy, the experience completely changed his views on abortion. Clancy now describes himself as pro-life and hopes his photo will change hearts in the same way Samuel Armas reached out to capture his.

Michael Clancy:

My parents are alcoholics, and I didn't really ever want to have children. It just seemed like too difficult a task, and so I didn't want kids of my own. And I'd really never made up my mind [about abortion], you know, I feel bad for a pregnant woman that's been left alone.

So that was my situation before, but once I saw Samuel reach out like that and realized that I had just taken a picture that was probably one of the most powerful pro-life icons that is available, and I started thinking about it, "If I do not do the right thing, I will not be able to live with myself." And I'm just trying to do the right thing. And I'm a journalist and that's what I do. I tell stories with pictures. Like I said, my parents were alcoholics. I ran away from home at 16 years old. I'm nobody and I got a miracle picture. The only way the academic community will ever acknowledge this is if somebody comes forward and gives it credibility. It's the earliest interaction ever recorded; proof that at 21 weeks in utero the child is a reactive human being. To me it's the most important evidence that we've got.

Both Michael Clancy and Dr. Thorp were called upon to testify to Congress in 2003.

Michael Clancy:

Now I know the Lacy-Conner law was a huge thing, and that's what prompted *Newsweek* to run the update on Samuel. And the cover was—of the June *Newsweek*—"Does a Fetus Have Rights?" Because we testified September 26, four months later, after Senator Brownback saw it on the floor of the Senate. That's where he saw it. And actually he held it up in front of [pro-choice] Barbara Boxer and asked her, you know, how can you explain this child reaching out like this, and she said she wouldn't address that question. But I testified before the Senate September 26, 2003, and Samuel was at the table with me along with Dr. Thorp and Samuel's parents. And, you know, just to be in the room with Samuel, you know, the kid's my hero!

And then weeks after that I got a call from the White House inviting me to the signing of the ban on partial-birth [abortion]. And I didn't erase it off my caller ID for a couple months either! And I just hope that this story gets out there and this kid gets the credit he deserves.

Dr. Thorp:

One point that I tried to make in front of the Senate was that, regardless of what laws are enacted in the states or what the Senate would decide or what the Congress would decide or what the

President would decide, the very fact that medicine and physicians themselves have initiated these treatments essentially personifies a fetus and gives the fetus the rights of a human child. The more that we treat the fetus inside the womb, the more we are treating it like a child.

So whatever anybody else decides, I think our medical community and my colleagues and myself—regardless of their persuasion, regardless of whether they are pro-choice or pro-life or agnostic or deistic—the very fact that they've spent significant proportions of their careers treating a fetus in the womb makes a statement that this fetus is a patient, is a child.

During that session Sen. Brownback observed that "there is little debate about whether the child in utero is alive; the debate is over whether or not the child is a life worthy of protection."

Michael Clancy:

And then a woman—was she head of NARAL? I can't remember who it was for sure, but she said images such as the picture of Samuel reaching out is what is going to turn this back into a culture of life.

It's said that a photograph is worth a thousand words. This one photograph of an unborn child reaching from his world into ours has already demonstrated the power not only to change hospital policies and scoop a major magazine, but even more importantly, to challenge the basic assumption of the entire pro-choice movement that a fetus and a baby are completely different things.

Clancy sums it up this way:

You know, I just think that this child is a hero. This child changed the cover of *Life* magazine, the act of an unborn child. People have to acknowledge he is a hero because he acted. This child has saved children's lives. But I really believe that this is a very important moment, and I've got to just keep fighting to tell this crazy story.

Typical of any discussion involving abortion, it's interesting to note how the controversy over this photo centers around a peripheral issue: whether or not a sedated unborn baby actually had the power to do what the photo shows him doing. Of course, only those present in the operating room know for sure whether Samuel himself or Dr. Bruner removed the arm from the womb. Only the doctor knows for sure the level of grip Samuel applied but in any case, the unavoidable truth is that every day, nonanaesthetized babies in the womb are constantly moving—just ask any expectant mother! The real objection to these photos is not whether the baby grasped or did not grasp. The real objection is that the photos graphically show what we already instinctively know anyway—that a fetus in the womb only halfway through pregnancy has a perfectly formed arm, hand, and fingers that look amazingly human and knows how to use them.

Even from the beginning, pro-choice advocates have fought against the use of photographic evidence demonstrating the humanity of the unborn child. On page 177 of her book, Sarah Weddington writes:

> Anti-abortionists began using words and images in new ways, emphasizing graphic depictions of what they claimed was the developing fetus, even playing tapes of what was said to be the heartbeat of a fetus. Experts questioned the accuracy and validity of this "evidence," but reason could not erase the impact of those tactics. (Weddington, 177)

So while pro-choice *arguments* are reasonable for Sarah Weddington, pro-life *evidence*, even photographic or audible evidence of a fetus in the womb or the results of an abortion, is, for her, questionable at best. Its interesting that Weddington fails to identify any of the generic "experts" she cites, nor does she find it necessary to offer any supporting statements from these unnamed "authorities." Rather she simply asserts it as unverifiable fact.

Another noteworthy absence from Weddington's assertion is any attempt on her part to set the record straight. If the "graphic depictions" that pro-life proponents "claimed was the developing fetus" were not really images of a developing fetus, then why not show actual counterevidence and point out the discrepancies? The reason, of course, is that the images were accurate, and any attempt to counter them would be doomed to failure. Of particular, almost comical irony is her assertion that "reason could not erase the impact of those tactics." More accurately, Weddington might as well simply admit that pro-choice propaganda could not erase the truth depicted in the images. As Randy Alcorn pointed out in our discussion, the unreasonable approach is the one that attempts to deny reality:

> How can I say this graciously? I mean that's just false. When you talk about experts questioning the accuracy and validity of this

evidence, I will never forget standing at a pro-life gathering where I had a picture—blown up pictures of preborn children at different stages of development. And so here's the first trimester, here is the child at eight weeks, here's the child at ten weeks sucking his thumb, and then here's a picture of the second trimester, third trimester, and all that.

Now, I had a young woman come up to me, a graduate student at Portland State University, and she came up and she looked at those and she said, "Do you think you're going to fool anyone with this trick photography?" Well these photographs, the *same* photographs, are in Harvard University Medical School textbooks. They're in *Life* magazine, in Lennart Nilsson's photograph. They're in all of these different places where they are published, and I looked at her and I said, "You're saying that this isn't real?!" And she said, "Well no, you've made that up. Some artist has done this and you've just rearranged things and made it look like this is a baby." And I said, "You know what you're saying is, 'This is clearly a child.' And so you're admitting that this is a child, and what you're saying is, 'Therefore it can't be real because I'm not going to choose to believe that these are real babies.'"

And, in fact, if you look on the back of the *Why Pro-life* book, there's a 3-D ultrasound of the baby just 21 weeks after conception, halfway through the pregnancy, in the middle of the second trimester. And here it's just very clear, you've got the child rubbing his right eye with his right hand. You have a cheek that's very pronounced; you've got the eye, you've got, count 'em, the five fingers of the left hand. You've got . . . I mean the photographic evidence is just incontrovertible! No wonder Sarah Weddington is uncomfortable with it! But to deny that it's real is silly! I mean it's not one of these debatable things in which I take a different position than Sarah Weddington; it's that she is being ridiculous.

It seems unreasonable to conclude that an intelligent attorney like Sarah Weddington could be completely oblivious to the fact that a human fetus actually has a heartbeat or is possibly dumbfounded that a human heartbeat could be audibly recorded while still in the womb.

Why then does Weddington question that twenty-first-century medical science has the ability to obtain recordings of the human heartbeat before birth? The audio production of this work includes an audio recording of an actual fetal heartbeat, which, nowadays, are readily available. As Randy Alcorn points out, it is the same heart that will continue beating until the death of the individual:

It's an indisputable scientific fact that each and every surgical abortion in America stops a beating heart and stops already measurable brain waves. (Alcorn, 30)

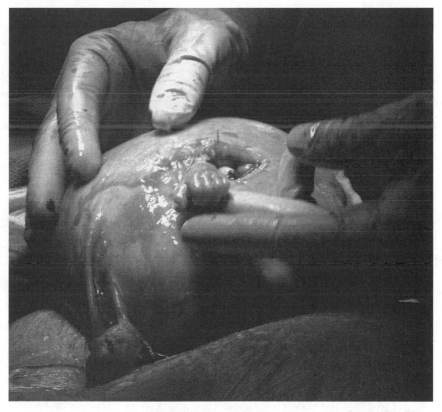

Photo by Michael Clancy

CHAPTER 25

A Spoonful of Gruesome

Human kind cannot bear much reality.
—T.S. ELIOT

O n page 249 in her book Sarah Weddington writes:

> [Abortion] opponents describe abortion procedures in an outrageously gruesome manner, often dwelling on techniques used only in extraordinary circumstances. (Weddington, 249)

But pro-life proponents wonder how a procedure that either fatally poisons, severs, dismembers, or pulverizes an unborn fetus *could* be described in *any* detail *without* being gruesome? As Dr. Mildred Jefferson explains, from the perspective of the unborn, abortion is gruesome.

Dr. Jefferson:

> You cannot discuss the science, the actual steps, without it sounding gruesome because it's a gruesome procedure. When you are going to introduce a cannula into the womb, the cervix, you've got to dilate the cervix because it's not going to be normally open. And that is a procedure that requires gradually increasing gentle force. When you remove the uterine contents, at that point where the little skull is beginning to be a little bit stiffer, where the cartilage is being infiltrated with calcium, it's not going to break up as easily, so that when you speak of suction aspiration in the first 6 to 8 weeks, then you're homogenizing the small body to mush when you use the

suction catheter. It's abhorrent but it's factual. You can pretend it's not happening that way but that doesn't deny the reality.

And if it's a little bit later and that little cartilaginous skeleton which is now getting cartilage in it so that it's harder, if it doesn't break up, the parts of the unbroken up skull and fragments of these bones have to be removed with the surgical instruments. And that is a reality.

When someone speaks of—in the saline or salting-out abortion—of that shudder, that convulsion when that strong salt solution hits the baby's skin, the operator on the end of a needle at the end of the tubing feels that shudder. The mother feels that shudder. That's not being gruesome or exaggerating; that is a fact. And to try to *deny* that is denying informed consent to the person who's undergoing the procedure and will have to live with that reality the rest of her life.

And with the abortion hysterotomy you can't quite hide it as well because the woman is left with a scar on her abdomen and a scar on her uterus and who knows what scars on her heart and soul.

A conspicuous absence in both oral arguments in *Roe v. Wade* as well as Weddington's book, is *any* description, gruesome or not, of any of the various techniques used by abortionists. Weddington mentions the D and C procedure in her book by name, dilation and curettage, when describing her own abortion in 1967. The Mexican doctor explains the D and C procedure to Weddington, but she fails to pass that information on to her readers.

Randy Alcorn:

She's simply just trying to pretend that abortion is okay. She has tremendous vested interest in it, and if you'd just ask her exactly what happens in an abortion I don't know what her response would be, but it might be something like, "it is the removal of unwanted tissue," or whatever she would say. Well that's all just semantics to take away from the fact that a little child with its own distinct DNA, never before reproduced, never again to be duplicated, that unique human being who has within himself or herself all that's necessary to become the full child, full adult that that person is going to develop into, is destroyed in an abortion. That's just a fact and Sarah Weddington doesn't want to believe that, obviously, but regardless, it's true.

The tactic of alleging that pro-life proponents "describe abortion procedures in an outrageously gruesome manner, often dwelling on techniques used only in extraordinary circumstances" is not unique to Sarah Weddington. It's a common grumble among those wishing to retain the unrestricted liberty to terminate the lives of fetuses. In the case of late-term abortions, where the fetus is irrefutably unappendix-like, complaints about gruesome descriptions are rarely attempted since any attention to detail is counter-productive. In the spirit of holocaust deniers, abortion advocates of the early 2000s apparently determined it was safer to portray abortions done late in pregnancy as something occurring only in the overactive imaginations of pro-life proponents rather than debate the level of gruesomeness.

Commenting on the controversy surrounding efforts in the late 1990s to ban what came to be known as "partial-birth abortion," provocative pro-life author Ann Coulter noted that pro-abortion proponents, in a *60 Minutes* news story, simply denied the existence of the procedure. After quoting the dialogue of an interview with late-term abortionist Dr. Warren Hern, who flatly states that "there's no such thing," Coulter reports that:

> *60 Minutes* also sought to assure viewers that despite all the hullabaloo about partial birth abortion—whatever the hell that is—such abortions are extremely rare, performed only in extenuating circumstances. You know, like pregnancy. Consider the lunacy of both denying that "partial birth abortions" exist and then discussing the frequency of that nonexistent procedure. [Ed] Bradley interviewed two women who had had partial birth abortions on horribly deformed babies who could not have lived outside the womb.
>
> One woman told Bradley, "In terms of misinformation, the biggest one is that they are—there are thousands and thousands of these abortions being done in the third trimester on normal babies with healthy mothers carrying normal babies. Well if that's the case, where are they?"
>
> Yes indeed! Why aren't more of those dead babies speaking up? (Ann Coulter, *Godless*, New York: Three Rivers Press, Random House, 2007, 81, hereafter "Coulter")

Coulter's characterization of the pro-abortion response as "lunacy" is spot on. PBA was a no-win scenario for pro-choice advocates since establishing that fetuses at 24 weeks are something radically different from babies is difficult, to say the least. But, as Coulter notes, the art of reality dodging while reporting statistics of an allegedly nonexistent procedure (banned as of 2007) was just getting underway:

> Bolstering the claim that partial-birth abortions are extremely rare, [60 Minutes host Ed] Bradley insisted, "Of the one and a half million abortions performed every year, only a tiny percentage, somewhere between 600 and 1,000 are performed in the third trimester of pregnancy." To talk only about how many abortions are performed in the "third trimester" is just another way of lying about abortion. It is like talking about only the number of partial birth abortions performed by left-handed abortionists with hairy moles on their faces. The third trimester begins at 26 weeks. Babies can take a breath outside the womb at around 19 weeks. At 14 weeks, they have eyes, ears, hair, toes, fingers, and fingernails. I think what repels most people about partial birth abortions . . . is the fact that that baby is having its brains suctioned out.
>
> A few months after Bradley assured viewers that the nonexistent partial birth abortion occurs only about 600 to 1,000 times per year, the *Record* (Bergen, New Jersey) reported that a single abortion clinic in Englewood, New Jersey, performs about 1,500 partial birth abortions every year on babies 20 to 24 weeks old. (Coulter, 81)

That "there's no such thing" as partial-birth abortion likely came as a surprise to the man who had invented it. Complaints about how opponents of abortion describe abortion tend to lose their punch when the descriptions come from the doctors themselves:

> With a lower [fetal] extremity in the vagina, the surgeon uses his fingers to deliver the opposite lower extremity, then the torso, the shoulders and the upper extremities. The skull lodges at the internal cervical os [the opening to the uterus]. Usually there is not enough dilation for it to pass through. The fetus is oriented dorsum or spine up. At this point, the right-handed surgeon slides the fingers of the left hand along the back of the fetus and "hooks" the shoulders of the fetus with the index and ring fingers (palm down). . . . [T]he surgeon takes a pair of blunt curved Metzenbaum scissors in the right hand.

He carefully advances the tip, curved down, along the spine and under his middle finger until he feels it contact the base of the skull under the tip of his middle finger. . . . [T]he surgeon then forces the scissors into the base of the skull or into the foramen magnum. Having safely entered the skull, he spreads the scissors to enlarge the opening. The surgeon removes the scissors and introduces a suction catheter into this hole and evacuates the skull contents. ("Dilation and Extraction for Late Second Trimester Abortion," by Martin Haskell, M.D., National Abortion Federation, 1992, as quoted in: Testimony of Douglas Johnson Legislative Director, National Right to Life Committee on the Partial-Birth Abortion Ban Act [H.R. 929, S. 6] at a Joint Hearing Before the U.S. Senate Judiciary Committee and The Constitution Subcommittee of the U.S. House Judiciary Committee, March 11, 1997, http://www.nrlc.org/abortion/pba/ test.html)

In addition to innovating the "procedure," one might suspect that Dr. Martin Haskell just might have a fairly good idea of how to describe it given the fact that he performed well over a thousand of them.

The controversy over what to call this—by any account, *gruesome*— procedure was a sideshow designed to distract attention away from what actually occurs in the procedure itself—sort of like debating whether to call Auschwitz an extermination or concentration camp.

The difficulty for those attempting to defend abortion in light of what actually occurred in partial-birth abortions was that no one needed to manufacture or enhance "gruesomeness" when the doctor's own uncensored words were sufficiently chilling. Relying on the layman-level language of the doctor's assistant made matters worse. According to Brenda Pratt Shafer, a registered nurse who accompanied Dr. Haskell as he performed partial-birth abortions in 1993, an example of one of those abortions involved "a baby boy" at 26 and a half weeks (over six months) who was alive and moving as the abortionist:

> . . . delivered the baby's body and the arms—everything but the head. The doctor kept the baby's head just inside the uterus. The baby's little fingers were clasping and unclasping, and his feet were kicking. Then the doctor stuck the scissors through the back of his head, and

the baby's arms jerked out in a flinch, a startle reaction, like a baby does when he thinks that he might fall. The doctor opened up the scissors, stuck a high-powered suction tube into the opening and sucked the baby's brains out. Now the baby was completely limp. ("Effects of Anesthesia During a Partial-Birth Abortion," Hearing Before the Subcommittee on the Constitution of the House Judiciary Committee, March 21, 1996, Serial No. 73)

One hardly needs pictures to enhance grisliness in light of the testimony of those onsite as this "procedure" went down. Apparently, the details of partial-birth abortion were sufficiently appalling to make a notable impression on the United States Supreme Court, which banned the procedure in its April 2007 *Gonzalez v. Carhart* decision.*

Losing the battle over partial-birth abortion was not good news for abortion advocates as it signaled a potential shift in abortion policy coming from both Congress and the United States Supreme Court. Once you start banning abortions because you think it might be a bit too "gruesome" for the fetus, you've revealed an "emotional" attachment which can only end in compassion for embryos.

Abortion advocates vociferously cry foul because the ban allows for no exceptions, not even to save the life of the mother. But this is also a sideshow. Partial-birth abortion is *never* needed to save the life of the mother. Those who so advocate demonstrate either a willingness to deceive or an "I'll naively repeat whatever my side says" mentality. The sole purpose of partial-birth abortion is to kill the semi-born child before birth is complete. By the time a partial-birth abortion is performed, the child is viable, meaning he or she can live outside the womb, and is nearly delivered. The mother can therefore be free of the unwanted pregnancy *without* killing the child. The child is killed only because the mother prefers a dead child over choice: as in the choice of whether to parent or give the child into adoption.

Unfortunately, although the ban is noteworthy and will likely save lives, determined mothers can still find abortionists who are willing to perform late-term abortions for the right price. The net result is that in order to remain legal, late-term abortion procedures must take annoying precautions to ensure they occur within the legal security of the womb—more cumbersome, certainly, for the abortionist, less "gruesome," perhaps, for the assistant, still as deadly for the unborn child.

Footnote:

*For more information behind the conflicting claims regarding partial-birth abortions see American Medical News (the official AMA newspaper) and Cincinnati Medicine, "Shock-tactic Ads Target Late-Term Abortion Procedure," by Diane M. Gianelli, American Medical News, July 5, 1993. Also, "Second Trimester Abortion: An Interview with W. Martin Haskell, M.D.," Cincinnati Medicine, Fall, 1993.

CHAPTER 26

Sweet Little Lies

*We fed the public a line of deceit, dishonesty, a fabrication of statistics
and figures. We succeeded because the time was right and
the news media cooperated. We sensationalized the
effects of illegal abortions, and fabricated polls which
indicated that 85 percent of the public favored unrestricted abortion,
when we knew it was only 5 percent. We unashamedly lied, and
yet our statements were quoted as though they had been written in law.*
—Dr. Bernard Nathanson

During the downtime between the two Roe hearings and fearing that the final outcome of *Roe* might not be favorable to abortion, Sarah Weddington lobbied the Texas legislature in favor of passage of a greatly liberalized abortion law. In her book, *A Question of Choice,* she describes the debates among pro-choice factions about the types of materials to include in their presentations to lawmakers. Some wanted to include photos of women who had died in illegal abortion procedures, while others disagreed. After describing one such photograph, Weddington writes:

> We expected the anti-abortionists to use grotesque and misleading photographs; they usually did. Some on our side felt we should show graphically the problems that resulted when abortion was illegal. Others argued that we would be sinking to the level of the opposition—a level we disdained—if we did the same. We decided to use reason instead of pictures. (Weddington, 78)

Weddington's expressed logic against using photographs that "show graphically the problems that resulted when abortion was illegal" is necessarily shallow. It wasn't "the level" of graphically illustrating a point that pro-choice proponents disdained. Weddington herself had used an admittedly doctored photograph of a "pregnant" Clarence Thomas during his Senate confirmation hearings for admission to the Supreme Court. There was no aversion on her part of "stooping to that level" in order to make a point by using a fake photo. (See Thomas photo in *A Question of Choice* between pages 160–1.) Obviously, what really bothers Weddington and her friends is the *effectiveness* of photographs featuring unborn children and the graphic impact made by photos illustrating the gruesomeness of abortion.

No doubt Weddington and her fellow pro-abortion advocates realized that showing photographs of botched abortions would be counterproductive to their agenda. In the first place, no one disputes that a pregnant woman is a living human being. In the second place, no one disputes that women can be and sometimes are physically harmed or even killed by abortion—whether legal or not. Certainly, no pro-life advocate disputes the emotional harm done by abortion not only to pregnant women but to those who love them as well. By revealing photographs that "show graphically the problems that resulted when abortion was illegal," Weddington would simply be illustrating the evils of abortion itself. Such photographs were not likely to have the desired effect. That is, after exposure to photos of women who had died as a result of abortion, the public would not be likely to conclude that the underlying problem was that abortion was not common enough or that giving women the freedom to choose legal abortion would solve the "problems that resulted when abortion was illegal." On the contrary, upon seeing such graphic photos, the public might actually desire even stricter regulations for access to and tighter regulations of legal abortion—something Weddington would have viewed as counterproductive. This is the likely reason we find no photographs of botched abortion attempts in Weddington's book.

An effective set of photos is used by the government to discourage what has become an almost epidemic use of the drug "meth." It is a simple before-and-after set of photos of meth users (see: www.anti-meth.org/photos2.html) with a tagline asking, "Life on meth, isn't it beautiful?" One can clearly see the negative effects of the drug in the "after" photos. The reaction of nearly all viewers is not to think, *Wow! How terrible! We should legalize meth to solve the problem.* Yet, Weddington and her peers had apparently hoped for just such a reaction to photos that "show graphically the problems that resulted when abortion was illegal." Undoubtedly the decision not to use such photos was reached not because pro-abortion advocates "disdained" the use of photos to make a point, but because they realized that even when the subject of the photo was the pregnant woman rather than the unborn child, the desired point was still likely to be obscured.

Regardless, even granting Weddington's stated logic, one is left to wonder how it could be that (according to Weddington) photographs that illustrated harm to women told the truth about the dangers of *illegal* abortion, while other photographs were "grotesque and misleading" because they exposed the reality of *legal* abortion and featured dead fetuses as their subjects. Weddington seems convinced that any photographs of the unborn child— whether dead or alive—are actually fakes created in pro-life photo labs. Given her own propensity to use doctored photos to promote her agenda, such a conclusion on her part is no great surprise. Still, it stretches credulity to imagine that Weddington is unaware that genuine photographs and even real-time videos of living human beings in the womb are easily obtained in this digital age.

Can anyone doubt that the visual effects of fatal salt poisoning or dismemberment of unborn humans could be anything but gruesome? Would it even be possible to find a picture of an aborted baby that was not shocking? And wouldn't it be misleading to give the impression that the effects of abortion on the intended victims were anything less than grotesque? Contrary to Weddington's assertions, the truth does occasionally hurt. Pro-life advocates like Professor William Brennan are quick to point out that:

Dr. Brennan:

> I find it ludicrous in our visual world where a picture is worth a thousand words, where pictures cut through all the rhetoric and show things at the most basic level, to say that these pictures are offensive or not reasonable I think, really, is irrelevant in many ways. These are the realities that a lot of people are not aware of, and every civil rights movement has used photographs to show the harsh realities of what took place against the victims that they were campaigning to protect.

Dr. Carolyn Gerster:

> We couldn't afford ever, ever, ever to be giving erroneous information; it would destroy our movement. We have to be telling the truth at all times. You know what the baby looks like at a certain age, and you know what must happen with dismemberment of the baby.

Dr. Mildred Jefferson:

> I don't know of any pro-life people from bona fide organizations who have ever produced any misleading or inaccurate photographs. So that's simply creating a propaganda line that can be useful.

If it is true that a fetus is not a baby, and if that alleged truth is as obvious as pro-choice advocates and by extension the United States Supreme Court propose, why, then, is the uproar so great among the pro-choice community when confronted with photographs and videos featuring the developing unborn child? If a fetus is not a baby, and not even a person or a human being, it would seem logical that a picture of an unborn child or, for that matter, even an aborted fetus, would cause no major concern. Could photographs of a removed appendix generate sympathy from the general public for the plight of unwanted appendices? No matter how gruesome the appendectomy is described or illustrated and no matter how sympathetic the language applied to the discarded appendix, it is difficult to envision a public propaganda campaign powerful enough to create an emotional connection in the national conscience between an unwanted appendix and a human baby. Nor is it likely that such a campaign could attract more than a handful of deluded devotees— in stark contrast to the millions of everyday people who believe abortion on demand is morally wrong.

In a revealing analogy, Weddington attempts to make the case that it is the language itself and the method of delivery that gives an unnecessarily gruesome impression of what she apparently feels is actually something else:

> Yet there is no medical procedure that can't be described in a way to make people shudder. If I used the technique of the opponents to describe a tonsillectomy I would say, "The menacing doctor grips a cold steel instrument and pries open the mouth, exposing a column of pink flesh. The doctor then takes an instrument resembling an ice

pick and chips away at the offending mound of tissue until the body reacts in pain. Satisfied with his work, the doctor takes a pliers-like tool and thrusts it into the pink column, and with a cold glint in his eye grabs the bloody mass and jerks it away from the exposed flesh. He carelessly tosses the human tissue aside and goes on to his next patient." Getting one's tonsils removed is a very safe legal procedure, but I'm not sure how many people would want to go through it if they had to read an account like that. (Weddington, 250)

Putting aside the most conspicuous logical flaw for the moment, it is noteworthy that while attempting to present a "menacing" version of a tonsillectomy in what is intended to be an analogous comparison to the way Weddington claims pro-life proponents describe abortions, Weddington fails to present *any* description—accurate or not—of what she believes an acceptable abortion procedure actually entails. Such details are noticeably absent from her book, despite her account of the difficulties she faced in obtaining her own illegal abortion. One would be hard pressed to conclude that such an oversight was purely coincidental. Rather than provide what she believes to be *an accurate description* of what occurs during an abortion, even to the woman, much less the fetus, she chooses instead to present a parody of a tonsillectomy.

Be that as it may, the larger problem in Weddington's analogy is that there is a conspicuous difference between a tonsillectomy and an abortion, regardless of the manner in which either procedure is described. Though tonsils are certainly *part of* a living human, as are fingernails, teeth, toes, etc., they are by no means *the embodiment of* that living human. When one cuts one's toenails in other places, one is not committing suicide. Similarly, removing one's tonsils does not typically end one's life. Certainly, the tissue making up the tonsil dies, but that tissue could never either continue living on its own or become a separate individual human. In fact, a tonsil is indeed "part of a woman's body" as the genetic markers are identical to every other cell in the woman's body. The DNA of the fetus she carries is radically different, and the fetus is indeed the total embodiment of that unique individual.

By stark, and what should be obvious contrast, an induced abortion always ends the life of the individual it targets. If it does not, then it was not a successful abortion. Weddington rightfully describes the discarded tonsil as "human tissue"—a term pro-abortion advocates often apply to a human fetus. But a human fetus is clearly much more than mere "human tissue." Her analogy fails.

But it shouldn't fail if a fetus is something similar to a tonsil. If that were truly the case, then abortion would indeed amount to little more than an appendectomy or a tonsillectomy. The lack of straightforward accounts of what exactly occurs during an induced abortion in pro-choice propaganda is a clue to what we have suspected all along: that abortion is not a public good to be defended on its own merits.

CHAPTER 27

Visualize Womb Peace

To ignore evil is to become an accomplice to it.
—DR. MARTIN LUTHER KING JR.

Photographs of aborted fetuses never fail to elicit passionate rebukes from the pro-abortion community coupled with allegations of "foul play." They are routinely censored from television, magazine, and newspaper reports as being offensive, gruesome, misleading, manipulative, and revolting. If the fetus is not a baby, as pro-abortion proponents insist, then photographs of aborted fetuses or even nonaborted fetuses should make the pro-choice case obvious. Instead, they have the opposite effect.

The reality is that abortion proponents react passionately against the use of prebirth photographs precisely because a fetus looks an awful lot like a baby. In moments of unusual candor, even pro-choice proponents admit as much. Take for example Connie Paige's description in her retelling of the Edelin case: "The fetuses, while unnaturally tiny and obviously immature, still looked like infants" (Paige, 11).

While such admissions from a pro-choice perspective are rare, Paige is simply stating the obvious. Paige seems oblivious to the possibility that the fetuses to which she was referring "still looked like infants" precisely because *they were,* in fact, infants who happened to be located inside a womb.

In an extraordinarily candid manner, pro-choice feminist Naomi Wolf created some controversy among her peers when she made these statements in the October 1996 issue of the *New Republic*:

How can we charge that it is vile and repulsive for pro-lifers to brandish vile and repulsive images if the images are real? To insist that the truth is in poor taste is the very height of hypocrisy. Besides, if these images are often the facts of the matter, and if we then claim that it is offensive for pro-choice women to be confronted by them, then we are making the judgment that women are too inherently weak to face a truth about which they have to make a grave decision. This view of women is unworthy of feminism. (Naomi Wolf, "Our Bodies, Our Souls," *New Republic*, October 16, 1996, 26 [see also: The Ethics of Abortion, Baird/Rosenbaum, 184, hereafter "Baird"])

Wolf's article is remarkable for its candor. She is one of an extremely small number of pro-choice feminists who concede that abortion is in fact killing and the killing doesn't look very pretty—especially when the fetuses that are killed by abortion tend to resemble babies.

The authors of a website called abort73.com present a compelling case for the use of photographs in the abortion debate. Commenting specifically on the pro-choice charge that the photos are fakes or misleading they ask:

Why would anyone make these photos up? If these pictures were all a big hoax, if abortion wasn't really destroying tiny little people, why would so many people sacrifice huge amounts of time and money to oppose abortion? It just doesn't make sense. Abortion advocates have a significant financial stake in abortion's continued availability. It's easy to see why they argue the pictures are fake. The pro-life community, however, doesn't make money in opposing abortion. We lose money. Why would we do that in defense of a hoax? The pro-life community exists because these pictures are real, because abortion does kill people, and that's a hard reality to argue with.

(www.abort73.com/abortion/where_do_abortion_pictures_come_from/, Oct. 2010)

It was a wise investigator who admonished his apprentice to "follow the money" in a quest for truth. One does not need a degree in rocket science to figure out that the abortion *industry* makes money by performing abortions—a lot of money. And one does not have to look very hard to see that abortion clinics do not offer free abortions as a public service. While abortion advocates vociferously champion free or low-cost abortions for poor women, they don't expect Planned Parenthood to absorb the costs. Instead, they want taxpayers to pick up the tab.

In a noteworthy combination of candor and eloquence, Naomi Wolf doesn't hold back while admonishing her pro-choice peers in the aforementioned article:

> The pro-choice movement often treats with contempt the pro-lifers' practice of holding up to our faces their disturbing graphics. We revile their placards showing an enlarged scene of the aftermath of a D and C abortion; we are disgusted by their lapel pins with the little feet, crafted in gold, of a ten-week-old fetus; we mock the sensationalism of *The Silent Scream*. We look with pity and horror at someone who would brandish a fetus in formaldehyde—and we are quick to say that they are lying: "those are stillbirths, anyway," we tell ourselves.
>
> To many pro-choice advocates, the imagery is revolting propaganda. There is a sense among us, let us be frank, that the gruesomeness of the imagery belongs to the pro-lifers; that it emerges from the dark, frightening minds of fanatics; that it represents the violence of imaginations that would, given half a chance, turn our world into a scary, repressive place. "People like us" see such material as the pornography of the pro-life movement.
>
> But feminism at its best is based on what is simply true. While pro-lifers have not been beyond dishonesty, distortion, and the doctoring of images (preferring, for example, to highlight the results of very late, very rare abortions), many of those photographs are in fact photographs of actual D & Cs; those footprints are in fact the footprints of a ten-week-old fetus; the pro-life slogan, "Abortion stops a beating heart," is incontrovertibly true. (Baird, 183)

To be honest, I was taken aback when I first read these words from a prominent, pro-choice feminist. One simply does not run across such brutal honesty every day within the pro-choice movement. That Wolf is confronting what could accurately be described as an epidemic of denial and self-delusion among her pro-choice peers is obvious.

Without a doubt her candor is both refreshing and called for, but, as might be expected, it did not fail to elicit a backlash.*

In fact, Naomi Wolf's article stands out among the pro-choice literature I encountered while doing research for this project, not only for its candor but also for its sincerity and eloquence. The first thing that struck me as refreshingly unique was Wolf's willingness to use the term "pro-life." Rarely does a pro-choice proponent—especially one of prominence—use that term. The preferred term is "anti-choice." When feeling generous, some will use the term "anti-abortion," but rarely do you see a pro-choice proponent freely using the term "pro-life." This is an indication—to me at least—that Wolf is approaching the issue with a deeper understanding of the pro-life position than most of her peers. There is a good chance Wolf has actually taken the time to consider pro-life arguments and, even though she apparently disagrees, at least she understands the logic and respects it for what it is.

Wolf is to be commended for her truthfulness. While we in the pro-life movement would dispute that any of the photographs pro-life proponents use have been doctored, Wolf at least recognizes that the majority are real. It is noteworthy that she fails to cite any example of a "doctored" photo but instead questions the sincerity of highlighting "the results of very late, very rare abortions." Wolf is likely referring to depictions of a D and X abortion, more popularly known as "partial-birth abortion." While such procedures may indeed be rare (and are now illegal), no doubt she understood, at the time she wrote the article, they were anything but fictitious.

The most poignant truth that emerges from Wolf's chastisement of her fellow pro-choice advocates is the ironic desire of pro-choice proponents to assign the gruesomeness of abortion to those who are, in fact, against it. The prevalence of this paradox—especially among the media—is truly remarkable. It's as though those who would display photos of the horrors of Treblinka, Sobibor, and Auschwitz are somehow responsible for the hideousness of the content. As Randy Alcorn writes, "The question we should ask is not, 'Why are pro-life people showing these pictures?' but "Why would anyone defend what's shown in these pictures?'" (Alcorn, 45).

The reality is, abortion *is* gruesome, and photos are an uncomfortable but effective way of communicating the gruesomeness. Naomi Wolf is simply courageous enough to admit that. Pro-life proponents are not responsible for the shocking nature of abortion. That the message is bad is not the fault of the messenger. Wolf puts a large part of the blame for the evil of abortion on a prudish lack of education about and access to various forms of contraception. While that may be one contributing factor to high rates of unwanted pregnancies in a society that has devalued marriage and embraced fornication, she can't jump from that to then lay the blame for abortion at the feet of those who despise it.

Footnote:
*Phrases like "created a sensation," "caused a stir," "a stunning surprise," and "international uproar" have been used to describe Naomi Wolf's 1996 article. For example, in a letter to The New Republic in the summer of 1996, Jane M. Johnson, Planned Parenthood's acting copresident, wrote, "We'd rather grapple with enemies we know than so-called friends in Wolf's clothing" (quoted in *Human Life Review*, "A Decision Between a Woman and God," Roy Rivenburg, Summer 1996, Vol. 22, Issue 3, 59).

Another example is Adam Young's posting on March 24, 2005, in which he writes: "In the mild-'90s, Naomi Wolf created a stir among abortion defenders and opponents with her essay in The New Republic. In that piece, entitled 'Our Bodies, Our Souls,' she made the provocative assertion that pro-choicers should frankly admit that abortion is an evil, although a necessary one, because it ends a human life." Young points out that Wolf's tactic "has not caught on, mainly due to its bad public relations for the abortion rights movement and its dangerous implications for equality before the law, which turns around and strikes at the very foundations of the abortion argument" (Abortion Revisited: The Libertarian Case for Abortion, posted March 24, 2005, http://www.strike-the-root.com/51/younga/younga8.html).

Or read Michael Shermer, who suggests that Wolf's article "shocked the pro-choice movement by claiming that the fetus at all stages is a human individual and therefore abortion is immoral (although she still supports free choice)." Shermer goes on to complain that Wolf's article presents "not a single scientific fact" in support of "her claim for fetal human individuality" but "instead we get emotional references to 'lapel pins with little feet,' 'framed sonogram photos,' and 'detailed drawings of the fetus'" from a popular pregnancy book (The Science of Good and Evil, New York: Henry Holt & Company, LLC, 2004, 307, fn 19). Ironically, Shermer's response epitomizes the very "callous" attitude so prevalent among pro-choice proponents that Wolf was criticizing in the article. Even more ironic: the very icons Shermer chooses to highlight from Wolf's article are the ones Wolf frankly admits annoy "abortion rights" proponents! Besides inadvertently demonstrating Wolf's point, Shermer also seems to fail to grasp the simple concept that Wolf was not attempting to make any scientific "claim" for "human individuality," though I have no doubt she is more than capable of making such a case should she ever choose to. Ironically, Shermer treats Wolf as though she is pro-life!

In context, one would not expect Wolf to provide "a single scientific fact" in support of "fetal human individuality," since her goal was not to argue in favor of the humanity of the fetus but to chastise her pro-choice peers for their patently "callous" denial of reality and to suggest that continuing on that course without contextualizing the discussion in terms of morality will be detrimental to the pro-choice cause. She suggests that it is precisely such an attitude of denial and self-delusion that is losing the "mushy middle" to the pro-life cause. That a fetus is a baby is not even contested by Wolf. She readily concedes the point when relating a personal encounter with a pro-life proponent who asked whether her own fetus at four months gestation was not a baby. "Of course it's a baby," Wolf retorted. Having been pregnant herself—a condition one suspects Michael Shermer likely has no personal experience with—Wolf sees it as undeniable that a fetus is a baby. Wolf has no need of relating scientific facts in support of what she clearly sees as obvious. What is more interesting is that Shermer seems to have completely missed (or avoided) the point of Wolf's essay: that a "callous" insistence on the part of pro-choice proponents that a fetus is nothing but protoplasm will eventually cost the pro-choice movement its very "soul."

CHAPTER 28

Tell It Like It Is

With the pro-choicers, even their talking points are lies.
—Ann Coulter

Wherever censorship does not prevail, pro-life advocates do indeed use words, photographs, videos, and audio recordings to make their case for a simple reason: unlike people, the evidence doesn't lie. Photographs of the aftermath of abortion are indeed very disturbing for the simple reason that aborted fetuses look remarkably similar to mutilated or severely burned babies. This appears to be the real reason pro-choice advocates (other than Wolf) are so passionately opposed to photographic evidence.

Randy Alcorn:

> The descriptions that I have in my books and that I've seen—most of those are direct quotes from Warren Hearn, a leading abortionist in Colorado. He has a medical textbook; a training textbook on how to perform abortions. And I quote from him in my books. I don't make up these descriptions. The decapitations, the different things that he describes are just simply: This is the fact of abortions and how these abortions are done. Now if [Weddington] is talking about partial-birth abortions then, yes, that's a well-developed child and in early abortions, because the child isn't as big, it's not necessary to crush the child, it's just necessary to cut the child up or vacuum the child out. Well no matter what the procedure is, if some are more or less gruesome than others, the point is still the same: the child is

being killed. Also, if somebody is making up the gruesomeness of this that would be one thing, but when the most vivid gruesome terms are from a doctor who trains other doctors how to perform abortions, then let's let him be the expert.

In an online article in 2003, Dr. Hern openly questioned whether his particular version of a late-term abortion violated the Partial-Birth Abortion Act:

> Earlier this year, I began an abortion on a young woman who was 17 weeks pregnant. Because of the two days of prior treatment, the amniotic membranes were visible and bulging. I ruptured the membranes and released the fluid to reduce the risk of amniotic fluid embolism. Then I inserted my forceps into the uterus and applied them to the head of the fetus, which was still alive, since fetal injection is not done at that stage of pregnancy. I closed the forceps, crushing the skull of the fetus, and withdrew the forceps. The fetus, now dead, slid out more or less intact. (Warren M. Hern, "Did I Violate the Partial-Birth Abortion Ban? A doctor ponders a new era of prosecution." Updated Wednesday, Oct. 22, 2003, at 4:17 PM PT)

Despite the lonely voice of Naomi Wolf, the overwhelming majority in the pro-abortion community has actively worked to cover up the reality of abortion. Euphemisms have been perfected. Pro-choice ideas that highlight the perils of the mother while ignoring the fetus have been implanted into the minds of the public by a media all too willing to promote the pro-choice agenda while censoring evidence to the contrary. Thought has indeed been corroded on a national level. But photographs of aborted babies rapidly destroy the false reality presented to the public which promotes abortion as little more than an appendectomy.

Dr. Carolyn Gerster:

> But your average person [who] thinks they are pro-abortion if they viewed an abortion I think they'd change markedly. But they say, well that's because they're squeamish about the blood, it's like watching an appendectomy. But the appendix is an organ and not a very complex one at that. So, you can't compare that at all.

Dr. Thorp:

I would disagree with a statement that a 16-cell stage or a 32-cell stage or a four-week embryo or a two-week embryo is nothing more than an appendix because an appendix in a natural process does not have a potential for human life, whereas that embryo does.

In the same article in which she reprimands her fellow pro-choice proponents for their failure to rationally confront the content of pro-life photographs, Naomi Wolf also asks her readers to "imagine how quickly public opinion would turn against a president who waged war while asserting that our sons and daughters were nothing but cannon fodder" (Baird, 187). The relevant point she makes is that abortion proponents do exactly that when they claim abortion is little more than the removal of tissue. While Wolf's willingness to face the truth about the humanity of the fetus is commendable, her decision to remain a pro choice proponent despite that realization leaves her essay with severe cognitive dissonance:

War is legal; it is sometimes even necessary. Letting the dying die in peace is often legal and sometimes even necessary. Abortion should be legal; it is sometimes even necessary. Sometimes the mother must be able to decide that the fetus, in its full humanity, must die. But it is never right or necessary to minimize the value of the lives involved or the sacrifice incurred in letting them go. Only if we uphold abortion rights within a matrix of individual conscience, atonement and responsibility can we both correct the logical and ethical absurdity in our position—and consolidate the support of the [political] center. (Baird, 187)

Wolf's very sincerity boxes her in. Rather than correcting the "logical and ethical absurdity" in the pro-choice position, her honesty serves to expose it.

The only possible nonbarbaric justification for abortion on demand is that there *must be* a radical difference between a human fetus and a baby. Wolf seems to instinctively understand the "logical and ethical absurdity" of asserting such a position given the "well-known facts of fetal development." Her own experience with pregnancy seems to have settled the question of whether the kicking inside her body was coming from a baby. She readily concedes the point. (When relating a personal encounter with a pro-life proponent who asked whether her own fetus at four months gestation was not a baby, Wolf retorted: "Of course it's a baby.") But in so doing, she reveals the inevitable fallacy. A nineteenth-century equivalent would be a slave owner who frankly acknowledges that there is something uncomfortable—indeed, evil—about slavery but still advocates for the "necessary evil" of owning slaves. No doubt Wolf would agree it is morally wrong to attempt to justify owning another human being as a slave on *the assertion* that there is some radical moral difference between a black person and a white person that effectively annihilates the rights of the black person—especially when, in reality, the crucial difference amounts to nothing more than a judicial decree. We agree that such thinking is incorrect and immoral. Nevertheless, the U.S. Supreme Court attempted to rationally argue that black humans were inferior to white humans and, on that basis, whites were morally entitled to own blacks as slaves. To eliminate that rationale, however flawed it may be, while still attempting to make a rational case for owning slaves leads to an irrational conclusion. On that basis Wolf would surely agree that a law defining slave-owning as a "fundamental right" of whites is inherently immoral and should be condemned and overturned. No doubt she would not advocate for the "necessary evil" of owning slaves. How much more glaringly obvious should it be that such a law is immoral, then, if even its proponents were to frankly admit that *there is no moral difference* between races? Without the assertion (however ludicrous) of a radical difference between black humans and white humans, *there is no moral basis* for slavery.

Similarly, by eliminating the only rationally justifiable basis on which to build so-called "abortion rights," Wolf pulls the rug out from under herself and the pro-choice movement in the process, hence the disapproval of her peers. If a fetus is not inferior to a baby—and radically so—then what possible justification is there for abortion other than a genuinely life-threatening situation for the mother?

A fetus must somehow be radically, morally inferior to a baby. Otherwise, abortion in most cases is simply cruel and unusual punishment for existing in the wrong place at the wrong time. While Wolf is certainly more honest about the killing part of abortion, the conclusion she draws given that realization seems unnecessarily brutal. War, as she asserts, may indeed be "a necessary evil," but no one attempts to hold war up as a fundamental right that equalizes women to men! Wolf may or may not suggest that abortion is necessary to equalize the playing field, but the movement she claims allegiance to surely does.

When Wolf asserts that sometimes "the mother must be able to decide that the fetus, in its full humanity, must die," one is left to ponder under what possible conditions a mother might be allowed to decide that *her child, in all its humanity*, must die. We clearly and rightfully reject this line of thinking when applied to mothers who leave their babies in dumpsters or strap their toddlers into car seats and push the car into a lake. Barefaced, brutal barbarity is surely where Wolf's logic ends. Recognizing the humanity of unborn humans does not cure the problem unless the realization prompts us to *stop killing* unborn humans. All we've done otherwise is to stop fooling ourselves about who we're killing. The blinders of Wolf's peers serve a function.

CHAPTER 29

Smiling Icons

If it isn't a baby, you're not pregnant.
—Unknown author

Even today with pro-choice language in full effect, there is still no mention of a "fetus," a "product of conception," or a "pathological specimen" when the pregnant mother wants to keep her baby. In that case, even abortion advocates are placed in the awkward position of having to resort to common yet pro-life terminology. It's not socially acceptable to ask, "Have you felt your fetus kicking yet?" Or even worse, "How's your product of conception today?"

A classic example of this occurred during the now infamous Scott Peterson murder trial. Peterson was convicted of killing his pregnant wife, Laci. The Petersons' unborn child was regularly referred to by everyone from reporters in the typically pro-choice media to high-profile, pro-choice feminists as "baby Conner." While pro-life proponents are quick to spot the inconsistency, pro-choice advocates often fail to see any double standard in using separate vocabularies to describe an unwanted fetus versus a wanted yet still unborn baby.

Yet hard-core feminists like former Planned Parenthood President, Gloria Feldt, understand the problems that can result when the inconsistency is not addressed. In her book, *The War on Choice*, she confronts the problem head-on:

> In reporting about the Laci Peterson murder, most stories refer to the fetus she was carrying as "the baby." Several news articles have even referred to the fetus as "Conner," the name Peterson told people

she had picked out. Similarly, many news articles refer to the incident as a "double murder." (Feldt, 176)

In an attempt at damage control, Feldt attempts to set the record straight by informing her readers that:

Laci's murder has nothing—nothing—to do with fetal rights; it's unequivocally about violence to women. (Feldt, 93)

Actually this tragic incident and Feldt's response to it reveals that pro-choice groups like Planned Parenthood simply do not want any of the attention ever to be on the unborn child. Even though Laci wanted to keep her baby and was looking forward to his birth, Feldt makes it clear that in her judgment, Conner's rights amounted to absolutely nothing. For Feldt, baby Conner wasn't a baby, he was merely a prematurely named, subhuman fetus without any rights. Even the fact that he was wanted by his mother couldn't change his status for Feldt.

If pro-choice advocates can't bring themselves to acknowledge the humanity of a *wanted* fetus, what prevents them from dehumanizing an *unwanted* baby?

Planned Parenthood promotes the phrase, "Every child a wanted child." They attempt to make the case for abortion by arguing that "unwanted" children get lower grades in school and are less than half as likely as wanted children to pursue higher education.

Dr. Jefferson:

Unwantedness is supposed to be something that can doom you to capital punishment. Well I certainly don't like that; I'm one of a people that's been unwanted at different times and places and I know very well that it doesn't matter whether someone else wants you or not. Our responsibility as a society is to see that each child learns to love and want himself. And if the child cannot love himself he's not going to, very likely, be able to love someone else, but he shouldn't have to die because the parents who may have conceived him cannot want or love that child.

Pro-choice proponents argue that no woman should be forced to carry an unwanted pregnancy. But while the pregnancy may be unwanted, the baby should not be killed as a result—especially in a country where nearly 1.3 million American families want to adopt each year. Unfortunately, because demand is so great and, thanks to abortion, supply is so low, a scenario has developed where babies are sold on a black market (Alcorn, 87).

Randy Alcorn:

> I think adoption is a threat because the worse they can make adoption appear then the better abortion is. If adoption is really a good choice all around, which I believe that it is; it's, of course, not without its problems and challenges and everything else, but if it's a really good thing, then it helps make abortion look like a worse thing. And I just think there's a lot of people that don't even want to come to terms with that. But it is so sad. I have a friend who for years was a counselor at an abortion clinic and she would advise women about their options, except all of their options, in her mind and in what they were trained, had to do with abortion. And she said we never even *ever* brought up adoption as a possibility, *ever*. It's just not even a possibility we put on the table with the woman.

Another part of the unwanted argument holds that by eliminating unwanted children, abortion helps to reduce the incidence of child abuse.

Randy Alcorn:

> Killing, and actually very mercilessly killing a child so that that child is not born into a world where they could potentially become a statistic of child abuse . . . so in other words, it's: Let's abuse the children earlier so that now they don't show up in statistics of children who are abused later. In other words, it's a very bizarre logic!
>
> But the other part of it is, even though it would seem to fit common sense that if there's more abortion there will be less child abuse later because it fits the idea that people don't want these children. And if you don't want a child, you are therefore more likely to abuse that child. But I cite a study that Edward Lenoski from the University of Southern California did—a landmark study of 674 abused children. He discovered—and this is remarkable—he discovered that 91 percent of the parents stated that they wanted the child they had abused.
>
> So, it actually works exactly the opposite. Not only is abortion itself a form of child abuse, but if you abort a child you are far more likely to abuse later children. Therefore, abortion increases child

abuse not only because it is child abuse but because it changes our mentality toward children.

In 1972 the Rockefeller Commission on Population Growth (http://www.population-security.org/rockefeller/001_population_growth_and_the_american_future.htm) produced a report favorable to legalized abortion. Grace Olivarez, a dissenter of the opinion and an Hispanic commented on the concept by stating:

> To talk about the "wanted" and the "unwanted" child smacks too much of bigotry and prejudice. Many of us have experienced the sting of being "unwanted" by certain segments of our society.... One usually wants objects and if they turn out to be unsatisfactory, they are returnable.... Human beings are not returnable items.... Those with power in our society cannot be allowed to "want" and "unwant" people at will.... The poor cry out for justice and equality and we respond with legalized abortion. (Grace Olivarez, "Separate Statement" Rockefeller Commission Report, *Population and the American Future*, 1972, 161)

In his book *Why Pro-life?* Randy Alcorn writes:

> Everyone agrees that children should be wanted. The only question is this: Should we get rid of the *unwanting* or get rid of the children? (Alcorn, 89)

Randy Alcorn:

> When I've been in debates with Planned Parenthood people I say, well, let's take your slogan, "Every child a wanted child." Now how do you finish that sentence? And they look at me like: Well what do you mean? And I say, well it's really not a complete sentence: "Every child a wanted child" so ... so, what? What does that mean? To me, I would say "every child a wanted child," so let's learn to want children more and let's get them into the homes of people who want them. Okay? But when you say "every child a wanted child" what do *you* really mean? How do you finish the sentence? And the answer is this—and they never give me the answer, so I have to supply it—is well, what you mean is "Every child a wanted child," so let's identify children who are unwanted and kill them before they're born. So essentially "every

child a wanted child," what that really means is, "Every unwanted child a dead child." Now that doesn't look good on a bumper sticker.

Taking the life of an already living human being simply because his or her mother does not want the responsibility of parenthood seems a bit extreme, even for many hard-core pro-abortion advocates to rally behind. To solve that problem, when pressured for answers pro-choice proponents have simply insisted that a fetus is something less than fully human which then, at least in theory, makes any abortion morally acceptable.

During a 1991 Phil Donohue show produced live in Wichita, Kansas, in which she was being interviewed alongside Randall Terry of Operation Rescue, then president of Planned Parenthood, Faye Wattleton, was backed into a corner when presented with a difficult question from a member of the audience. The awkward delay in Wattleton's response was more than just an indication of a weak spot in pro-choice philosophy; it also signaled an atypically candid response by Wattleton in the making. The question was: *What happens to the baby that was aborted and lives?*

Wattleton eventually broke the silence by stating, "I do not accept that a fetus is a baby; it is a fetus." A chorus of boos immediately filled the auditorium while Wattleton composed herself and then fell back on recitation of typical pro-choice mantras:

> . . . and we have taken the position that the state, in fact, can intervene to protect potential life but never if a woman's life or health are jeopardized. Those are difficult issues that must be decided by the woman and her physician and not by Randall Terry and other people trying to make that decision for her.

And with that the pro-choice portion of the audience erupted in applause.

So, just as Sarah Weddington had argued in *Roe v. Wade*, when pressured to do so, Faye Wattleton was also forced to concede that the moral basis for abortion does not ultimately rest in a choice made by a pregnant woman but rather in the concept that a fetus and a baby are not the same thing. Abortion is therefore justified for *any* reason, according to pro-choice logic, since it merely kills a fetus and not a baby.

This seems to satisfy many Americans. But the specific question presented to Wattleton that day goes deeper than her answer would indicate and demands further clarification. Once we accept the argument that a fetus is not a baby, a new set of moral questions arises. The obvious first question is: *At what point in its development does a human fetus change into a baby?* Obviously, the morality of abortion cannot be determined until this question is adequately answered. And beyond that, one wonders *what exactly are* the fundamental, biological, scientifically classifiable differences between a fetus and a baby that justify the killing of the former and the legal protection of the latter?

Considering the question presented to Wattleton leads us to the difficult realities of abortion. The fact is, Wattleton's questioner was not theorizing in the hypothetical realm. There are cases in which babies have actually been aborted and lived to eventually speak about it. The reality of abortion is then brought out from the obscure setting of an abortion clinic to the light of day, and the real victims of abortion are then given names and faces.

One such noteworthy abortion survivor is today a pro-life advocate and singer. Gianna Jesson has mesmerized audiences the world over with the story of how she survived a saline abortion attempt on her life when her biological mother was seven months pregnant. During the abortion, saline was injected into her mother's womb completely surrounding and burning Gianna.

Though rarely used today because of its failure rate, the desired result of a saline abortion is to cause the death of the unborn child within 24 hours. It is typically a slow death, followed by spontaneous abortion. Gianna was indeed expelled from the womb but miraculously survived the procedure to the shock of both her biological mother and the nurses in attendance. Rather than risk prosecution for infanticide, the nurses administered first aid and worked to keep Gianna alive. She still suffers from cerebral palsy as a consequence of the abortion attempt on her life. Even to this day Gianna's mere existence is a threat to pro-choice advocates who often find themselves speechless when confronted with the breathing, smiling symbol of what is wrong with their philosophy.

I myself witnessed this phenomenon firsthand while attending a pro-life rally in Lawrence, Kansas, in 1991. Positioning themselves on a hill at the entrance to the stadium were a vocal group of pro-choice proponents carrying signs and chanting slogans. They made their presence known all day, regardless of who was speaking, doing their best to disrupt the rally—that is until the keynote speaker, a small, then 16-year-old Gianna slowly made her way onto the stage. At that moment, I glanced over my shoulder. I took it as no coincidence that the formerly boisterous pro-choice crowd, who had hung in with us all through the rally up to that point, chose that moment to begin packing up and heading home *en masse*. We listened to Gianna speak without any further heckling.

Lack of words is often the best approach for pro-choice proponents when confronted with Gianna Jesson and those other very few abortion survivors like her, since any attempt to comment often creates more PR damage than good for the pro-choice cause.

Judy Maggio, for example, with the Rockford Illinois Coalition for Reproductive Choice, described Gianna's appearance at pro-life rallies as an "appeal to the emotionalism of a second trimester abortion" (as quoted in Jessica Shaver, *Gianna: Aborted and Lived to Tell About It*, CO: Focus on the Family Publishing, 1995, 130, hereafter "Shaver"). Maggio misrepresents the facts by implying that Gianna was a victim of a second-trimester abortion, when, according to Gianna's birth weight, it was actually a third-trimester abortion. Beyond that, Maggio fails to explain why the survivor of an abortion should not be celebrated, while the stories of women who do not survive abortion attempts are exploited in pro-abortion propaganda.

Feeling the need to comment, Planned Parenthood eventually issued a paradoxical statement about Gianna in 1992 in which they expressed their "enormous compassion for this young woman . . ."

> Certainly her case is a tragedy in that she has suffered. However this doesn't mean that every decision made to have an abortion is wrong. Women choose abortions for many reasons, sometimes out of despair. It is not possible to judge an entire issue based on this 14 year old's experience. . . . Gianna is a symbol of triumph over adversity, not a symbol of why abortion should not be available. (Planned Parenthood of NW & NE Indiana—the Munster, Indiana, *Sunday Times*, March 1, 1992, as quoted in Shaver, 131)

The glaring irony in this statement by a leading proponent of legal access to and provider of the procedure *that caused* Gianna's suffering and nearly took her life is impossible to miss.

How is it that the nation's leading abortion advocacy group could label Gianna a "symbol of triumph over adversity" when the very adversity she triumphed over was a failed attempt at what they otherwise passionately promote as a fundamental right for women and provide for hundreds on a daily basis? If we were to take this statement at face value, should we not then expect Planned Parenthood to proclaim pro-life efforts to save the lives of other unborn children by stopping abortion as similar triumphs over adversity? Should it not follow that *every* abortion attempt that fails or, better still, was never attempted in the first place, must be equally triumphant in the eyes of Planned Parenthood? Where is the brave soul at Planned Parenthood who will look into the eyes of Gianna Jesson and explain why she *is not* a symbol of why abortion on demand should not be a fundamental right?

Using Wattleton's and Weddington's logic, one is left to wonder when exactly did Gianna Jesson and those other rare abortion survivors like her *become* a baby? (See for example, the similar story of Melissa Ohden at melissaohden. com.) Did that transformation occur before, during, or after the abortion? Given that Gianna was clearly viable at the time of the abortion, was she, at that point, a "person in the whole sense"? And in what morally significant way(s) did she change from a mere "fetus" into a baby? Could she legally have been killed after she drew her first breath outside the womb? Are we to conclude that there was some crucial biological difference between the Gianna who was surrounded by the poisonous saline solution while inside the womb and the Gianna who miraculously hung onto life moments later outside the womb? Should we conclude that a mysterious and apparently undetectable fundamental change occurred in Gianna's biological makeup the moment someone decided she could no longer legally be killed? Or are we to say that, just as in real estate, location and desirability are the critical factors on which to base the value of human life? Pro-choice proponents have no answers for these questions. Their typical response is either silence or to change the subject.

By ignoring the biological aspect of the question of when human life begins and instead focusing on the vague, philosophical notion of the beginning of "personhood," the result was to arbitrarily fix the moral and legal distinction between meaningful and nonmeaningful human life on a convenient but morally meaningless legal peg otherwise known as birth. In doing so the Supreme Court opened the door to the irrational and ambiguous standards of location and desirability as the ultimate determining factors of worthy and nonworthy human life. On a practical level, the lasting physical consequences of the destructive but legal actions done to those lives when deemed unworthy by the state and located in the wrong place remained well after a tiny minority survived the abortion attack on their lifes—more than adequately proving the "meaningfulness" of their own existence. But these stories, dramatic as they are, are rare indeed because the vast majority of abortion attempts in the modern era, are "successful."

The questions raised by the acceptance of the unsupported and unverifiable pro-choice concept of radical and necessarily significant moral differences between a human fetus and a baby does not provide a satisfactory moral basis for unrestricted abortion; instead, it merely adds to the controversy. And yet, because abortion necessarily involves killing, freedom to choose abortion must ultimately rest on *some* moral basis or acknowledge its own savagery. In the end, "civilized" pro-choice logic demands that somehow and in some as yet undefined but profound way, an unwanted fetus and a wanted baby are as fundamentally different as an appendix and a full-grown woman.

CHAPTER 30

Because the Law Says So: The Edelin Case

[T]hat was a very stomach-turning kind of existence.
—Dr. Anthony Levantino (former abortionist)

From the perspective of *Roe v. Wade*, desirability coupled with location is the critical dynamic in determining the legal status of the entity in the womb. But, practically speaking, even remaining alive outside the womb does not necessarily guarantee protection for the survivor of abortion. Unfortunately, cases like Gianna Jessen's, in which the abortion survivor is allowed to continue living, are rare. More often, abortion victims who refuse to die in the womb end up being killed either directly or indirectly through neglect outside the womb.

Babies who don't cooperate with abortionists by dying in the proper location create a dilemma for abortion advocates for the simple reason that birth was defined as the peg on which personhood was legally, though certainly not logically, determined to rest. According to the post-*Roe* interpretation of the law, when abortion is desired, any action that kills a fetus in the womb is viewed as a necessary part of the abortion liberty. A legal quagmire resulted, however, when an action designed to kill the fetus in the womb succeeded *after* a live birth. Since defining personhood at birth completely lacks any physiological basis in terms of the life being extinguished by abortion, courts have been forced to confront the question of infanticide in cases resulting from unsuccessful abortions.

In an effort to protect doctors from prosecution, the laws covering infanticide had to be reconsidered after *Roe v. Wade* went into effect. What it currently boils down to is that any *wanted* child who is killed outside the womb is, by definition, a victim of infanticide whose killer will surely be prosecuted, while an unwanted fetus who manages to survive an abortion—while, in theory, obtaining a legal right to retain life by virtue of emerging from the womb alive—in practicality is rarely granted the opportunity.

A key case that set the stage for this involved Dr. Kenneth Edelin, who would later go on to become president of Planned Parenthood. In 1975, Dr. Edelin was the chief resident in obstetrics and gynecology at Boston City Hospital. While there he became embroiled in a legal battle which involved manslaughter charges resulting from an abortion he had performed on a baby who refused to cooperate.

Of course, most cases of babies surviving abortion only to subsequently die are simply not made public. But through an unusual set of circumstances, the body of a black baby boy was discovered in Boston's Southern Mortuary during the course of an investigation into experiments conducted on unborn children believed to have been carried out at Boston City Hospital.

Dr. Mildred Jefferson, who became the first witness called by the prosecution (led by District Attorney Newman Flanagan) in the court case that followed, explains:

> There were two doctors who had gone on trial. The trials grew out of the fact that we had determined through an article in the *New England Journal of Medicine* that experiments were being done on pregnant women and girls using very strong antibiotics. And on reading the article in the medical journal those of us, led by Dr. Joseph Stanton, questioned why, among the subjects of these experiments, there was a 15-year-old girl. And the question was raised immediately: Who signed the consent form for her? What were they told? What did they understand? What did they understand about the dangers of the drug on the patients themselves, and what was explained to them with regard to the unborn children?
>
> Now from the standpoint of the researchers it was ideal because [the unborn children] were going to be aborted anyway. And that old rationale that comes out of the socialist era of Nazi Germany—

that since they were going to die anyway they may as well be of some benefit to society—neatly bypassing the idea that if you weren't going to kill them they wouldn't be going to die.

Dr. Edelin was identified as the doctor who had delivered the baby. Edelin had estimated the baby's age at between twenty and twenty-two weeks.

Dr. Jefferson:

> The cases that became the Edelin trial grew out of that investigation when they found that there were bodies in the morgue—babies' bodies—that had not been discharged. Because, under the laws of the Commonwealth of Massachusetts, if you are born at 20 weeks or older and have any visible sign of life, then both a birth and death certificate has to be signed before you can be discharged to the funeral director.
>
> Needless to say we had very high regard for that District Attorney of Suffolk County, Newman Flanagan, and when he was the District Attorney we could be certain that we had someone who would interpret the law in a simple, clear way according to the traditional posture of the law.

The child's mother had come to Edelin to obtain an abortion. Dr. Edelin made three unsuccessful attempts at a saline abortion, but the "fetus" simply refused to die. Mildred Jefferson points out that even those three attempts weren't the only attempted abortions performed on that infant.

Dr. Jefferson:

> There may have been three by Edelin, but there were also unsuccessful attempts by other people. So that creates of itself a dangerous circumstance for the patient undergoing the procedure. It's a dangerous process to begin with, but the more times you have to penetrate the abdominal wall to get into the amniotic sac, each time you do that you increase the risk of infection. So when they were unsuccessful in doing the salting-out, which is a questionable procedure in a 17 year old anyway, they then had to do the abortion hysterotomy.

Edelin made an incision into the womb and detached the unborn child's placenta from the womb.

Dr. Jefferson:

> Hysterotomy involves opening the uterus and removing the baby from the amniotic sac. The matter of someone trying to guarantee that it's dead before it's lifted out is not part of the standard operation known as hysterotomy. It may be a modification which has been added by an abortionist to guarantee that they carry out the contract they are provided under *Roe v. Wade*.

The medical examiner had determined the infant's cause of death to be anoxia or lack of oxygen.

Dr. Jefferson:

> And the accusation against him grew out of the fact that someone who was in the operating room testified that he kept the baby submerged in the amniotic fluid long enough to guarantee that it would not be breathing when it was lifted out of the uterus. And that's all part of what the trial grew out of. Did he do that? If he did, that was a direct act of asphyxiating the baby by drowning.

According to the testimony of his assistant, Edelin kept his hand in the womb for at least three minutes by the clock. He then pulled the baby from the womb, felt the boy's chest with his rubber-gloved hand for three to five seconds, noticed no heartbeat, and placed him in a stainless steel basin held by the nurse who emptied the baby's body into another container in the back room (Noonan, 129).

According to experts for the prosecution, examination of the boy's lungs revealed he had been born alive but had died sometime after birth and before reaching the mortuary.

In order to prove Dr. Edelin guilty of involuntary manslaughter, the Commonwealth of Massachusetts "had to prove him guilty of 'wanton or reckless conduct' causing death" which consisted of "'indifference to or disregard of the probable consequences to the rights of others' by one who had a duty to those affected by his indifference" (Noonan, 130).

It was the Commonwealth's position that by removing the source of oxygen from the baby in the womb (the placenta) and keeping him from breathing air by holding him in the womb, Dr. Edelin's actions caused a grave injury to the baby resulting in his subsequent death and should therefore be found "reckless and wanton" by the jury.

Yet, Dr. Edelin's testimony was that he believed the fetus was dead at the time he emerged from the womb. "He denied that he had delayed three minutes in extracting the fetus, and his experts denied that the three-minute delay would have killed" the fetus (Noonan, 131).

Dr. Jefferson:

> I had been invited by the prosecution to define the terms that would be used in the trial, and I was invited to do that because I had established, over the time of my, even pre–medical school experience, a record as someone who could explain scientific terms to laymen in a way that they would understand. So my being the lead-off witness was to establish familiarity, among the jurors, with the stages of development of the unborn child; not every single one of them but with the understanding that we have a scientific term for every stage of the development once the fertilized egg, which is called a zygote, comes into existence.
>
> And a brief chronology of the development of that first division of the zygote when it goes from one cell to two cells until the many cell stage and indicating what the different stages were as it makes its trip down the fallopian tube to be implanted within the mother's womb.
>
> And the descriptions and definitions I gave were the same that any honest person would give and it wouldn't have mattered whether I was invited by the prosecution or the defense; the definitions would have been the same. And if you read testimony of doctors called by the defense toward the end of the trial their definitions, as I recall, stack up almost the same as mine.

Basing his logic on *Roe v. Wade*, the trial judge instructed the jury that termination of pregnancy was legal in Massachusetts *during the entire term of pregnancy* and "'that the abortion process and its effectuation must be left to the medical judgment of the pregnant woman's attending physician; that a person existed only 'after birth,' and that the jury could convict Dr. Edelin only if 'satisfied beyond a reasonable doubt' that he had caused 'the death of a person' born alive outside the body of his mother" (Noonan, 131–2).

In so doing, the judge had already interpreted *Roe v. Wade* to mean that an injury inflicted on the child in the womb during an abortion that subsequently resulted in death outside the womb was not a prosecutable offense (Noonan, 132). Therefore, none of Dr. Edelin's actions prior to birth were punishable.

Given those conditions, the case hinged on whether or not the baby had still been alive when he emerged from the womb. Dr. Edelin believed he was not, while Massachusetts believed he was.

Even given the restrictive instructions, the jury found Dr. Edelin guilty of manslaughter.

Dr. Jefferson:

> The doctor convicted himself because the evidence in that photograph is the thing that swayed the jury, not what anybody said. When the jury saw the picture of that little, dead, premature, baby boy lying on his side with his hair long enough to curl, you couldn't tell them that he wasn't a person.

The judge imposed probation and the case was immediately appealed to the Massachusetts Supreme Judicial Court. The court remained silent on the case through the 1976 election season, and finally handed down an acquittal of Dr. Edelin on December 17, 1976. Though the margin of victory was narrow, the net effect was viewed as a triumph for the pro-choice cause, which immediately labeled the whole process a pitiful attempt to challenge the *Roe* doctrine.

Dr. Jefferson:

> The problem in that acquittal is, again, in the opinion written by Justice Braucher who denied that the state, the Commonwealth, had proved that the little boy was born alive. He said, "Oh there may have been some spontaneous gasps," but what is breathing at any point but a series of spontaneous gasps? So that in the words of the opinion that resulted in the reversal of the jury, the justice himself has established that the baby was born alive.

Writing from a decidedly pro-choice perspective, reporter Connie Paige offers this sympathetic, though incredible, version of events:

> In the split second after the fetus emerged, Edelin realized once again how uneasy these later abortions made him feel. He loved the work of an obstetrician, delivering a robust baby to a satisfied mother. The fetuses, while unnaturally tiny and obviously immature, still looked like infants. He always had to remind himself that if they

had lived at that stage of development, which was highly unlikely, they would end up blind, retarded—vegetables really. And without a mother, or with a mother who more often than not hated them. If they were black, like this one, they might have yet one more strike against them. (Paige, 11)

This quote nearly defies a rational response, yet it is representative of pro-abortion reasoning. First, Paige acknowledges that aborted human fetuses have an uncanny resemblance to "infants." One is left to ponder why that might be true. It seems to elude Paige that the natural state of any infant extracted from the womb prematurely would in fact be "tiny and immature."

Next, assuming the thoughts of Dr. Edelin, Paige informs her readers that if these unfortunate fetuses had, in her words, "lived at that stage of development, which was highly unlikely, they would end up blind, retarded—vegetables." Of course the implication, though not directly stated, was that there was something inherently wrong with fetuses at this stage of development *continuing* to live and develop. Dr. Edelin had actually done the poor thing a favor.

What Paige fails to point out is that the only unnatural part of the entire process—the repeated abortion attempts on the life of the unborn child—were perpetrated by Dr. Edelin in the first place at the request of the pregnant woman. Indeed, it was the healthy development of the pregnancy that was the problem as the mother simply did not want the result of a healthy pregnancy.

What does the phrase "lived, at that stage of development" mean? What point was Paige attempting to make with this peculiar use of words? The unborn boy had obviously been living and developing quite normally inside the womb until subjected to saline poisoning and finally asphyxia. And, apart from the damage done through the failed abortions, why would "living" at that stage of development have ultimately led to blindness, retardation or worse?

Dr. Jefferson:

In the '70s the experience in saving these babies safely was not as good as it is now because one of the things that caused the blindness was administering too much oxygen to these premature babies. But I just don't have a viewpoint that could comprehend someone making such a comment. Because, in general, babies of African descent are somewhat more mature at the earlier stage so that they might survive it even better. But from my medical standpoint, [the opinion of Paige] is an unfortunate point of view.

Was the public to assume that defects were the inevitable result of allowing an unnatural, tiny, immature, unwanted fetus to continue to live? Was Paige implying that the mature form of a tiny unwanted fetus was blindness or retardation? Or was her ambiguity a subtle acknowledgment of the fact that unsuccessful abortion attempts, though themselves rare, do often result in birth defects?

Of course, the truth is that the baby boy Edelin aborted was a perfectly normal unborn baby until he was attacked more than three times unsuccessfully in the womb through saline poisoning and finally killed through asphyxia. That any unborn baby could survive such circumstances is indeed "highly unlikely"! That physical impairments could result after more than three abortion attempts was also certainly a real possibility. That anything *other* than a normal childbirth would have occurred if the baby had simply been left alone was also highly unlikely.

Finally vindicated, Edelin commented that he had done nothing illegal, immoral, or of bad medical practice. Everything he did, Edelin proclaimed, was in accordance with the law.

And yet while perhaps "legal," at least from his point of view, the Edelin case serves as a stark reminder of the irrational set of circumstances created by *Roe v. Wade* and *Doe v. Bolton*. While the trial judge informed the jury that a person only existed after birth, he did not, nor could not, offer any logical or rational reasons why that same person did not exist moments prior to being prematurely extracted from his mother's womb. It was, after all, the same entity inside the womb that had been examined outside the womb. Yet, the law asserted that in some inexplicable way, the person examined outside the womb simply did not exist moments before. It was so because the law said so.

Pushing Weddington's legal "peg" to the next level, Connie Paige makes this noteworthy statement while referring to the prosecution team in the Edelin case:

> The Supreme Court decision had definitively stated that the
> fetus was not a person, but Flanagan rested his legal argument on
> the presumption that it became a person at the exact moment of

birth—no matter how premature or in what fashion—and thereby was subject to murder. (Paige, 20)

Since Weddington had specifically argued for legal rights, including the right to life, *attaching at birth,* one can understand how Newman Flanagan might have reached that conclusion. Yet Paige implies that birth actually has little to do with the mysterious acquisition of "personhood."

Here then is one key component in the paradox of pro-abortion philosophy. On the one hand this philosophy, as first expressed in *Roe v. Wade,* maintains that a fetus gains a potential for "meaningful life" by reaching a point in development where, with the aid of medical technology, it could theoretically survive outside the body of the woman. And because of this alleged morally relevant change in the status of the fetus, the state was then, in theory, free to begin restricting the woman's right to choose abortion. Yet for Paige and many in the pro-choice community, it was an unacceptable inconvenience to be accordingly bound by viability. As a result, like Paige, such pro-choice advocates end up unexpectedly *agreeing* with the pro-life concept that *birth is of little relevance* to the humanity or personhood of the unborn child no matter when it occurs in relation to the development of the fetus.

CHAPTER 31

Of Doctors and Oaths

Whenever a doctor cannot do good, he must be kept from doing harm.
—HIPPOCRATES

The story of *Roe v. Wade* is full of both major inconsistencies as well as trivial little ironies. One of those seemingly inconsequential quirks of fate was brought to center stage in the *Roe* discussions, ironically, not by the pro-life attorneys arguing on behalf of the right of the unborn human to continue living, but rather the Supreme Court justice who would later author the Roe majority opinion.

In one of those rare incidents where the ultraprepared Sarah Weddington was caught off guard—perhaps because she rightly viewed Justice Blackmun as an ally—Weddington seemed to struggle for an answer to this question:

> JUSTICE BLACKMUN: Now you referred a little bit to history. And let me ask you a question—

> MS. WEDDINGTON: Okay.

> JUSTICE BLACKMUN: —based on history. You're familiar with the Hippocratic oath?

> MS. WEDDINGTON: I am.

> JUSTICE BLACKMUN: I think—I may have missed it, but I find no reference to it in this—in your brief, or in the voluminous briefs that we're overwhelmed with here. Do you have any comment about the Hippocratic oath?

MS. WEDDINGTON: I think two things could be said. The first would be that situations and understandings change. In this case, for example, we have before the Court a medical amicus brief that was joined by all the deans of the public medical schools in Texas. It was joined by numerous other professors of medicine. It was joined by the American College of Obstetricians and Gynecologists.

JUSTICE BLACKMUN: Of course there are other briefs, on the other side, joined by equally outstanding physicians.

MS. WEDDINGTON: None of them has—

JUSTICE BLACKMUN: Tell me why you didn't discuss the Hippocratic oath.

MS. WEDDINGTON: Okay. I guess it was—okay—in part, because the Hippocratic oath—we discussed basically the constitutional protection we felt the woman to have. The Hippocratic oath does not pertain to that. Second, we discuss the fact that the state had not established a compelling state interest. The Hippocratic oath would not really pertain to that. And then we discuss the vagueness jurisdiction. It seemed to us that the fact that the medical profession at one time had adopted the Hippocratic oath does not weigh upon the fundamental constitutional rights involved. It is a guide for physicians, but the outstanding organizations of the medical profession have, in fact, adopted a position that says the doctor and the patient should be able to make the decision for themselves in this kind of situation.

JUSTICE BLACKMUN: Of course, it's the only definitive statement of ethics of the medical profession. I take it from what you just said that your ... you didn't even footnote it, because it's old? That's about, really, what you're saying?

MS. WEDDINGTON: Well, I guess it is old. And not that it's out of date, but that it seemed to us that it was not pertinent to the argument we were making.

As Dr. William Brennan points out, Weddington's logic is simply a veiled way of stating: *We didn't talk about the oath because the oath condemns the liberty we were attempting to forge into the Constitution.*

Dr. Brennan:

> Weddington, when she was asked by one of the justices, "What about the Hippocratic oath? I don't see any references to it in any of the briefs," she really hemmed and hawed but she said, "Well, the Hippocratic oath does not pertain to the situation," that this was something that was inaugurated many centuries ago and it doesn't pertain to the situation today. But the problem is that she left out the whole history of the Hippocratic oath and its significance for the issue of abortion and the killing of the unborn and how this has even spilled over to the postnatal phases. And I can give you some idea of the historical significance of the Hippocratic oath.

> Let me begin by saying this, if we look at this historically, when Hippocrates came upon the scene it was more than 2500 years ago. It was a superstitious world where the sorcerer, who is a physician, was both a killer and a healer. But Hippocrates's code marked a turning point in the history of civilization and the medical profession. It was the first time a complete separation was effected between killing and healing. From that point on, physicians were never again to be killers but preeminently healers. Hippocrates's code has explicit condemnations of killing both inside and outside the womb.

Specifically, the oath had the physician promise not to "give a deadly drug to anyone who asked for it, nor will I make a suggestion to this effect. Similarly, I will not give to a woman an abortive remedy. In purity and holiness I will guard my life and my art" (Ludwig Edelstien, *The Hippocratic Oath: Text, Translation, and Interpretation*, Baltimore, Johns Hopkins University Press, 1943).

It was the specific condemnation of abortion that caused Weddington to ignore the oath. While the pro-choice lobby could effectively create the illusion that nineteenth-century abortion laws were created without any concern for the fetus in mind, the explicit mention and condemnation of abortion in the oath was simply too blatant to casually explain away. Until called specifically on the question by Justice Blackmun, Weddington simply chose to ignore it.

Dr. Carolyn Gerster:

In medical school—in the early days of antiquity when I was in medical school (laughs), when I took OB/GYN—they said, remember, when a doctor attends a pregnant woman the doctor has two patients. And the unborn child is as much a patient as the mother. I graduated from the University of Oregon Medical School, and it's rather ironic since that's the only state in the union to legalize euthanasia. But there was about a hundred in our graduating class, only seven women of course in those days, but we knelt and said that oath aloud. And I can remember that second paragraph that said that, *I will abstain from all that is harmful and injurious. I will give no man a poison, even though asked, nor will I suggest such a counsel. In like manner I will not give a woman an instrument to produce an abortion.* And that was, what? 2500 years ago? The man certainly didn't come from the Vatican! He didn't even have the benefit of the Judeo Christian ethic because he was a pagan. But he just believed that the doctor should cure; that no doctor should become a killer.

Dr. Brennan:

This has been the standard of medical ethics for centuries. Now, two times, both in the twentieth century, has the Hippocratic oath been assaulted relentlessly: during the 12 years of the Third Reich and today. In Nazi Germany, the doctors no longer took the Hippocratic oath. It was dropped from their medical school curricula, and they took an oath to the Fuehrer rather than to Hippocrates. And at the Nuremberg Doctors' Trial in 1946 and 1947, when they were asked by the prosecuting attorney, how can you reconcile your involvement in killing the unborn, euthanasia victims, victims of racial genocide, etc.; how can you doctors justify that involvement when it's not in line with the Hippocratic oath? And each doctor on trial at Nuremberg said, the Hippocratic oath is obsolete, it doesn't pertain to the situation. This is almost exactly what Sarah Weddington said about the Hippocratic oath when she was asked in the oral arguments before the Supreme Court in 1973.

Of course in hindsight, the irony of Harry Blackmun bringing up the Hippocratic oath as a challenge to Sarah Weddington is worth mentioning.

It suggests that, at least at the time, Blackmun may have been struggling with the morality of abortion—or at least wrestling with the physician's justification for it. Because of his experience as legal counsel for the Mayo Clinic, he was well aware of the Hippocratic oath and obviously wondered how Weddington would attempt to get around its explicit condemnation of abortion.

> MS. WEDDINGTON: As to the Hippocratic oath, it seems to me that the oath was adopted at a time when abortion was extremely dangerous to the health of the woman. And, second, that the oath is to protect life. And here the question is: What does life mean in this particular context? It's the sort of same vagueness, it seems to me, that you're—well, okay. Life there could be slightly different, because of the constitutional implications here. It seems to me that—

> JUSTICE BLACKMUN: Well, the Hippocratic oath went directly and specifically to abortive procedures.

> MS. WEDDINGTON: To providing a—

> JUSTICE BLACKMUN: However life was defined.

> MS. WEDDINGTON: That's correct.

As it turned out, this was one area of challenge that had apparently been either overlooked or underdeveloped by Weddington and her preparation team. As Dr. Brennan points out, her immediate response to Blackmun's pointed question was uncharacteristically nervous laughter followed by a brief stammering for words. Even after recovering a confident composure, the logic she used in response to Blackmun's challenge was essentially useless to him. It may well be that Justice Blackmun understood the moral quagmire that would have resulted had he adopted Weddington's cavalier dismissal of the oath as simply not pertaining to the current situation. Even without considering the similarity to Nazi logic at Nuremberg, such a "justification" could conceivably be used to excuse any gross civil violation if allowed to stand. A rapist could justify his actions by claiming that laws mentioning rape do not pertain to his specific situation. A police interrogator who engages in torture could argue that the moral standards presented at the Geneva Convention, while fine for the context in which they were expressed, do not pertain to this specific interrogation.

Blackmun was apparently searching for a better means of disposing of the oath. Though given little assistance from Weddington, Blackmun was, nonetheless, undeterred in his quest to reconcile the *Roe* majority opinion with the oath of Hippocrates.

Dr. Brennan:

The major core of the Hippocratic oath is: Do no harm. Do no harm to anyone whether they are born or unborn. And Margaret Mead said, *This is a turning point in the history of medicine.* From Hippocrates on, doctors were never again to be killers but preeminently healers. This is a watershed thing that occurred with the Hippocratic oath. In fact, you see the significance of the oath in 1948; the World Medical Association enacted what they call the Declaration of Geneva. And this was a modern reaffirmation of the Hippocratic oath. And they enacted this and the AMA [American Medical Association] was a member of the World Medical Association and they indicated that we have to, again, reaffirm the ethic of the Hippocratic oath because of the tremendous violations by Nazi doctors. And they indicated that the Declaration of Geneva states— and it's a modern reaffirmation of the Hippocratic oath—and it states: "I will maintain the utmost respect for human life from the time of its conception. Even under threat I will not use my medical skill contrary to the laws of humanity."

You notice they said "from the moment of conception" I will maintain the utmost respect for human life, not from viability, not from quickening but from conception. And this was a restatement of this. Now we look at the situation today, how quickly memory fades with the passage of time! Today we have the doctors saying the Hippocratic oath is no longer relevant. They're using the same rationale against the Hippocratic oath today—doctors who favor abortion, infanticide, euthanasia—as the doctors on trial at Nuremberg used to justify their atrocities.

Given the nature of the oath as being openly opposed to abortion and given the fact that Blackmun himself had thought it significant enough to raise the question during oral arguments, how did he reconcile the *Roe* majority opinion with the oath of Hippocrates?

Dr. Gerster:

When they got to the Hippocratic oath they said, well, actually Hippocrates was an elitist, and he didn't represent the mores of his time, which was true, because abortion, infanticide, and euthanasia were very legal in Greece and commonly practiced. So he was worse than an elitist, he was a dangerous social activist.

Dr. Brennan:

What [Blackmun] did, I think basically, is say that the Hippocratic oath was not the standard of all doctors at that time; it was more sort of a subsample of doctors. He called them the Pythagoreans, and they were not representative of medicine as a whole. And he depended upon an interpretation by Ludwig Edelstein, who indicated that when the Hippocratic oath came into being this represented just a minority of Greek physicians; they were not representative of all doctors and therefore they were biased. And he also said, well, at that time there were all kinds of other things happening too: infanticide, euthanasia, the Spartans with their children, getting rid of those who were defective after birth, and that type of thing. He said, therefore, the Pythagoreans came in, and what they tried to do was impose their view of morality on the rest of Greek society. (chuckles) So he was maligning—actually maligning—the Hippocratic oath! But it was a very, very selective and erroneous view of Hippocrates and his rationale.

You see, Hippocrates was not a religious sectarian; he was a pagan! And his enacting the Hippocratic oath, formulating it, developing it, was based not on any religious, dogmatic interpretation but on the whole idea of medicine and the doctor being a healer and not a killer. They said the doctor should never be a killer of anyone whether unborn or born. And then of course Blackmun tried to connect that with Christianity and saying, well, the oath is sort of a relic of Christianity also because Christianity took up the oath and made it part of its ethical orientation towards human life.

Just as Blackmun eventually concluded that the oath was simply a form of religion imposing itself onto society, modern defenders of the abortion liberty direct exactly the same criticism toward all who dare challenge that liberty today.

PART 4.

Is Pro-Choice
a Neutral Position?

CHAPTER 32

Both Sides Can't Be Right

He who denies that human life begins with conception does not need to contend with religion, but science. To deny this certainty of biology is not to express a lack of faith, but a lack of basic knowledge of human genetics, something that is even known by the general public.
—ECUADORIAN FEDERATION OF SOCIETIES OF GYNECOLOGY AND OBSTETRICS

Whether or not society has been convinced that what is killed during an abortion is not a human being, the effect of *Roe v. Wade* has been to establish a social doctrine based on that conviction. That this ideology was created without any attempt to offer scientific support or verification made it simply a subjective moral philosophy. That decades of biological science and medical instruction had authoritatively stated the exact opposite, made it unsubstantiated. That the Constitution had mysteriously hidden the abortion liberty somewhere deep within its amendments for over a century only to emerge during the sexual revolution of the 1960s made it highly suspect. Not surprisingly, as a result, the reaction to *Roe v. Wade* has been dramatic and intense.

Just a few years after *Roe v. Wade*, John Noonan wrote an accurate summation of the continuing social dilemma:

> Abortion has not gone away. Today it divides the country. Neutrality for a legislator is impossible. Each side believes with deep conviction that it is right. Both sides cannot be right, and conflict in theory means conflict in practice. Legalized as a private act, abortion has become a public issue. (Noonan, 1)

Noonan makes a very important point: Both sides simply cannot be right because the philosophies of each rest on incompatible ideas. Either the life of a living human is worthy of legal protection by virtue of the fact that it is a living human, or the right to life of each living human is subjectively obtained at some point during its development.

In American politics compromise is the name of the game. But compromise when human life is at stake is dangerous. At its core the abortion debate is not about a woman's "right to choose" abortion. It is about whether or not a human life is destroyed as a consequence of the mother's choice. No woman has the "right to choose" to destroy her offspring when the child is located outside her womb. Both sides cannot be right.

Planned Parenthood President Gloria Feldt asks:

> Why do religious fundamentalists...and their political operatives ...think that they are entitled to force their personal belief systems on the rest of us? (Feldt, 17)

According to Sarah Weddington:

> The level of passion that abortion evokes in some who oppose it, particularly those who participate in the assault waves against clinics and women seeking services, has puzzled me. Why are they so passionate about forcing women to go through every pregnancy? (Weddington, 246–7)

Of course the converse is true as well for pro-life advocates who are often quite puzzled by those who, like Weddington and Feldt, have a perplexing but passionate disregard for the intrinsic value of human life when that life is located in the womb of a woman yet suddenly begin to recognize it after birth.

Weddington speculates about what motivates pro-life proponents, reporting that a friend of hers believes that they are often people who feel "powerless" and that "they seek to gain or regain power and control by trying to control women and their decisions" (Weddington, 247).

The utter nonsense of this approach is revealed by considering the public response to the actions of mothers like Susan Smith, who *made a conscious choice* to strap her living toddlers into their car seats and roll the car into a lake.

Those who find Smith's behavior unfathomably reprehensible are not accused of being religious zealots and misguided power seekers who merely want to control women like Smith. Those who feel such actions are rightfully illegal are not charged with attempting to force their religious or moral beliefs onto Smith or the rest of society. For those in the pro-choice movement to so characterize abortion opponents (whose only "sin" is sharing an equal concern for toddlers and unborn children) demonstrates the complete lack of regard pro-choice proponents hold for the value of unborn human life as well as their lack of understanding, tolerance of, and sensitivity to the sincere conviction that the unborn child is a human being worthy of legal protection—which, as all genuinely pro-life advocates agree, is *the* motivating factor for the pro-life movement. To argue, as Weddington and Feldt do, that pro-life proponents are secretly motivated by a desire to control women rather than the expressed desire of protecting the fetus, is clearly nothing more than blatant pro-choice propaganda. And yet, sadly, the pro-life movement, and the very term "pro-life" often conjure negative images for average Americans.

Dr. Mildred Jefferson:

Abortion is the issue of our opponents. Our issue is the defense of the sanctity of life and a defense of the political principle of the right to life. And the right to life is the cornerstone and foundation of our democratic/republican form of government and therefore is the foundation of the Constitution and the laws of our country. So that to try to twist it in terms of individual and personal choice is not only to create social anarchy but it creates legal and political anarchy.

CHAPTER 33

The Gospel of Choice

I just happen to believe that simple morality dictates that unless and until someone can prove the unborn human is not alive, we must give it the benefit of the doubt and assume it is. And thus, it should be entitled to life, liberty, and the pursuit of happiness.
—RONALD REAGAN, REMARKS AT THE ALFRED M. LANDON LECTURE SERIES ON PUBLIC ISSUES, MANHATTAN, KANSAS, SEPTEMBER 9, 1982

The abortion debate is not about control; it is not about the subjugation of women to men. Such notions are past their expiration date. Ultimately, the abortion debate is about the value of human life. That pro-choice proponents refuse to accept this simple truth does not make right-to-life advocates insincere.

But Weddington perpetuates the idea of secret and sinister pro-life motivations by insisting that while adherents to pro-choice philosophy are "generally 'live and let live' people" (Weddington, 242), pro-lifers, by contrast, simply want to force their religious beliefs onto the rest of society:

> . . . we aren't trying to convince those on the other side to agree with us. We are simply trying to keep them from forcing their beliefs on us. (Weddington, 242)

The fallacious implication of this and oft-repeated similar statements is that the pro-choice position is the ideal since it is somehow neutral, nonpartisan, devoid of any religious basis, or at least accommodating of any religious basis or none at all; whereas, one allegedly cannot be pro-life without resting that position on religious convictions. In a society that increasingly leans toward the separation of church and state, the pro-choice position is packaged and presented as the only acceptable secular position. As John Noonan succinctly points out, in the ensuing legal and philosophical battles following *Roe*, ironically, "the facts of biology were treated as though they had a religious coloration" (Noonan, 58), while the metaphysical notion of personhood attaching at some point during pregnancy, birth, or even beyond, was presented as secular rationalism.

The resulting double standard is difficult to conceal, especially when championed by the attorney who had successfully preached and established a radical new gospel of choice by converting seven Supreme Court justices to the new abortion orthodoxy. The seven new disciples on the high Court demonstrated their newfound zeal by granting validity to a variety of unsupported doctrines, such as the alleged uncertainty regarding the beginning of human life, the erroneous dogma of the original purpose underlying pre-*Roe* anti-abortion laws, a questionable interpretation of the Constitution, and an overreaching philosophy of privacy while simultaneously eradicating, in one swift blow, over one hundred years of established abortion law across the country.

Weddington goes on to state that:

> To me, the current public controversy over abortion is primarily a religious conflict. Religious faith is of course important, but it is upsetting when religion is invoked as the source of authority for imposing one set of ideas on people who do not share them. (Weddington, 243)

Remarkably, Weddington characterizes the conflict over abortion as primarily religious yet implies that only the opinions of those who oppose her point of view amount to a religious imposition. In what might be considered a masterful piece of propaganda, Weddington casually stacks the deck in her favor by implying—rather than directly stating—that the pro-choice cause is essentially secular in nature and therefore devoid of religious concepts. She attempts to reinforce this notion with her earlier assertions that "life" is a continuum with no clear beginning or end.

Yet, the reality is that Weddington and the pro-choice movement have failed to explain how repeatable observation of actively developing human life from fertilization onward is somehow a religious phenomenon. Weddington also fails to explain how her own wholly unsupported notion that a fetus was not "equal to a 'human being'" (Weddington, 97) until birth *was not* a "religious" assertion. Never mind that the latter conclusion requires faith that necessarily contradicts what even Justice Blackmun acknowledged as the "well-known facts of fetal development." As John Noonan writes:

> To say that the Christian position rested on a theory of ensoulment and to proceed therefore to disqualify it in the realm of secular law was to imply that Christians had no right to be heard on killing in general. The Christian opposition to genocide, to urban air raids, to the war in Vietnam was no more and no less theological than the Christian opposition to abortion. (Noonan, 53)

Going back in time prior to the advent of microscopes, one could rationally have argued—from a position of ignorance—that a fetus is not a living human being until the mother first feels the unmistakable indication of life in the form of movement within her body. In this age of ultrasound imagery and fetal surgery, such an archaic appeal to ignorance is simply inappropriate. There is *no question* that the life of the individual human has begun well before the mother can feel the baby's acrobatics inside her womb.

Randy Alcorn:

> In any dialogue over any moral issue people muster their arguments. So, if the arguments are bad, then refute them. But to say that a person with a religious viewpoint can't, with any validity, bring scientific evidence to the table and medical evidence to the table, is clearly inappropriate. You have atheists who are pro-life just as you have religious people who are pro-abortion. The question is not the beliefs of these people but the actual evidence that they're putting on the table. So, while I have definite spiritual beliefs, call them religious beliefs, that are an important part of my life, the arguments that I'm making in my books are almost never religious. I mean they are occasionally for those who, to whom religious arguments are of value that, of course, we are created in the image of God, but even if someone doesn't believe we're "created in the image of God," they can still believe that human beings have certain rights.
>
> And so, this is not imposing somebody's religion. If you take away

all the laws that are defended by and, in fact, historically rooted in, for instance, the Ten Commandments, take: "thou shalt not kill" and "thou shall not steal;" let's just take those two. All right, well, there you go! Those are religious issues! So let's repeal laws against killing and stealing because, after all, those are religious arguments that are made historically and religious people believe them and so why should they, you know, foist their beliefs on us? Well, those beliefs are best for society, and they conform to natural law, and they are right, and the great majority of people believe them to be right.

Dr. Jefferson:

The point of transmission of the life that's the individual that's the target of the abortionist is the point known as fertilization, popularly known as conception. And as long as you have a healthy egg cell and a healthy sperm cell and appropriate lab conditions, you can demonstrate that. It's not a matter of religious faith. It's a matter of what has been demonstrated by advances in science and technology.

Dr. Brennan:

Weddington assumes that the belief, the so-called belief, that's being imposed on her is a strictly Christian belief, a sanctity-of-life ethic that's derived from the Judeo-Christian ethic. But actually, one can even use this on strictly a reason-based level. This is not to say that faith is not important and faith and reason are really compatible with one another, but I think you can look at this in terms of an equality-of-life ethic. Whatever the roots of this are, whether they are secular or religious, they all point to an equality-of-life ethic. And I think on that basis you can say that this is not imposing anything on anyone. It's protecting the equality of all human beings. That is the ethic we're talking about. And this can be also an ethic that some atheists may agree with. Some atheists may agree that we should have equal protection under the law.

Dr. Magill:

Well that raises a very difficult question and that is how any society works in terms of protecting all of its members. No matter how diverse your society may be, at the end of the day there are always going to be different groups with different beliefs; some of them will be secular beliefs, some of them will be religious beliefs. The plurality and diversity of beliefs is not going to leave society, so society has to learn to traverse a terrain of beliefs clashing against each other. And therefore, it has got to try to resolve those clashes at very foundational points. And it seems to me in a civilized society one of the most foundational points is the protection of human life. You might want to argue about what color of car you're allowed to have, but whether you're allowed to take life is certainly a hallmark of civilized society. And so in terms of the pluralist nature of society, whether it be a religious belief or a secularist belief, the idea of not having those foundational black-and-white protective lines seems to me as a compromise of the civil reality. So for people who would say this is religion imposing itself upon society, [that's] simply false. It's rather a very logical, rational stance asserting itself to enhance civility in society.

There was a time in America when taking a "very logical, rational stance" in order to "enhance civility in society" by protecting unborn human life was taken for granted as something virtuous. Nowadays, it is often seen as an unacceptable form of religious imposition.

Remarkably, people from all walks of life within the pro-choice community have fallen into the erroneous line of thought that the beginning of human life is not a settled matter. The simple reality is that the beginning of *biological* human life is an observable phenomenon. It is factual, not hypothetical. It's worth noting that the process of fertilization occurs at a specific point and shortly afterwards (the first seven to fourteen days following conception) when the developing new human *is not* attached to the mother's body, but rather, is simply residing inside it. From that point on, growth and development is continuous and internally self-directed. The point is that the beginning of human life can be *repeatedly* observed, scientifically. There is simply no getting around this.

Of course, the disagreement Justice Blackmun references among theologians and philosophers is also true. But that debate can only realistically center around the hypothetical notion that *something greater than* actual biological human life *must* (theoretically) be present for humans to actually be worthy of a continued "right to life." In other words, being human and alive must not be intrinsically valuable in and of itself. Certainly, such a notion is *indeed* a religious concept. If what I really am is more than the sum of the physical cells, processes, and chromosomes that make up my body, then, granted, it *may well be* that the essential element that constitutes the real "me" comes into existence or is implanted into my body at some point beyond fertilization. *This* is where legitimate debate and lack of consensus enter the picture.

But such an idea cannot be factually demonstrated from either perspective. It is purely hypothetical. More importantly, it is the pro-choice position that requires an unsettled debate centered around the metaphysical concept of "personhood" in order to keep itself alive, not the pro-life position. It might be that the genes contain "personhood" or "ensoulment" encoded within them from the beginning. Or it might be that "ensoulment" or "personhood" begins later in physiological development. Either of these options is *possible*. Neither is demonstrably provable, which is what keeps pro-choice philosophy in business. What *is* provable is that the human being is biologically alive and uniquely human from conception onward. In short, pro-life philosophy accords with reality. Pro-choice philosophy depends on metaphysical speculation.

The critical point pro-choice proponents miss when they point triumphantly to ignorance as a basis for abortion is that they themselves are espousing an essentially "religious" doctrine that says it is permissible to kill *what we know biologically to be* a living human on *the chance* that whatever it *may hypothetically be* that makes us legitimate "persons" and gives us intrinsic value is *probably* not yet present in the living human body that must be killed by abortion. Yet, this wildly speculative "theory" is touted as being acceptable because of its *assumed* neutrality!

The widespread idea that the pro-life side of the abortion debate is a religious imposition while the pro-choice side is not is particularly offensive in light of the reality that the only side supported by concrete facts when it comes to the entity most drastically affected by abortion is the pro-life position. Hypothetical entities are not killed by abortion. Real ones are. In the absence of an option to simply deny the existence of unborn human life, the pro-choice side necessarily attempts to *minimize the value of* the life that is killed by abortion. This minimization is purely speculative and must therefore be accepted on faith. Attempts to ground this subjective minimization in something logically based end up resembling religious dogma.

While the more familiar attempts to "justify" acceptance of abortion on demand are framed in terms of secular-sounding but inherently metaphysical concepts like "personhood" or "meaningful life," other attempts to accomplish the same goal employ an overtly religious framework.

Rev. John V. Stevens Sr. is one such religiously motivated abortion advocate. Pastor Stevens interprets Psalm 139 to mean that:

> Although God sees and knows the developing baby in the womb and matures it for birth, that does not qualify an unborn baby as being a person. The key explanation is found in the reference in the text, "The days fashioned for me, when as yet there were none of them." This clearly refers to the fetus as a non-existent person. The 90th Psalm revealed man's lifespan long before our time, about 1000 B.C.: "The days of our lives are seventy years; and if by reason of strength they are eighty years, yet their boast is only labor and sorrow, for it is soon cut off." Days are the measure of the span of life, from birth to death. In the 139th Psalm the developing baby has no days; hence, it has no life, other than mother's borrowed life, and no personhood. (John V. Stevens Sr., *The Abortion Controversy*, Founders Freedom Press, 173, hereafter "Stevens")

In fact, the thesis of Pastor Stevens's entire book is an explicitly religious justification for legal abortion through birth (!) based on the notion that "there is no life without breath, nor personhood without life that comes from breath" (Stevens, Table of Contents, Chapter 12).

The diabolical irony in Stevens's use of the phrase "developing baby in the womb" while simultaneously arguing in favor of legal abortion through birth is shockingly brazen—especially when you consider that even Sarah Weddington felt uneasy about late-term abortions. Not only are Pastor Stevens's views religiously inspired, they clearly contradict observable biological facts. Why then are Pastor Stevens's views *not* presented as an unacceptable imposition of religion onto society?

If I develop a religious doctrine that born babies are not worthy of legal protection until they have the ability to communicate through language—therefore infanticide is justified until the baby learns to talk—is such a doctrine morally acceptable? One would certainly hope not. Yet such a doctrine is more factually rooted than that of Stevens, which actually *contradicts* observable biological facts. Stevens's religious doctrine that *there is no life* without breath "other than mother's borrowed life" is demonstrably inaccurate. This would be like saying a scuba diver borrows his life from an oxygen tank while diving. On the contrary, the oxygen tank merely serves to temporarily sustain the diver's preexisting life by supplying it with one crucial element not otherwise readily available in the current environment. By the same token, the mother provides nourishment and oxygen to her unborn child, which are necessary *to sustain preexisting life*, but she doesn't loan the fetus a portion of her own life for nine months any more than an oxygen tank loans life to the scuba diver. We can all agree, one would hope, that killing a scuba diver while underwater is as immoral as killing the same individual when he or she is taking in air directly from the atmosphere.

Stevens's unconventional interpretation of Psalm 139 and his further attempts to justify abortion on demand are a clear example of religious dogma attempting to impose itself onto society with drastic consequences. But because his views are categorized as falling under the broader context of "choice," they are generally tolerated on the basis that if you disagree with him, don't have an abortion. If this is sound logic, then I would have equally sufficient grounds to respond accordingly to those who might object to the infanticide epidemic resulting from the widespread acceptance of my philosophically based language doctrine.

In the event that *Roe* were overturned, one could, of course, employ the retort in reverse such that women who disagree with anti-abortion laws should simply not get pregnant. The pragmatism of such an approach is seldom accepted by those who view abortion as a fundamental right. Regardless, there is an intrinsic difference between not getting pregnant and killing an unborn human.

Stevens's attempts to rationalize abortion on request from a religious perspective are not unique. In fact, a Clergy Consultation Service made up mostly of Protestants, which basically amounted to an abortion referral agency, was established early on in the fight to liberalize abortion in the years before *Roe*. As pro-choice historian David Garrow freely acknowledges, the group, created in 1967, was "not so much an organization as a network" that "publicly advertised abortion counseling *and* abortion referral information" (Garrow, 333, emphasis in original).

Consider the resulting double standard: The Catholic Church is repeatedly charged with attempting to force its morality onto society by simply opposing abortion and working legitimately within the legal system to discourage abortion while a mostly Protestant "Clergy Consultation Service" had been actively working within the pro-abortion movement as a referral agency for a procedure *still illegal* in most states at least six years prior to *Roe v. Wade*. Yet this active involvement, formally recognized as "clergy" willing to refer abortions, was *not* charged with attempting to force its religion and/or morality onto society. Why not?

Recounting the triumph of legal abortion in her book, *Roe v. Wade: The Untold Story of the Landmark Supreme Court Decision That Made Abortion Legal*, Marian Faux reveals how religion was skillfully exploited in Texas to advance the pro-abortion agenda in the months leading up to the *Roe* decision. Describing the shrewd tactics of the Dallas women who, with Weddington, had attempted to push for repeal of the Texas abortion law in that state, Faux notes that:

> They also devised ways of approaching what everyone euphemistically called the "religious issue," a reference to the Catholic Church's opposition to abortion. The women were not above trading on the anti-Catholic feeling that seemed almost indigenous to Texas, a state settled by Anglo-Saxon Protestants who had carried their evangelical puritanism west with them and made it their unofficial "state" religion.
>
> Texas also took states' rights seriously and separation of Church and State very seriously. Members of the clergy were barred from holding office in the state legislature. The women learned to phrase their comments in a kind of code that was clearly understood by the legislators to whom they spoke. They emphasized for example, that restrictive abortion laws seemed to support the view of one particular (unnamed) religion.
>
> The women knew that the legislators, including several Protestants with large Roman Catholic constituencies, had been scared away from the 1969 reform bill, when the church had organized an unexpectedly forceful mail campaign that pleaded, begged, and threatened the legislators if they voted to liberalize abortion. (Faux, 202–3)

Apparently Faux fails to see the irony in a pre-*Roe* group of abortion proponents in a state that took "separation of Church and State very seriously" using "a kind of code that was clearly understood" by the mostly Protestant legislators to emphasize that the laws they opposed coincidentally seemed to "support the view of" the Catholic religion. In order to further their own pro-abortion agenda, Faux discloses that these "women were not above trading on the anti-Catholic feeling" prevalent in Texas by exploiting a preexisting ill will between Protestants and Catholics. Evidently, for Faux and the pro-abortion women she writes about, religion can only force itself onto society if it happens to disagree with the pro-abortion agenda.

While religious groups have worked to advance political agendas on both sides of the abortion debate since its inception, the only groups that have taken heat for it are those lining up in support of the pro-life movement.

Faux provides a textbook example of this double standard as she describes the amici curiae (friend of the court) briefs filed for both sides in Roe v. Wade. Faux asserts that "the pro-choice briefs were most impressive" (Faux, 270), while "[i]n contrast," she claims, "the amici curiae briefs for the opposition were propagandistic as well as inaccurate" (Faux, 271) despite the fact that they centered on biological facts, the facts referred to by Justice Blackmun as "the well-known facts of fetal development." Why, according to Faux, were the pro-life briefs "propagandistic"? Evidently because one of them was written by Dr. Jack and Barbara Willke, a Christian couple who "taught sex education to church groups across the country" (Faux, 271).

Faux also found fault in the fact that they focused attention on the developing organism in the womb and referred to it as a "baby":

> The state's brief was also more propagandistic than legal. Almost half was given over to examination of the developing fetus, which was often erroneously referred to as a "baby." This section contained several misleadingly labeled and greatly enlarged photographs of developing fetuses and made numerous misleading statements, such as one indicating that after the eighth week until adulthood, "the changes of the body will be mainly in dimension and in gradual refinement of the working parts." (Faux, 271–2)

Notably, Faux's main complaint centers around the notion that nearly half of the state's brief was "given over to examination of the developing fetus," which she felt should not be referred to as a baby. Given that the state was arguing for personhood from conception, it is hardly surprising that much of its evidence would center on "examination of the developing fetus" or that it might refer to a fetus as an unborn baby. Also no less surprise is the fact that the state would choose to use photographs to support its case. Faux's complaint is not that the photographs contained inaccurate information but that they were "enlarged." Faux suggests that, "it might have been helpful to know that a three-month-old fetus is less than two inches long" (Faux, 272). Exactly what conclusion that information might have been "helpful" to reach is unclear, but the implication is that the size of a human life is morally significant.

There is nothing misleading about the statement that after the eighth week until adulthood, "the changes of the body will be mainly in dimension and in gradual refinement of the working parts." In fact, it's an accurate statement.

Faux then complains that the briefs asserted that "every child shows a distinct individuality in his behavior by the end of the third month" and that the "child hears and recognizes his mother's voice," a contention Faux suggests cannot be known for certain, but Faux cites no authorities who dispute the claim. In fact, evidence steadily obtained since 1973 supports the accuracy of these assertions (See, for example, chapter 44, "Dreams and Hiccups").

In what may qualify as the clearest example of the pot calling the kettle black, Faux writes: "Unbiased antiabortion experts seemed remarkably hard to come by" (Faux, 272). Again, it is noteworthy that Faux does not dispute the "well-known facts of fetal development" in any substantive way. She simply implies that the term "baby" is inappropriate, complains that the photographs were "enlarged," and objects to the idea that an unborn child can learn to recognize his mother's voice despite supporting observational evidence.

Faux's criticisms illustrate a larger problem. Her protests imply that if the state has its facts correct, then abortion is immoral. If Faux were to eventually come to realize that her criticisms of the Texas briefs are baseless, would she then change her mind about abortion? Probably not. The truth is, many pro-choice advocates do not *want* a fetus to be the moral equivalent of a baby, so they latch onto whatever seems to support that preconceived notion.

Despite all of this, the salient point is that biology is observable while personhood is essentially a metaphysical concept. Because it centers on the notion of "personhood" vs. "nonpersonhood," pro-abortion philosophy rests on a patently metaphysical framework. By insisting either that human life in the womb is not meaningful enough or that the problems of the mother or the harm she might do to herself in obtaining a "back alley" abortion outweigh the right of her unborn child to continue living, pro-choice proponents demonstrate their loyalty to a metaphysically based political cause.

By contrast, anti-abortion philosophy rests on biological facts. That biological human life is present from conception onward—whether or not it is viewed by those of us on the outside as possessing a "soul" or is viewed by courts as being a "person in the whole sense"—is simply indisputable. Clearly, there is no religion involved in observing life in its earliest stages. Religious dogma *does* come into play, however, when those who wish to destroy existing human life in its earliest stages attempt to justify this desire—as did the *Roe* majority—based only on the unsubstantiated assertion that unborn humans are "not persons in the whole sense," or that what is growing in the womb of a woman is merely "potential life," or that (when conceding actual life) the life of the unborn is not "meaningful" enough to warrant legal protection.

The subjective nature of each of these attempts by the *Roe* majority to find a rational justification for abortion on demand is emphasized by the fact that, upon reflection, they actually contradict one another, with the result that pro-choice proponents can't get their story straight.

Either human life is present in the womb or it isn't. There is no middle ground. If what is located in the womb of a woman is merely potential life, then actual life is not yet present. Potential life ceases to be potential life when actualized. At that point, it is simply actual life with a lot of potential. If actual life is not present in the womb, then nothing needs to be killed by abortion. If nothing needs to be killed by abortion, there is no controversy and we can all pack up and go home. The reality is that if the actual, living fetus *is not killed*, pregnancy continues. Clearly then, actual life is present, which renders the "potential life" argument adopted by the U.S. Supreme Court utterly ridiculous.

The remaining ideas fare no better. By using the term "meaningful life," the court was tacitly acknowledging that indeed *something* needed to be killed by abortion. Furthermore, there could be no dispute that what needed to be killed was human. The moral basis, then, for allowing prenatal human killing (on what would prove to be a massive scale) was that, although actual, it was not yet *meaningful*. But the term itself is highly subjective. Human life in the womb is undoubtedly meaningful to any mother who wants to keep her baby or, for that matter, to any father who wants the child. It is also meaningful to any of us who've managed to make the journey outside the womb. Without that developmental period in our lives, none of us would now exist. That in itself renders the prenatal period quite "meaningful" to the entity residing in the womb. Though unseen in its early stages without the aid of science, human development in the womb is nothing short of miraculous. To argue that the life of the unborn human lacks meaning to such an extent that it is unworthy of legal protection is simply a callous attempt to rationalize the desire to be rid of the obligation to care for it. The same argument could be—and has been—made to justify infanticide.

The third idea enunciated by the *Roe* majority—that, although clearly living, unborn humans were "not persons in the whole sense"—was simply a declaratory statement with no rational, real-world support. Essentially, unborn humans were not "persons" because the court said so. Rigging the playing field, the Court had defined personhood as having nothing to do with the "well-known facts of fetal development." Personhood as used by the Court amounted to little more than a convenient but arbitrary legal label with no underlying basis in the real world. If it had had the courage, the Court might have cited its own prior "logic" as precedent, for, in exactly the same way, it had previously concluded that black humans were not persons in the whole sense under constitutional protection because the *Dred Scott* majority had held it to be so. Michael Stokes Paulsen states it this way:

> A decision to fashion a right to abortion out of the words "due process of law" [Fourteenth Amendment] would share much in common with *Dred Scott*, which is, methodologically, the single best supportive precedent for such an invention. . . .
>
> Were it not for the fact that *Dred Scott* is so thoroughly discredited, its substantive due process methodology so plainly indefensible, its result so illustrative of the dangers of judges assuming quasi-legislative authority, *Dred Scott* would be the precedent most nearly in point for the proposition appellants [Sarah Weddington and the pro-choice lobby] assert. (Michael Stokes Paulsen, as quoted in Balkin, 203)

Regrettably, as Paulsen notes, relegating a powerless segment of society to the status of nonpersonhood for the purpose of running roughshod over their rights was not uncharted territory for the United States Supreme Court. And it was a tactic for which the Court either believed it needed no rationalization or could simply find none. Coherent logic resting on observable data was apparently an unnecessary nuisance. Either way, in the absence of massive public protest, the Court's decree alone was sufficient. It was free—so it believed—to whimsically declare the unborn to be less than "persons in the whole sense" and then proceed with abortion on demand.

CHAPTER 34

Whose Morality?

Morality cannot be legislated, but behavior can be regulated.
Judicial decrees may not change the heart, but they can restrain the heartless.
—Dr. Martin Luther King Jr.

Justice Blackmun aptly demonstrated his devotion to the Weddington/ Lucas/Means choice gospel by formally writing out the new canon which decreed:

> We do not agree that, by adopting one theory of life, Texas may override the rights of the pregnant woman that are at stake. (*RvW*, 162)

The irony of prohibiting Texas from operating under a factually supported "theory" that personhood is present when biological human life begins while permitting itself to operate under the opposite assumption based on admitted ignorance (or purposeful avoidance) of those same facts is palpable. Consider once again this exchange between Texas attorney Robert Flowers and Supreme Court Justice Potter Stewart:

> MR. FLOWERS: Your Honor, it seems to me that the physical act of being born—I'm not playing it down. I know it's a very momentous incident. But what changes? Is it a nonhuman, and changing by the act of birth into a human? Or would . . .
>
> JUSTICE STEWART: Well, that's been the theory up until now in the law.

Putting aside, for the moment, Justice Stewart's dubious assertion that the legal theory up until *Roe* had been that unborn humans were "nonhuman" until birth, Stewart, nevertheless, freely acknowledges that the Court was indeed ready to base its own ruling on *a theory*. What Stewart didn't acknowledge was just how incoherent the theory would turn out to be, vaguely holding either that human life begins at birth or that meaningful human life begins at viability. And while adopting this dual hypothesis as though it represented reality, the Court also flatly admitted in the *Roe* majority opinion that it was not in any position *even to speculate* whether its own novel "theory" had any rational correlation to biological fact. Nor was it even interested in searching for a possible connection. It simply fashioned a law (rather than interpreting an existing one) holding birth (i.e., separation from the mother) as the key distinguishing point between "meaningful" and "nonmeaningful" human life. Viability was noteworthy in that it was a "point" wherein birth could theoretically be induced with a reasonable chance of survival for the unborn child. But viability ultimately proved to be an essentially hollow legal barrier to the on-demand destruction of the fetus given the liberal "health" override provision of *Doe*. The Court never provided any rational basis for codifying its own inimitable "theory of life"—which amounted to little more than an admission of ignorance—while denying Texas by fiat any opportunity to do the same thing based on the "well-known facts of fetal development."

The new Lucas/Weddington/Means/Blackmun abortion orthodoxy was then thrust upon society in the form of a radical gospel of choice as enumerated in the *Roe v. Wade* canon and marketed as the only allegedly acceptable nonreligious way to think about abortion.

Dr. Jefferson:

> We are in a civic arena, and when the branch of the government that does not derive its power—its just power—from the consent of the governed undertakes to act as a super-Congress to force its own social law upon the country, and a law that is based in the secular humanist religious philosophy, those who object to our Judeo-Christian religious principles simply have no ground and no worthy challenge. And whether Weddington acknowledges it or not, she is advancing the core theory and beliefs of the secular humanist philosophy in everything that she has uttered in *Roe v. Wade* or in justification of *Roe v. Wade*.

Dr. Brennan:

> And whose morality are you using? And here we get into the whole area of ethical relativism, which is rampant in our society. It's not just morality in general but the question is: whose morality will be imposed? The other side says, well, you're imposing your morality on me, but they fail to say that their morality is being imposed on you or on the unborn or on the vulnerable groups of individuals. So, you can't get away from that.

But the new "choice gospel" ran into some snags. First, it seemed to contradict the spirit of the Founding Fathers' stated ideals involving protection of the weak from the questionable morals of an all-powerful state. Consider the language of the Declaration of Independence for example:

> We hold these truths to be self-evident that all men are created equal, that they are endowed by their creator with certain unalienable rights, that among these are life, liberty and the pursuit of happiness.

Where Weddington could only state with relative certainty in her book that "life began once" and is a continuum, by contrast the writers of the Declaration viewed it as fact that each human life is not only created, but endowed by the Creator (as opposed to Supreme Court justices) with certain unalienable rights, chief of which is *the right to life*. This fact was so obvious to our Founding Fathers as to be proclaimed *self-evident*. These basic, unalienable human rights superseded the government. They superseded the Constitution. They superseded the Supreme Court. In order for *Roe v. Wade* to find itself in harmony with the Declaration of Independence, one must assume the "Creator" of life does not "endow" his creations with life until birth—a concept even Weddington apparently finds questionable as expressed by her uneasiness with late-term abortions.

A second snag involved the reality that pro-choice logic essentially rests on an unsupportable and arbitrary *assumption,* despite the fact that its proponents accused their opposition of being anti-abortion for unavoidably religious reasons. Nevertheless, advocates of abortion have been generally effective in convincing the public that any position maintaining personhood to be present at conception—or even merely suggesting that unborn human life is worthy of retaining its life long enough to be safely removed from the womb regardless of the onset of any metaphysical idea called "personhood"—is somehow exclusively a religious notion not to be forced onto others who do not share it. Yet the fact that the opposite position maintaining that an unquantifiable but critical amount of "personhood" *is not present* until birth or that unborn human life does not have enough value or meaning, itself a patently religious concept in that it must be accepted by faith, is overlooked.

CHAPTER 35

Live and Let Die

I am not religious. I do not believe that personhood is conferred upon conception. But I also do not believe that a human embryo is the moral equivalent of a hangnail and deserves no more respect than an appendix.
—CHARLES KRAUTHAMMER

Obviously science cannot verify claims of "personhood" when personhood is defined as having nothing to do with the very thing science *can* observe: the "well-known facts of fetal development." If fetal development were to have been used as a factor in determining a moral response to abortion and abortion laws, the outcome of *Roe v. Wade* would necessarily have been radically different.

As it is, since the "personhood" claims of neither side in the debate can be measured scientifically, it becomes apparent that both sides are essentially "religious" or at least hypothetical/philosophical in nature when the debate centers exclusively around the notion of "personhood" while ignoring biology. But are the opposing claims in regard to personhood *equally* hypothetical? Upon careful review, pro-choice claims turn out to be much more tenuous and arbitrary than pro-life claims.

The ethic that says it's okay to kill a fetus (when the mother is not in a life-threatening situation) can only find moral justification by insisting that the human fetus is radically subhuman. As we've seen, the idea that a living fetus is merely "potential life" is absurd on its face, and the idea of "meaningfulness" attaching at viability is simply another way of arguing that birth—removal from the womb with an ability to survive—renders human life meaningful.

With respect to "meaningfulness," viability is simply the vehicle through which birth might be safely accelerated. If the fetus has truly reached viability, however, then there is no longer a need for abortion. Yet this tends to be true only in theory, since abortion advocates have a propensity to argue for a "right to abortion" irrespective of viability. Unfortunately, in most cases of unwanted pregnancy, the mother prefers a dead baby (while denying its existence to morally justify the act of abortion) rather than to simply be delivered of the pregnancy where the problem of a live baby remains.

The remaining ethic adopted and promoted by the Court centers on the idea that a fetus is not a "person in the whole sense." But personhood, according to the Court's own logic, can have nothing to do with concrete, observable data in the form of the "well-known facts of fetal development." Thus, what might have been a boon for the pro-choice cause (assuming the "well-known facts of fetal development" could have been exploited in support of pro-choice ideology) turns out to be a conspicuous weakness. Instead of harboring its philosophical assumptions within the security of actual biological data, the Court chose instead to situate its ruling on an abstract, capricious idea the Court itself had invented: that unborn humans "are not persons in the whole sense." There was no correlation to reality justifying this pronouncement nor even a superficial attempt to find one.

By contrast, pro-life claims do indeed rest on observable scientific data— namely, the "well-known facts of fetal development." In short, the fact that you see pro-life proponents using biological facts in support of their argument tells you something about their argument.

Pro-choice arguments—if they touch on biological facts at all—typically attempt to suggest that personhood is directly correlated to brain function, and brain function does not occur until later in pregnancy. But that premise is highly untenable. The *Roe* Court never attempts to make brain function the centerpiece of its denial of a right to life for good reasons. First, development of a brain is a process in which one is hard pressed to find any postconception point in human development in which cognition differs significantly from what it had been in previous moments. Second, cognition itself is difficult to measure and impossible to determine a precise beginning. Third, the process varies slightly from individual to individual and continues to develop in complexity throughout childhood and even into adulthood. But the larger problem is that no concrete correlation between "personhood" or one's being a "person in the whole sense" and brain development exists. It is simply *an assertion* to argue that one must have a functioning brain before one can be a person. One can just as easily rationally assert the opposite idea: that all humans are persons by virtue of being human regardless of the level of brain functionality and that, unless something abnormal occurs, all persons in the womb are actively developing functioning brains.

In his book *Abortion and Unborn Human Life*, Patrick Lee eloquently and logically argues for fetal personhood by emphasizing five foundational truths:

1. The human embryo or fetus is, from conception onward, a distinct individual.

2. The human embryo or fetus is, from conception onward, human.

3. The human embryo or fetus is, from conception onward, a complete human being.

4. Every whole human being is a person.

5. It is wrong intentionally to kill an innocent human person.

(Patrick Lee, *Abortion and Unborn Human Life*, DC: The Catholic University of America Press, 3–6, hereafter "Lee")

Of course the conscientious advocate of abortion on demand will object to the notion that a human fetus is a "distinct individual" from conception onward or that "every whole human being is a person," but that is exactly the point. In so objecting, the abortion advocate merely *asserts* a negative in both cases. Proving that negative is impossible. Essentially pro-choice logic in this specific case boils down to this: Despite the fact that we all agree that individual humans do exist and that babies *are* individual humans, we (pro-choice proponents) *don't believe* that human fetuses are individual humans even though all babies were fetuses up until their emergence from the womb.

Put another way, *every* known example of an individual human was at one time a living human fetus. Therefore, to argue that human fetuses *are not* individual humans is clearly a negative formulation (without known support) that rests on pure assertion. The burden of proof falls squarely on the pro-choice advocate to adequately demonstrate by what criteria a living human fetus *is not* an individual human despite the fact that it *is* at birth and to explain the rational reasons for so concluding.

If this sounds like splitting hairs, it is. But this sort of hairsplitting is what results when older human beings attempt to find a rational basis from which to deprive younger human beings of their right to continue living.

Similarly, the pro-abortion proponent must also demonstrate what societal benefit underlies the negative assertion that *not* every whole human being is a person and deal with any possible unforeseen negative consequences. Why must we even ask whether such a distinction is plausible? In other words, what good reason is there to ponder such a question? Except for radical thinkers like Michael Tooley or Peter Singer, the vast majority of pro-choice advocates agree that babies are "persons in the whole sense." Irrespective of Tooley and Singer, the *Roe* majority agreed that because of the Fourteenth Amendment, all born humans are persons.

When considering pro-choice philosophy outside the legal context, one must ask whether pro-choice proponents can point to any example of any born human and demonstrate that that human is not also a person? Radical and typically complex attempts to do this have been made by philosophers such as Tooley and Singer, but the majority of people in the U.S.—even most of those who describe themselves as pro-choice—find Tooley's and Singer's arguments as barbaric as pro-lifers do. This is what begs the question: What societal benefit arises if the notion of "personhood" can logically be separated from the notion of "human being," and what negative consequences might it produce? What "good" might be achieved even if the idea were not merely imaginary? Other than the desired immediate "benefit" of pregnant women to abort their unwanted pregnancies, these questions were not even considered by the *Roe* Supreme Court. The problem, of course, with this is that it logically follows that all kinds of undesirable humans may be defined as nonpersons for the purpose of ridding society of them. If this sounds reminiscent of Nazi philosophy, it is not by coincidence.

Thus, one suspects that the very idea of a possible extraction of "personhood" from "human being" came about as an ad hoc response to the desire for abortion on demand. Simply stated, science did not make a breakthrough discovery that "personhood" and "unborn human" were separable entities, and from that abortion on demand logically followed. On the contrary, the desire for abortion on demand arose, which was then followed by the requisite theoretical extraction of an intangible concept labeled "personhood" from the targeted group of tangible human beings.

Even if pro-choice philosophy became unified around the wild notion that personhood commences only after the establishment of an arbitrary amount of social relationships (or some other equally subjective criteria), the fact would still remain that "personhood" is immaterial and mutable. What one generation sees as "personhood" could easily be transposed on the whim of the next. The root problem remains: The negative assertion that *not* all whole humans are persons or even "individual human beings" is impossible to demonstrate and cannot be morally justified. One must keep in mind that the Court invented the notion of living humans who are not "persons in the whole sense." *No known examples of humans who are not also persons exist.* This is crucial. To have any possible moral justification for its "logic," the Court must demonstrate that the concept it rests its judgment on is a plausible concept. It has failed to do so. The Court might just as demonstrably have proclaimed: "Colts are not horses in the whole sense." But it gets even worse than this. In previously pronouncing that black humans are not "a part of the people," the U.S. Supreme Court illustrated its propensity for reaching unsound conclusions in exactly the same moral area. Therefore, not only is the Court's current judgment unsupported by real-world data, its previous similar judgment involving the same logical line of moral reasoning is now universally rejected. In short, the Court has a dismal track record in exactly the same area of moral reasoning.

By contrast, pro-life proponents point to genuine examples of living humans (not guilty of capital crimes) and ask whether society allows any of them to be legally killed? With the controversial exception of assisted suicide, which brings with it a unique set of ethical considerations, the answer is no. But even in these highly controversial cases or in cases of capital punishment, no one is suggesting that assisted suicide is permissible or capital punishment is permissible on the moral grounds that the human in question is not a "person." The question of personhood, then, after birth, becomes *irrelevant* because at that point personhood *is taken for granted.* By what criteria should we *assume* that personhood *is not* present before birth, and what proof is there to justify making such a radical assertion? Naturally pro-abortion advocates point to the *Roe* majority opinion in response, but doing so merely results in circular reasoning. Humans in the womb are not "persons in the whole sense" only because the Supreme Court, who has already failed in previous similar judgments, says so. We agree that virtually all of these same humans are persons when located outside the womb. Given that, the burden of proof rests with those who wish to assert the negative idea that some living humans are not "persons in the whole sense" as a direct consequence of their location and level of development, and only because of a desire on the part of others to be rid of them. Not surprisingly, there is no way to demonstrate this assertion objectively. Attempts to do so amount to metaphysically based rhetoric that must simply be accepted by faith.

In addition to the solid case that can be made for the existence of biological human life in the womb, its undeniable beginning at conception, and the resulting immorality of killing it by induced abortion (in the absence of dire circumstances), Patrick Lee also makes a rational counterclaim to the pro-choice idea that a fetus is not a "person in the whole sense." Lee writes:

> Human embryos and fetuses are rational and free agents because they are identical with the things which at a later time reason and freely choose, and they are actively developing themselves to the point where they will perform such acts. The important point for morality is that life, knowledge, friendship, and so on, are possibilities or potentialities for *this very being* even though it may take this being many years to actualize those potentialities. Indeed, these beings are even now *actively developing* themselves to the point at which they will realize these perfections.
>
> Finally, the point is not that they *potentially* have those characteristics which confer personhood. To have such characteristics only potentially would mean that they have personhood only potentially. Nor is the point that they are potential persons and therefore have rights. Rather, being a thing which has the potentiality rationally to pursue these various goods is what confers *actual* personhood, and human embryos and fetuses have that characteristic actually, not just potentially. (Lee, 61, emphasis in original)

These are extremely potent points. Not only are pro-choice proponents unable to prove the most critical assumption of their theory, Lee provides strong moral justification for believing their assumption is incorrect. Essentially pro-choice logic wishes to assert that what is killed by abortion is *a different entity entirely* than the entity that later emerges from the womb. If this basic assumption were accurate, then pro-choice logic would begin to make rational and moral sense. But as we will see when we examine the question in more detail in later chapters, this assumption is simply not accurate.

Clearly then, when comparing philosophical assertions, pro-choice philosophy is far more tenuous and arbitrary than pro-life philosophy. Yet for unclear reasons, pro-choice philosophy is packaged and promoted as though it were the only acceptable nonsectarian worldview when it comes to abortion, despite the fact that its tenets are inherently weaker and drastically so with much more serious consequences.

Despite the pro-choice representation of its own beliefs as tolerant and nonreligious, John Noonan points out that pro-abortion disciples were quick to force the new orthodoxy of what I call the "gospel of choice" onto those in society who openly oppose abortion by requiring hospitals to offer abortion services, medical students to pledge allegiance to choice, and the government and even college students to fund it:

> Just as the slaveholders had once wanted the cooperation of their critics in returning their slaves, so these libertarians wanted their critics to cooperate in doing what their critics believed was evil.
>
> The personal decision of the pregnant woman for abortion had social consequences for college students, medical students, hospitals, doctors, parents, towns, cities and states. The dedicated defenders of choice were dedicated to making everyone else agree with the choice of abortion. The defenders of conscience—the ACLU foremost of all—recognized only their own consciences as right. The liberty [of abortion], so peculiarly private in legend, was ubiquitously social in reality. (Noonan, 64)

Noonan goes on to document how even in its earliest stages, the pro-abortion movement sought not merely to be let alone but to actively promote abortion on demand and require cooperation from the rest of society. While working to repeal restrictive abortion laws, Harvard law professor Laurence Tribe, for example, had defended the principles of abortion in the name of "no establishment of religion." Pointing out that restrictive abortion legislation rested on a definition of what is to be regarded as "a human being," Tribe concluded that such a definition unavoidably "depended on a statement of religious faith upon which people will invariably differ" (Laurence H. Tribe, "Foreword to the Supreme Court—1972 Term: Toward a Model of Roles in the Due Process of Life and Law," *Harvard Law Review* 87, 1973, 20–3). Since restrictive abortion laws were consequently an establishment of "religion," according to Tribe, the state (or the courts) should repeal all such restrictive legislation. In other words, it was only an unconstitutional religious imposition to enact laws that treated the fetus as a person, whereas laws that did not recognize fetal personhood were, according to Tribe, constitutional. If Tribe's logic sounds reminiscent of Weddington's, it was actually the other way around. Weddington drew from Tribe's reasoning despite Tribe's own rejection of the argument upon later reflection. Nevertheless, contrary to Weddington's expressed ideal of "live and let live," John Noonan points out that a "choose choice or else" mentality was rapidly developing in the aftermath of *Roe v. Wade*:

> What could convince them that they should rest content? This and this only: Cease to call abortion wrong, and join them in calling it right. And this must be done thoroughly—in acts as well as in words. Silence would not be tolerated; all must place themselves avowedly with them. To achieve this, private choice was to assault the structure of the family; override the consciences of trustees, legislators, and whole political communities; alter the law of infanticide; and assert dominion over the meaning of language itself. (Noonan, 89)

Despite Tribe's later rejection of his own argument, the damage had been done. The notion that to be pro-life is inherently and unavoidably religious was too tempting to be dropped flat out. If the anti-abortion point of view could be characterized as an unconstitutional establishment of religion, Weddington and her pro-abortion allies were more than ready to jump on the bandwagon. And because the most prominent and effective organized opponent of abortion liberalization was the Catholic Church, pro-abortion proponents set about to link any and all abortion opposition to the Catholic Church.

CHAPTER 36

Conception and Misconception

Don't force your beliefs on me.

—Unborn Fetus

A large part of the pro-choice attack on personhood focuses on the Catholic Church since it is and has been at the forefront of the pro-life movement since *Roe v. Wade*. Yet, as bioethics professor at Duquesne University Gerard Magill, himself a Catholic, explains, the idea that the Catholic Church teaches that personhood or ensoulment begins at conception is actually a commonly held misconception.

Dr. Magill:

> First of all, it's what we mean in the Catholic Church by "the beginning of human life." By that we mean the beginning of *ensouled human* life where the human person has a soul. What other people mean by the beginning of human life is an open question. So, we're really talking about human life with a soul.
>
> And secondly, and this is actually more controversial but I think it's really important that the pro-life—that is the people who protect life, the people opposed to abortion—the pro-life lobby often gets this wrong and actually misrepresents the subtlety of Catholic teaching. We *do not know* when human ensouled life begins. The Catholic Church formally teaches that, and it's because we don't know we must, with great vigor, protect human life from its very [biological] inception. Now the advantage of that nuanced teaching is, one, it

gives us a great deal of modesty because we cannot play God on that issue. Secondly, it forces us to really set the safest possible moment for protecting human life, that is, from fertilization onwards.

And in terms of how modern science is developing, that's giving us a great argument to protect ourselves against the claims of human cloning, that that's not fertilization, therefore it shouldn't be protected. If we taught that human ensouled life began at conception and taught that as a doctrine, then people could easily say to us, well, that's your doctrine! You know, you're stuck with it! Good luck with it. We don't happen to believe that as a religious doctrine.

The Catholic Church doesn't say that. What the Catholic Church says is that our doctrine is that we will *protect* life from its very beginning. It's an assumptive doctrine. In other words, our doctrine is not *that* [ensouled] life begins then because that's only God's ultimate knowledge; we don't know that. But because of the dignity of the human condition *we will protect life* from its very inception. So, our religious doctrine is based on actual reasoning. It's not based on revelation in this matter; it's based on reason. That is, because of the stakes of human dignity, we will *reasonably* argue that we must protect it from the very beginning and so our religious doctrine is based on that, and that's called natural law reasoning.

So, in fact, because of our stance of protecting life from its very beginning—because we don't know when it begins we assume the safest possible moment—that's a function of logic; that's a function of reason. And, therefore, it sidesteps people who say that's just a religious doctrine. It's actually not; it's a doctrine of reason. It's a doctrine based on reason, based on natural law analysis.

So from the point of view of rational and persuasive argument, the Catholic Church has got the strongest argument of all. No one denies the dignity and the immense importance of protecting human life; therefore, the church carries that argument to its best and strongest conclusion by saying, given that conclusion that is universally respected—other than by mad people or crazy, murdering people—that human life has to be protected from its earliest possible moment, and its earliest possible moment is its most fragile moment and requires that support. And so it's not only a matter of logic it's a matter of actual responsibility to look after life from its very beginning.

While Catholics may represent the most visibly organized religious body opposing abortion, it is wildly inaccurate to argue that one can only oppose abortion on demand from a Catholic or even religious basis, or even that all Catholics oppose abortion. Nevertheless, anti-Catholicism is very often at the heart of pro-choice philosophy. As Joseph Dellapenna points out (himself a Unitarian), one of the clearest examples of this can be found coming "from the word processor of law professor David Garrow":

> Garrow traces the history of the birth control, the abortion reform, and the abortion repeal movements in the United States in the twentieth century in great detail. He makes no effort to hide either his pro-choice prejudices or his anti-Catholic prejudices, presenting all opposition to his favored views as an expression of Catholic bigotry without acknowledging the possibility that some people might oppose abortion on purely secular grounds. Garrow, on the other hand, finds nothing remarkable about the major involvement of Unitarian groups in bringing about abortion reform or even in helping to make *Roe v. Wade* possible. (Dellapenna, 790)

Like Weddington, Garrow frames any opposition to abortion in terms of repressive Catholic dogma forcing its way onto normal society. While narrowing the focus onto one prominent, concrete enemy may help rally his fellow pro-abortion troops, like so many other facets of pro-abortion ideology, it is wholly out of touch with reality. While pro-life Catholics are to be commended for their bold, principled, and steadfast stand against what they correctly perceive to be a deeply immoral practice, I do not see them arguing that abortion is to be opposed *because it goes against Catholic dogma*. On the contrary, they rightly oppose abortion on demand for the same reason many atheists do: because it kills innocent human life.

CHAPTER 37

Abortion Dogma

The true hypocrite is the one who ceases to perceive his deception,
the one who lies with sincerity.
—ANDRÉ GIDE

Another tenet of the "gospel of choice" holds that in the years before *Roe v. Wade* hundreds of thousands of women were dying from illegal abortions. The only way to ensure that women will not die from illegal abortions, says the argument, is to keep abortion legal. This, of course, is contested since neither side accepts the numbers of the other side. Pro-lifers insist that the number of abortion-related deaths prior to *Roe* is grossly exaggerated, while the number of deaths, injuries, and health-related consequences of legal, *Roe*-protected, abortion is underreported.

On the other hand, the pro-choice side steadfastly maintains that the only safe abortion is legal abortion. Making abortion illegal, they contend, will not result in fewer abortions but will only force women of means to places where abortion is legal and desperate women into the "back alleys."

This logic is reminiscent of arguments in favor of legalized drugs which hold that since a certain number of individuals are inevitably going to break the law and use illegal drugs, society should legalize drugs, pass out taxpayer funded needles, and make drug use "safe." The end result, of course, is a rise in drug use as well as drug abuse leading to a rise in drug-related injuries and death. The logic completely breaks down, however, when substituting an indisputably morally repugnant vice, such as arguing that since some people are inevitably going to abuse other people we should tailor our laws to ensure that no one other than the intended victim gets hurt or killed while passing out the proper and "safe" instruments of abuse to abusers at taxpayer expense. Constructing the argument in these terms renders the fallacy readily apparent.

CHAPTER 38

Reproductive Rights and Wrongs

It is a poverty to decide that a child must die so that you may live as you wish.
—MOTHER TERESA, NATIONAL PRAYER BREAKFAST, WASHINGTON, DC, 1997

Yet another tenet of the choice gospel can be summed up in the phrase: "reproductive freedom." The concept is that women should have the freedom to decide what to do with their own bodies and since pregnancy interferes with the normal functioning of a woman's body, she should be allowed the freedom to choose how to respond to it. Abortion is seen as a liberating alternative to pregnancy and is therefore established as a fundamental part of equal rights for women.

Lest we underestimate the importance of this right, Gloria Feldt, former president of Planned Parenthood, informs us that:

> Reproductive self-determination is the most fundamental civil and human right a woman can have. It's the key to enjoying full equality, liberty and justice. And that's the very right that the right-wing extremists are fighting so hard to take away. (Feldt, 18)

In reality, precisely the opposite is often the result as the abortion "option" is often pushed on the woman by a man, whether her own father, brother, or even the father of the child who does not want to accept responsibility for his participation in the creation of life and who, himself, does not have to undergo an abortion to kill it. In spite of the fact that abortion is overwhelmingly perceived to be a women's rights issue, according to a 1991 Gallup Poll, a greater percentage of men than women are pro-abortion (Alcorn, 59).

Nowadays "choice" has been redefined by the women's movement to mean more than just the choice for abortion.

> The right to choose is not just about abortion. Not by a long shot. It comprises the right to have full access to family planning information, health care and products; the right to have children or not; sex education for young people that goes beyond abstinence-only education being promoted by the right wing; and the right to medically accurate information about sexuality for the general public, too. (Feldt, 4)

Certainly there are aspects of the abortion debate that spill into other areas. Many of those peripheral issues are also hotly debated and inspire passionate rhetoric. There is an appropriate place to discuss these issues that all touch to one degree or another on abortion. Unlike abortion, however, these issues do not involve the legal redefinition of a minority group of human beings for the express purpose of killing them. Were it not for this blatant injustice and its effect, there would be little controversy.

Ironically, though abortion is championed by high-profile feminists as the pinnacle in the hierarchy of women's rights, the net effect of abortion worldwide has been a reduction in the percentage of female live births as compared to males. Through the use of amniocentesis tests, mothers in places like China and India are choosing to destroy their unborn baby girls and deliver their unborn baby boys.

In the U.S., too many view the efforts to restrict abortion as an attack on women and women's rights. Left-wing women's groups like NOW (the National Organization for Women) have championed the idea that any challenge to *Roe v. Wade* represents an affront to women's rights and equality. Though it necessarily has a "restricting of liberty" by-product, the true goals of the pro-life movement are to protect the innocent, unborn child as well as the safety of the mother. But this restricting of liberty is nothing out of the ordinary. No one has the "liberty" to abuse or kill a child after birth. By their very nature, laws restrict rights. Neither women nor men who are tired of taking care of their toddlers have a legal right or freedom to dispose of them. No right is absolute.

It's telling that Beverly Wildung Harrison begins a chapter on "Evaluating the Act of Abortion" in her book with psychoanalysis observations of the pro-life mind-set, setting the stage for the inevitable implication that holding a pro-life position must be rooted in cognitive disorder and misogyny leading to a paternalistic desire to control and repress the lives of women. Citing pollsters and "social scientists" who search for behavior patterns among abortion opponents, Harrison concludes that:

> ... evaluations of abortion are, in fact, intimately interrelated with perceptions of the woman's sexual purity and that, therefore, sexual attitudes play a powerful motivating role in people's moral assessments of abortion. (Beverly Wildung Harrison, *Our Right To Choose: Toward a New Ethic of Abortion*, 190, hereafter "Harrison")

Harrison, like many other pro-choice feminists, sees abortion restriction as an extension of male chauvinism. Her failure to similarly psychoanalyze the typical pro-choice mind-set leads to the implication that it must be a normal condition in contrast to the pro-life mind-set, which, for Harrison, obviously needs professional evaluation.

When Harrison, Faux, Weddington, and others frame the abortion debate in terms of equal rights for women, the case they make would be more compelling if its thesis were shared unanimously among the gender they purport to speak for. As it is, at least as many women (if not more, depending on which poll you look at) do not regard abortion to be either a fundamental right or a medical procedure that restores female equality to men. This fact alone should eliminate the argument that abortion boils down to a question of women's rights.

Dr. Jefferson:

> It's nothing to do with women. And the fact that they have adopted it as a "women's rights" issue shows the delusional state they're operating from. No woman is in control of anything upon an operating room table with her feet in stirrups. And if she thinks she's controlling anything from that position, she is sorely deluded. The only thing that makes us distinct and different is the biological capability. The survival of nations and people depend upon its women, and to willingly destroy that shows a lack of judgment that has developed in our modern society among those who are of the female species.

But the pro-choice community tends to ignore that reality in favor of the ideal they have created. Most pro-choice leaders view abortion as the sacred cow of women's rights. For them, abortion is inextricably linked to other issues important to women's empowerment and equality. Certainly, in generations past, women were treated as being inferior to men. Employment opportunities and salaries were discriminatory. While some hold that the same is true today to a certain extent, women now hold key positions of power and authority in both government as well as the private sector. In the era of *Roe v. Wade,* none of the justices on the Supreme Court were women. Today, three women sit on the high Court.

Because *Roe v. Wade* has become such an icon of certain women's groups, any thought of returning to the "dark days" before *Roe* smacks of heresy to the gospel of choice. For them, subordinating a woman's rights to that of a fetus is unthinkable regardless of the scientific status of that fetus.

Arguing that "reproductive freedom" gives women power to control all other aspects of their lives, Gloria Feldt insists that it:

> . . . poses a threat to the status of the entrenched hierarchy. That's why the right-wing extremists are so focused on taking away reproductive rights. And that's why they are using every weapon in their arsenals to ensure that politicians, judges, government appointees, and public health care agencies follow the anti-choice agenda. They are determined to take away not only the right to abortion but all reproductive rights. That's right. *All* reproductive rights. (Feldt, 6)

Apart from the mere assertion, Feldt does not adequately explain how reproductive freedom for women poses such an enormous threat to the "entrenched hierarchy." The idea expressed by Feldt in her book is that women will have little time or energy to be a threat to the men in authority so long as they remain barefoot and pregnant. Lack of access to abortion is then simply another method for men to reduce competition from women.

While I've never personally heard of, much less seen in print, anything even remotely resembling this concept ever being promoted (or even secretly implemented!) by any of today's pro-life leaders, whether in public or private (nor does Feldt offer any documentation to support her claim), this tenet of the pro-choice gospel is articulated as though it were fact by its defenders. If there was ever any truth to this claim, it has long since vanished since there are now more women than men graduating from U.S. colleges and universities.

According to a 2009 U.S. Census Bureau survey, there are now a million more female college graduates than male for the first time in U.S. history. (See for example: http://adage.com/article/adagestat/women-earning-college-graduate-degrees-men/148888/)

Even though most Americans recognize the mythology of such a pro-life motivation, the argument is still effective in diverting attention from the real issue. The focus is once again on the woman and the alleged deprivation of her rights while the spotlight ignores the plight of her unborn child.

CHAPTER 39

Follow the Money

*The product, abortion, is skillfully marketed and sold to the woman
at the crisis time in her life. She buys the product, finds it defective
and wants to return it for a refund.
But, it's too late.*
—FORMER ABORTION CLINIC OPERATOR CAROL EVERETT,
PRO-LIFE ACTION LEAGUE CONFERENCE, NOVEMBER, 1987

According to the new gospel of choice, where funding of abortion was concerned, the state had a duty, enforceable by the courts, to provide the means to enable the choice. Supreme Court Justice Thurgood Marshall labeled the denial of funds for elective abortion by the state as one more attempt by the opponents of abortion to "impose their moral choices on the rest of society" (Noonan, 85). Marshall's selection of words is ironic in that while championing "choice" he condemns abortion opponents for not choosing correctly. The choice to *not* participate in the funding of abortion was unacceptable.

What began to emerge after *Roe v. Wade* was a scenario in which choosing not to participate in the new, liberal abortion phenomenon was impossible since, if it were to be made accessible to poor women, the public needed to pick up the tab.

Few incidents have more dramatically illustrated the compulsory funding tenet of the choice gospel as clearly as Planned Parenthood's public "shakedown" of the Susan G. Komen Foundation. Komen—the nation's largest nonprofit organization dedicated to the fight against breast cancer—suddenly found itself in *really* hot water after it had quietly attempted to eliminate future grants to Planned Parenthood, the nation's largest abortion provider, under the pretext that it would no longer approve grants to "organizations under investigation" (http://ww5.komen.org/KomenNewsArticle.aspx? id=19327354148). In addition to receiving over 480 million taxpayer dollars annually, Planned Parenthood also receives Komen grants to the tune of roughly $700,000 annually with the stipulation that none of that money will be used to help fund what Planned Parenthood is best known for: abortions. The money it had received from Komen was to be specifically targeted to providing women—especially underprivileged women—with potentially life-saving breast cancer screenings and mammograms.

Concern among pro-life members of Congress over Planned Parenthood's use of their annual taxpayer-funded windfall grew after an undercover investigation by a twenty-three-year-old college graduate revealed that Planned Parenthood doesn't actually provide mammograms. Instead, they offer a basic cancer screening and then refer women to other organizations for mammograms. The recent grad behind the exposé is California resident, Lila Rose, who has made waves for her involvement in several undercover "sting" operations not flattering to Planned Parenthood. Several Planned Parenthood staffers were fired in 2011 after Lila's hidden camera revealed their "Willingness to Aid and Abet Sexual Exploitation of Minors" (www.liveaction. org/traffick).

Then in March, 2011, Live Action (the pro-life organization started by Lila at age 15 in her kitchen) published its "Mammosham" investigation in which 30 phone calls were made to Planned Parenthood clinics in 27 states inquiring about mammograms. None of the clinics contacted offered mammograms. Instead, every one of them referred the caller to other non–Planned Parenthood facilities.

Concerned that Planned Parenthood might not be using its donations for its stated purpose, Komen officials concluded that the best response would be to implement "new granting strategies and criteria." Although no current grants would be affected, the change would definitely impact future grants. Noting that donors have not only given Komen their money, but also "their trust," Komen founder and CEO Nancy Brinker announced that:

> We are working to eliminate duplicative grants, freeing up more
> dollars for higher impact programs, and wherever possible, we want

to grant to the provider that is actually providing the lifesaving mammogram. (http://www.youtube.com/watch?feature=player_ embedded&v=I4oOh6JhayA, see also http://ww5.komen.org/ KomenNewsArticle.aspx?id=19327354148)

Brinker's statement came in the form of a three-minute YouTube video in which she hinted that "this strategic shift will affect any number of longstanding partners." Although Planned Parenthood was never mentioned by name, it was clear that the abortion giant would be the only potential grantee currently affected by the new policies.

Komen's desire to "grant [directly] to the provider that is actually providing the lifesaving mammogram" is certainly understandable. One might reasonably suspect Komen to be within its rights in determining to whom and under what conditions it was going to dole out hundreds of thousands of dollars in grant money. While Komen executives may have anticipated some negative repercussions from the move, they were completely thunderstruck at the intensity of the backlash.

Ironically, the primary motivation for the change in policy at Komen had been *to avoid* any possibly negative political ramifications that might develop as the public became aware of Komen's partnership with Planned Parenthood. The moment defunding news went public, however, a firestorm of pro-abortion outrage erupted among the media, and Komen quickly found itself between a rock and a hard place.

Left-leaning media outlets went into a frenzy, characterizing the move by Komen as an outrage and betrayal. Pro-choice Democrats in Washington jumped on the bandwagon. Representative Jackie Speier (D-CA), longtime Komen supporter, announced from the House floor that she would no longer support the organization. Senator Barbara Boxer (D-CA) expressed outrage and insisted that anti-abortion forces within the Komen organization were the driving force behind the decision. Even Howard Kurtz, commenting from the not-so-conservative *Daily Beast* noticed the blatant pro-abortion framing of the issue:

> . . . there is no question that the media have driven this story, forced the apology from the Komen Foundation and have been approaching the whole narrative from the left. ("There's no question the media forced the Komen apology," video posted Feb. 6, 2012,

http://www.thedailybeast.com/videos/2012/02/06/there-s-no-question-the-media-forced-the-komen-apology.html, hereafter "Kurtz")

Kurtz pointed out that "the turning point came when NBC's Andrea Mitchell interviewed the Komen Foundation founder, Nancy Brinker, on her cable show." In that interview, remarkable for its unabashed pro–Planned Parenthood slant, Mitchell, herself a cancer survivor and Komen supporter, effectively stepped out of her role as an allegedly unbiased journalist and brusquely characterized Komen's policy shift as "shocking." Openly suggesting that she was "channeling the anger" of those who were upset at Komen's decision, Mitchell asked incredulously, "How could this have taken place?" Apparently somewhat stunned, Brinker's rather conciliatory response was to assert that Komen's critics had mischaracterized the decision and that, in fact, Komen was still funding Planned Parenthood, at least through the end of the current grant cycle.

Not satisfied, Mitchell turned attention to Komen's 2011, "surprising hiring of Karen Handel," who, before accepting the position at Komen, had run for Governor of Georgia on a pro-life platform. Quoting Handel as saying, "Let me be clear, since I am pro-life, I do not support the mission of Planned Parenthood," Mitchell then asked:

> For a bipartisan organization such as yours, which has a broad-based advisory group, why hire a key staff person who is so strongly, fiercely identified against Planned Parenthood, one of your grantees? (Andrea Mitchell Interviews Susan G. Komen's Nancy Brinker, Feb. 2, 2012, MSNBC, http://firstread.msnbc.msn.com/_news/2012/02/02/10303379-andrea-mitchell-interviews-susan-g-komens-nancy-brinker, hereafter "MSNBC")

Brinker asserted that Handel "did not have anything to do with this decision," but that it was, "decided at the board level." This was Brinker's second misstatement in what would become a series of blunders. Handel later acknowledged being a key player, although not the sole voice, behind the policy shift.

Mitchell honed in on the abortion connection:

> MITCHELL: Their supporters say they are the only ones that have been singled out among these thousands—

BRINKER: No, that's not true. That's not true.

MITCHELL: —and that their grants for breast screening have nothing to do with any contraceptive or abortion counseling.

BRINKER: It's not—

MITCHELL: That they separate this funding completely.

BRINKER: The issue—that's not the issue. Because that's not our issue. Our issue is grant excellence. They do pass-through grants with their screening grants. They send people to other facilities. We want to do more direct-service grants. (MSNBC)

Remarkably, the conversation turned even more transparently partisan after Brinker noted that Komen had been a decades-long partner with Planned Parenthood, giving them a total of over $9 million, which Mitchell cavalierly acknowledged but, not appeased, suggested that,

> . . . the anger that's being expressed is going to hit you in the pocketbook. You have worked so hard to create a bipartisan organization. Look at your Facebook page. Your Facebook page has people cutting the pink ribbons in half. Your branding is at stake. (MSNBC)

In response, Brinker restated that the new metrics were necessary but stressed that existing grants would continue to be funded. Mitchell then wondered if Komen would "put out the evidence that you have that there's been anything flawed in the way they've [Planned Parenthood] delivered services to the vulnerable?" To this, Brinker simply restated that Komen was merely explaining the criteria for new grants, also noting that, "once they go through the Planned Parenthood program, they often have to come to us for additional therapy and care." Planned Parenthood had been a longtime partner, Komen had notified them of the change and, "frankly, we'd been very private about it and we have not said that we won't accept grants who meet our criteria."

What is most stunning about this conversation, is the notion, as expressed by Andrea Mitchell but shared nearly universally by her media peers, that *the very definition of being nonpartisan* is to *continue funding* Planned Parenthood. Howard Kurtz put it this way:

But when you look at the media's conduct here and you look at the way it was framed, this is what I mean: if the Komen Foundation were to continue funding Planned Parenthood, well that's not political. But if the Komen Foundation were to take money away from Planned Parenthood, well that's a blatantly political act. Now is that a little bit of a double standard? Yeah. A lot of people would say so. (Kurtz)

A "little bit of a double standard" is a little bit of an understatement. Kurtz has perhaps inadvertently put his finger on the tip of the iceberg. The media framing of the Komen meltdown makes sense when viewed from within the larger context of the abortion debate itself. The entire pro-choice agenda is packaged and presented as being the only nonpartisan, nonpolitical, nonreligious, nonbiased point of view on the question of abortion.

For the pro-abortion left, which includes most of the "mainstream" media, to be pro-choice is to be rational, tolerant, sophisticated, freethinking, apolitical, and nonpartisan; to be pro-life is to be backward-thinking, repressive, authoritarian, radically religious, insensitive to women, and intolerant. When viewed from that highly partisan perspective, the left slant of the Komen media coverage that even Kurtz (to his credit) notices makes perfect sense. Recognizing double standards, however, doesn't go very far toward alleviating the problem. Women's rights and women's health care are currently being sold to the public as necessarily including abortion. If that "all-inclusive" packaging bothers pro-life women, the standard answer is that they don't have to have abortions. The Komen saga simply illustrates how strong that pro-abortion undercurrent actually is.

Although Brinker left the interview under the assumption that she had stuck to her principles, the blitzkrieg was already taking its toll. In an effort to clarify the situation, Brinker produced a three-minute video in which she made what might qualify as the worst PR statement of her career:

We will never bow to political pressure. We will always stand firm in our goal to end breast cancer forever. We will never turn our backs on the women who need us the most. We do this because this is our promise. (http://www.youtube.com/watch?feature=player_embedded&v=I4oOh6JhayA)

Had she and her organization not "bowed to political pressure" within a week, the statement might be remembered as exemplifying her finest hour.

As it turned out, in an effort to restore sanity in the face of a pro-abortion media onslaught, Brinker retracted, apologized, and, as one blogger put it, "surrendered and kissed the abortion ring" (Wesley J. Smith, "Pyrrhic Victory for Planned Parenthood as Komen Kisses the Abortion Ring," First Things Blog, Secondhand Smoke, http://www.firstthings.com/blogs/ secondhandsmoke/2012/02/03/pyrrhic-victory-for-planned-parenthood -as-komen-kisses-the-abortion-ring/).

Not only did Brinker and Komen bow to political pressure, they completely reversed their earlier decision, admitted to handling things badly, apologized to their supporters, and agreed to continue the flow of Komen cash to Planned Parenthood (http://ww5.komen.org/KomenNewsArticle. aspx?id=19327354148).

With forthright candor, *Daily Beast* commentator Howard Kurtz captured the essence of Komen's defeat when he suggested that:

> . . . the pressure was so relentless, the publicity was so bad, the headlines were so negative, that the media pressure, in effect, forced the Komen Foundation—despite its initial insistence that everything was just fine—to reverse itself, to restore the funding, to apologize, to seek forgiveness from its supporters. (Kurtz)

This was a truly remarkable turn of events from more than one standpoint. It is perhaps a model of what *not to do* in terms of 501(c)(3) public relations. In the span of one week, the Komen Foundation had unintentionally managed to alienate both sides of the hotly contested abortion debate. The fiasco was also a testament to the power of the media and its pro-abortion bias. Additionally, it was an exposé on both the tactics of Planned Parenthood and the way in which it markets itself versus the services it actually provides. But what is perhaps most significant is the context in which Komen's decision was framed by those who favor abortion.

The Susan G. Komen Foundation is an entity dedicated to fighting breast cancer. As an organization, it rightfully has nothing to do with abortion. Though I am not personally aware of Komen officials ever explicitly acknowledging a newly discovered distaste for the idea that Komen grant money might have been funneled into abortions rather than breast cancer screenings and mammograms, virtually everyone outside the organization concluded that that was, in fact, the reason for the policy shift. Brinker herself noted that Komen simply wanted to shift grants to those entities that were actually providing mammograms instead of Planned Parenthood, which doesn't. Looking at this rationally, one is hard pressed to understand why Komen should be obligated to direct its grant money into an organization that must, in turn, refer women to other organizations—especially when that organization is tarnished with the dubious reputation of being the largest abortion provider in the United States.

Days after "Komen caved," Karen Handel resigned from her position as Senior Vice President for Public Policy. Now able to freely speak her mind, Handel acknowledged that she had indeed taken "the lead in developing alternatives and working through the process," but that "the decision was fully vetted at every appropriate level of the organization," and that she had been "hired to shepherd the organization to 'neutral ground' with respect to the abortion issue" (*Atlanta Journal Constitution*, Katie Leslie, February 7, 2012, http://www.ajc.com/news/handel-resigns-from-komen-1337241.html, hereafter "AJC").

In so stating, Handel reveals the real problem: for abortion rights supporters, continued funding of Planned Parenthood was the only acceptable "neutral ground." Handel did not mince words, however, noting that Planned Parenthood had, "unleashed a premeditated and vicious attack not only on Komen, but also on Ambassador [Nancy] Brinker as well." According to Handel, Planned Parenthood had been informed of the policy change in December and had been plotting a well-orchestrated "shakedown" during the ensuing month. In her resignation letter to Brinker, Handel noted that:

> The decision to update our granting model was made before I joined Komen, and the controversy related to Planned Parenthood has long been a concern to the organization. (AJC)

Contrary to the instant mythology that was developing around this story, Komen was not responsible for publicly "announcing" a new policy shift in terms of its granting criteria. On the contrary, the organization had hoped to quietly implement the shift while avoiding public controversy. It was not even unequivocally rescinding Planned Parenthood's license to apply for future grants. It was simply implementing "more stringent criteria" for earning future grant money—something well within its rights to do. Komen's biggest mistake seems to have been notifying its longstanding partner, Planned Parenthood, of the new criteria. Handel suggested that:

> What happened here, is that Planned Parenthood turned the issue into politics. And they hijacked, literally hijacked this great organization and conducted what is the most unbelievable shakedown that I think we've seen in a long time. (AJC)

"Shakedown" certainly has a ring of truth to it. What other grantee has the political power to coerce its benefactor into indefinite continued funding of unsatisfactory services? Reduced to pointing out the obvious due to the sheer absurdity of the situation, Handel noted that:

> And the last time I checked, this is a private non-profit organization that has every right, every right, to set its standards the way they choose to set it in the best interest of this organization. (AJC)

Apparently Handel was naïve to think so. As James Taranto pointed out in the *Wall Street Journal*, in the wacky world of pro-choice ideology, reality appears to operate under something akin to the preferred modus operandi of the Mafia:

> Planned Parenthood's bitter campaign against Komen—aided by left-liberal activists and media—is analogous to a protection racket: *Nice charity you've got there. It'd be a shame if anything happened to it.* The message to other Planned Parenthood donors is that if they don't play nice and keep coughing up the cash, they'll get the Komen treatment. ("Komen Get It: The Abortion Protection Racket," *Wall Street Journal*, James Taranto, Feb. 2, 2012, http://online.wsj. com/article/SB10001424052970203889904577199110913604418. html?mod=WSJ_Opinion_MIDDLETopOpinion)

In response to the now immortalized question of Rodney King, "Can't we all just get along?" the pro-abortion left replies: *Sure, so long as "getting along" includes abortion funding.*

CHAPTER 40

Radical Feminists

Abortion is the ultimate exploitation of women.
—ALICE PAUL, AUTHOR OF THE ORIGINAL EQUAL RIGHTS AMENDMENT, 1923

The abortion debate is not lacking in paradox. One of the more notable ironies is the surprising fact that the founder of what is today the largest abortion provider in the United States, Planned Parenthood Federation of America, was opposed to abortion. Margaret Sanger is credited with coining the term "birth control." The term itself is something of a misnomer, since the goal of "birth control" was actually contraception. Many modern-day, left-wing feminists who hold Sanger in high regard as the founder of Planned Parenthood (then called the American Birth Control League, 1921) would be shocked to learn that she looked to contraception as a key component *in preventing* what she openly labeled "the evil" of abortion.

Writing in her autobiography about her early days as a birth-control activist, at a time when speaking publicly about birth control could get one arrested for obscenity, Sanger describes what happened at the opening of her Birth Control Clinic in Brooklyn, New York:

> The morning of October 16th, 1916—crisp but sunny and bright after days of rain—Ethel, Fania and I opened the doors of the first birth control clinic in America, the first anywhere in the world except the Netherlands. I still believe this was an event of social significance. . . .
>
> Fania had a copy of *What Every Girl Should Know* on her desk, and if she had a free moment, read from it. When asked, she told where

it could be bought, and later kept a few copies for the convenience of those who wanted them.

Children were left with her and mothers ushered in to Ethel or me in the rear room, from seven to ten at once. To each group we explained simply what contraception was; *that abortion was the wrong way—no matter how early it was performed it was taking a life*; that contraception was the better way, the safer way—it took a little time, a little trouble, but was well worth while in the long run, because life had not yet begun. (*Margaret Sanger: An Autobiography*, 1938, 217, emphasis added)

Several days later Sanger was arrested on charges including dissemination of obscenity (in the form of contraceptive information, namely her pamphlet entitled: *What Every Girl Should Know*, which provided information about such topics as menstruation and sexuality in adolescents), as well as maintaining a public nuisance. She was later convicted and sentenced to 30 days in a workhouse. Sanger was arrested eight times in total.

While Sanger is rightfully criticized for her radical views on race and eugenics, modern feminists nevertheless hold her up as an icon of women's rights. Ironically, most of those same feminists would find themselves passionately at odds with Sanger on the topic of abortion. Some seek to explain Sanger's disdain for abortion as being necessary given that abortion was a crime at the time. They seem to forget that public distribution of birth-control information was a crime as well, yet that did not stop Sanger from opening a clinic dedicated to that purpose. If Sanger secretly believed that abortion was acceptable, she did a remarkable job of giving the opposite impression:

When motherhood becomes the fruit of a deep yearning, not the result of ignorance or accident, its children will become the foundation of a new race. *There will be no killing of babies in the womb by abortion,* nor through neglect in foundling homes nor will there be infanticide. (Margaret Sanger, *Women and the New Race*, 1920, 232, emphasis added)

Such graphic language no doubt prompts a bristle or two from Sanger's modern admirers. But Sanger was just getting started:

When, in spite of these unscientific practices, pregnancy follows, *abortion, the greatest disgrace of modern civilization*, is the only resort of the harassed mother, unless she will bear unwanted offspring. (Margaret Sanger, *The Case For Birth Control*, 1917, 185, emphasis added)

Oddly enough, modern pro-life advocates agree with the founder of Planned Parenthood when it comes to abortion! Writing in 1920, Sanger again characterized abortion as a disgrace:

While there are cases where even the law recognizes an abortion as justifiable if recommended by a physician, *I assert that the hundreds of thousands of abortions performed in America each year are a disgrace to civilization*. The effects of such operations upon a woman, serious as they may be, are nothing as compared to the injury done to her general health by drugs taken to produce the same result. Even such drugs as are prescribed by physicians have harmful effects, and nostrums recommended by druggists are often worse still.

Even more drastic may be *the effect upon the unborn child*, for many women fill their systems with poisonous drugs during the first weeks of pregnancy only to decide at last, when drugs have failed, as they usually do, to bring the child to birth. (Margaret Sanger, *Women and the New Race*, 1920, 126–7, emphasis added)

Writing in the *Birth Control Review* in 1917 (which was a Sanger publication) in response to a sermon by Dr. S. Parkes Cadman of the Central Congregational Church in Brooklyn, in which Dr. Cadman extols the virtue of women who permit themselves to bear children while condemning those who would attempt to limit the number of children they conceive, Charles Hiram Chapman, a Sanger associate, had this to say:

Dr. S. Parkes Cadman is long on sentimentality and short on common sense. . . . He does not even seem to know what birth control, or family limitation aims at. His remark that "more children are murdered than can be computed" shows his ignorance in all its glory. Family limitation seeks to stop *this child murder*, which Mrs. Sanger and the rest of us deplore as much as Dr. Cadman or any other preacher can. *Child murder is effected principally by way of abortion*. The prevention of conception when children are not desired would make abortion a useless crime. Is it possible that men such as Dr. Cadman perceive no moral difference between the prevention of conception and the murder of a living child? (*Birth Control Review*, 1917, 16, emphasis added)

It's interesting to note that Sanger believed that acceptance by society of birth control would "make abortion a useless crime." While birth control has, no doubt, had some effect at reducing the number of abortions, abortion continues to be a lucrative business for abortion providers like Planned Parenthood despite decades of readily available forms of birth control.

Given Sanger's passionate opposition to abortion and her characterization of it as the "killing of babies in the womb" and "child murder," it is no great surprise that the organization she founded, Planned Parenthood, was also opposed abortion in its early days. An official Planned Parenthood pamphlet asked the following question as late as 1964:

Question: Is birth control an abortion?

Answer: Definitely not. *An abortion kills the life of a baby after it has begun.* It is dangerous to your life and health. It may make you sterile so that, when you want a child, you cannot have it. Birth control merely postpones the beginning of life. (*Plan Your Children For Health and Happiness*, Aug. 1963, Planned Parenthood Publication, [emphasis added], Online photocopy at http://i81.photobucket.com/albums/j214/yodavater/PPPlanYourFamily63.jpg.)

How remarkably far from their original stance has Planned Parenthood come! Sanger would be appalled. Historian David Garrow notes that Margaret Sanger was not the only birth-control advocate who spoke negatively about abortion:

Even the American Birth Control League's *Birth Control Review* referred in passing to abortion as "the murder of the unborn child," and as late as 1939 Morris Ernst and Harriet Pilpel [who served as legal council to Planned Parenthood], also writing in the *Birth Control Review*, explicitly termed abortion "the antithesis of contraception." (Garrow, 274)

Harriet Pilpel would go on to be a driving force behind the legalization of abortion and a strong supporter of Sarah Weddington and *Roe v. Wade*.

While Sanger's views on race, sterilization, and eugenics were clearly radical, her anti-abortion perspective was not unique among early American feminists. In fact, near unanimity existed among key feminists and women's suffrage leaders such as Susan B. Anthony and Elizabeth Cady Stanton that abortion was an evil to be harshly condemned.

Anthony wrote in her suffrage newspaper: "I deplore the horrible crime of child murder. . . . No matter what the motive, the love of ease, or a desire to save from suffering the unborn innocent, the woman is awfully guilty who commits the deed" (Susan B. Anthony, *The Revolution* July 8, 1869, p. 4. As quoted in Alcorn, p. 57).

In a letter to Julia Ward Howe, Elizabeth Cady Stanton wrote: "When we consider that women are treated as property, it is degrading to women that we should treat our children as property to be disposed of as we see fit" (October 16, 1873, www.sba-list.org/suzy-b-blog/setting-record-straight-susan-b-anthony).

The notion that the Constitution was hiding a right to abortion somewhere deep within its unenumerated rights would have seemed absurd to these and other early female activists.

PART 5.

Where Do We Go from Here?

CHAPTER 41

What *Roe* Should Have Said

It is more honorable to repair a wrong that to persist in it.
—THOMAS JEFFERSON

W hile arguing that a fetus is not a baby, that a fetus is not a person, that a fetus is not a human being, that a fetus is not a life, pro-choice proponents inevitably fall back on the definitions laid out in the *Roe* decision rather than on the "well-known facts of fetal development" as the basis for their conclusions. The problem with that approach is the fact that *Roe refused to answer the critical question altogether.* Modern pro-choice philosophy, on the other hand, boldly goes into uncharted territory proclaiming as fact that a fetus is *not* a baby, yet through circular reasoning, typically refers back to *Roe* as the source of this profound knowledge.

Not surprisingly, with the exception of those in the pro-abortion movement, the *Roe* decision was not well received. Even legal scholars with little or no opinion on abortion were shocked at what amounted to little more than judicial legislation. In the words of Villanova law professor Joseph Dellapenna, "Despite the inordinate amount of time Blackmun took to produce the majority opinion, the opinion in *Roe* is so poorly written that defenders of its outcome usually begin their analysis by apologizing for the opinion" (Dellapenna, 687). Utah law professor Michael W. McConnell puts it even more bluntly:

> "The reasoning of *Roe v. Wade* is an embarrassment to those
> who take constitutional law seriously, even to many scholars who
> heartily support the outcome of the case. As Jon Hart Ely, former

dean of Stanford Law School and a supporter of abortion rights, has
written, *Roe* "is not constitutional law and gives almost no sense of
an obligation to try to be." (Michael W. McConnell, "*Roe v. Wade* at 25:
Still Illegitimate," as quoted in Baird, p. 137)

The attempt to justify the ruling through reliance on biased, pro-abortion
history, the adoption of an arbitrary trimester framework, and the usurpation
of legislative responsibility were invitations for criticism not just from abortion
opponents but also from what otherwise might have been friendly sources.
As if the topic of abortion were not controversial enough, the structure and
content of the majority opinion added fuel to the fire. In fact, outside pro-
abortion circles, *Roe* has been so poorly received that attempts have been made
to clarify what the Court really meant. As new justices replaced aging ones,
the Court itself rejected some its own prior logic in subsequent rulings but
stopped short of overturning *Roe*, much to the consternation of the Reagan
and Bush administrations as well as the pro-life community.

One example of an attempt to repackage *Roe* logic can be found in a
fascinating book published in 2003 (the thirtieth anniversary of *Roe v. Wade*)
with a title that speaks for itself: *What Roe v. Wade Should Have Said*. Edited
and coauthored by Yale law professor Jack Balkin, the book is an exercise in
hindsight honing with Balkin and ten other legal scholars offering their own
rewrite of *Roe* stating, in their respective opinions, what *Roe* should have said
with the caveat of referencing only material that would have been available
at the time of the ruling in 1973.

Because Balkin and those of his coauthors who are pro-choice present
a coherent case for "abortion freedom," I will address some of their more
salient points. As we move forward, the main question to keep in mind when
evaluating pro-choice logic is, would this line of reasoning fly if we were
to substitute the word "baby" for "fetus"? I recognize that most pro-choice
readers are committed to the idea that a fetus *is not* the moral equivalent of a
baby. The point is not in identifying which philosophical labels the pro-choice
community finds unacceptable but rather in hopefully bringing non-pro-life
people to a point where they can better understand the pro-life perspective.
In fact, there are a lot of sincere folks who passionately believe that there is
no moral difference between a fetus and a baby—certainly nothing of any
significance. If we were to leave it at that, then it might simply boil down to pro-
choice dogma vs. pro-life dogma, ending in a stalemate. But it doesn't end there.

Facts are on the pro-life side when it comes to the beginning of human life. In contrast, pro-choice logic must either redefine human life as something other than actual biological life or, if conceding to the presence of actual, biological human life, it must suggest that that life is not worthy of legal protection at its earliest stages. These appear to be the only acceptable, nonbarbaric avenues for rationally defending pro-choice logic. The problem is that both avenues boil down to assertions having little or no correlation to concrete reality and evidence.

The fact that what emerges from the womb of a pregnant woman is clearly a baby works in favor of pro-life logic. Were this not the case, pro-choice logic would be easier to defend. The difficulty for pro-choice proponents lies in convincing the public that the baby that emerges from the womb *did not exist* before emerging—yet *something* clearly did exist. The thoughtful observer will note that only one of two possibilities may be correct. Either:

the baby that emerges from the womb is a fundamentally different entity from the fetus that occupied the womb (e.g., potential human vs. human); or

the label "baby" and the label "fetus" are simply two words used to describe the same human organism in different stages of development and/or in different locations.

While nearly all pro-choice proponents operate under the former assumption, very few adequately describe or even agree on the key moral differences that allegedly justify abortion. What typically occurs is that a baby is compared with a zygote with the pro-choice advocate pointing out that the zygote has no brain, no nervous system, no arms, no legs, etc. This is problematic for at least two reasons. First, this observation does nothing to explain why a living human must currently possess a functioning brain, nervous system, arms, etc., in order *not to be exterminated*—especially given that the entity is actively working toward developing those attributes at a remarkable pace. Second, it is essentially a false or at least a misleading comparison, since most induced abortions take place at a point in pregnancy well beyond the zygote stage when the fetus, in fact, does have a rudimentary brain, nervous system, limbs, etc.

Pro-choice advocates rarely wish to discuss the differences between a "fetus" and a "baby," however, because doing so not only illustrates a fundamental defect in pro-choice logic, but it also focuses attention on the entity they prefer to ignore. The net result is that we are typically left with the mere *assumption* that the two entities are inexplicably but radically different.

Nearly everyone agrees that human babies possess an inherent right to life. Infanticide is rightfully viewed as unacceptable by nearly everyone in society with the rare exception of only the most extreme philosophers. On that basis, we can use the fetus/baby comparison for purposes of illustrating the underlying fallacies of pro-choice logic, even if (especially if) pro-choice proponents do not accept the interchangeability of the terms. At this point, we're not attempting to demonstrate that a fetus is the moral equivalent of a baby but to simply illustrate that *if pro-life advocates are correct* when they assert no significant moral difference between a fetus and a baby, *then* pro-choice logic *cannot stand* except perhaps in the most dire of circumstances. Of course, the critical issue boils down to which assertion is correct—is a fetus the moral equivalent of a baby or not? For now, the immediate point is that once the moral equality of "fetus" and "baby" is established, pro-choice logic in most cases must fall since killing babies is universally accepted (at least in Western society) as being morally wrong. With that in mind as we move forward, it is worth our time to consider the arguments Jack Balkin and his fellow role-playing justices raise as they explain what *Roe* should have said.

When Balkin addresses the argument in favor of a woman's right to choose abortion, he essentially restates with slightly more eloquence the pro-choice arguments that can be found in *Roe* but then goes on to reestablish the alleged "right to abortion" on the notion of sex equality, that is, equality of the male and female genders. It is notable, however, that he completely dispenses with the abortion history lesson presented in *Roe*. Whereas in 1973 Justice Blackmun felt compelled to offer a fairly lengthy, albeit substantially inaccurate, discussion of historical attitudes regarding abortion as justification for the radical new direction in which he was leading the Court and the country, by contrast, in this hypothetical rewrite three decades later, Balkin apparently sees no similar need to reexamine historical views and legal opinions on abortion in any detail except to casually note that "at common law abortion was not a felony before 'quickening.'" According to Balkin, this suggests that the word *person* was not "understood or intended to include fetuses" at the time of the ratification of either the Fifth Amendment (1791) or the Fourteenth Amendment (1868) (Balkin, 46). Balkin cites no reference in support of this claim, but the notion was argued almost word for word by Cyril Means Jr. in his two *New York Law Forum* articles and Roy Lucas in his 1968 essay in the *North Carolina Law Review* (see chapter 5).

As we have already seen, the notion that the word *person* was not directly associated with fetuses in the Constitution is a sleight-of-hand trick used by pro-choice proponents to reinvent history. The drafters of the Constitution had no need to use the specific word "person" in defining an unborn child since the Constitution did not address the subject of unborn children or abortion. Similarly, Congress had no need to identify unborn children as "persons," since no one was suggesting anything to the contrary within a legal context in the eighteenth and nineteenth centuries. Laws did include references to "unborn children," however. In what (in hindsight) appears to be a too-candid slip of the tongue during oral arguments in *Roe*, pro-choice Justice Stewart directly mentioned "unborn children" in reference to tort and estate laws, unwittingly revealing the common legal terminology of the day.

Moreover, the fact that the Constitution does not specifically address unborn humans works both ways. Balkin would be hard pressed to find language in the Constitution (or in any pre-*Roe* abortion law) asserting that unborn children *are not* persons! While neither Balkin nor Blackmun can locate a usage of the term "person" in the Constitution that they think might apply to unborn humans, it does not follow that the framers of the Fourteenth Amendment believed that unborn humans were not persons. In fact, the contrary proves to be true. As we already noted, at least as early as 1765, William Blackstone and his *Commentaries on the Laws of England* stated that a "person" was one "like us" who had been "formed by God" in the womb (*Commentaries on the Laws of England;* London, 1765; book 1, chapter 1, 125–6; book 4, chapter 14 as quoted in Noonan, *A Private Choice,* 5).

The same men who had drafted and passed the Fourteenth Amendment had also passed rigid anti-abortion laws in federal territories during the time frame when the most stringent anti-abortion laws were also coming on the books in various states across the country and as we've seen, the primary function of these laws was to protect unborn children from the "unwarrantable destruction of human life" (*RvW,* 142) caused by abortion. There was no disparity between federal and state laws on abortion at the time. The trend on both the federal and state level was consistently toward more stringent anti-abortion laws, not more lenient ones. These laws specifically referred to "unborn children." In fact, the Texas law that was under attack in

Roe specifically noted that "Destroying [an] Unborn Child" was a crime (Article 1195, Texas Penal Code, 1854). Balkin reprints this law for the benefit of his readers (Balkin, 57). One wonders how the specific reference to the destruction of an "unborn child" in the Texas law could result in a crime punishable by confinement "in the penitentiary for life or for not less than five years" if the fetus was not a "person in the whole sense."

As we have seen, the term "person" was specifically chosen by Justice Blackmun (and now Balkin) because the connotative ambiguity was useful. While the Court was free to rhetorically extract the abstract notion of "person" from the legal notion of "children" to arrive at the desired conclusion that "unborn" children were not "persons in the whole sense," such a conclusion, however, would have no real-world evidential support and would therefore amount to little more than a raw judicial decree. A larger problem resulted when the Court attempted to superimpose this radical, new interpretation on that of more reasonable nineteenth-century legislators for whom such an extraction would have been unimaginable. If the Court was correct in its attempt to rewrite history, then the notion that "a fetus is not a person" was conspicuously unexpressed in nineteenth-century abortion laws. Nevertheless, Balkin follows Blackmun's history as if it were gospel truth.

Balkin scores higher, however, as his argument moves into the origin of the right to privacy, previous cases in which it had arisen, how it had evolved, and how it had been applied to a right of married couples "to be let alone" when deciding whether or not to use contraceptives (*Griswold v. Connecticut*, 1965). Building on the privacy right, Balkin explains that it "was not simply a right to secrecy; it was a right to engage in deeply personal decisions about whether or not to have a child, a right with which the state should not interfere" (Balkin, 39).

With respect to privacy, especially as it applies to married couples' use of contraceptives, there is little in Balkin's logic with which to disagree. Common sense would suggest that unless a person is causing harm to himself or someone else or to property in private, married couples probably should have a right to be "let alone." A right to privacy, however, is not absolute. One does not have the right to abuse someone else in private or to ingest illegal substances in private. There are, in fact, many actions that cannot be justified merely because they are performed in private. So the question of whether a right to privacy can or should cover the alleged "right to abortion" is raised.

A flaw throughout Balkin's argument (which is common among pro-choice arguments) is the fact that it *presupposes* that a fetus is not the moral equivalent of a baby and builds on that dubious assumption without ever establishing it as fact. This tends to be the case because pro-choice proponents nearly always take it for granted whether consciously or not. In *Roe*, for example, Justice Blackmun had simply asserted that the "question of when human life begins" needed no answer, as if the assertion itself constituted sufficient moral ground to ignore the issue. Balkin follows suit. While applying a similar set of euphemisms such as labeling a fetus "a potential member of the human species" (48), Balkin, like Blackmun, suggests that:

> ...for purposes of this case, we may ask whether the state may assert an interest in the fetus's life based on a moral view of when human life begins, or, at the very least, an interest in the potential human life of the fetus. We agree that the state has such an interest, in addition to the interests in maternal health and in the proper regulation of the medical profession to secure public health. (Balkin, 48)

Why a state might have any interest (much less a compelling one) in protecting life that does not actually exist is unclear. It seems reasonably far-fetched to think that any self-respecting pro-choice advocate would permit the notion that a state has a vague interest in protecting mere *potentialities* to trump her desire to obtain *an actual* abortion. The very framing of the argument by Balkin (and Blackmun) stacks the scales in favor of abortion on request.

To be perfectly clear, the state has no interest in protecting *potential* human life—at least no compelling interest; it has an interest in protecting *actual* human life. Therefore, the question of when human life *actually* begins is critical. It is not, as Balkin frames the issue, that the state is obligated to take an interest in the life of a fetus based on its own abstract "moral view of when human life begins," but rather that *if* actual human life is present (regardless of when it came into existence), then the state *is morally obligated* to take an interest in protecting it from at-will extermination.

In addition to the blatant illogic of recognizing a state's "interest in the potential human life of the fetus" (as opposed to the actual life of the fetus) such a recognition, in practice, amounted to little more than a platitude under Balkin's logic because according to his rewrite of *Roe*, the state's interest was also subject to providing the woman with an ample amount of time to discover her pregnancy and then to choose how to respond to it. The result is an unspoken but very real underlying supposition that a fetus is *of necessity* not the moral equivalent of a baby. The notion seems to be taken for granted on an almost subconscious level by Balkin. Given Balkin's emphasis on an appropriate time frame in which a woman may respond, the question of when one entity (fetus) changes into the other (baby) is, surprisingly, never addressed, leaving the impression that birth must be intended. It is clear from the rest of Balkin's assertions, however, that at least from a moral standpoint, birth was not intended. Nevertheless, exactly what point during pregnancy Balkin finds critical to the morality of abortion is quite unclear.

Abortion necessarily involves an act of killing. Though pro-choice advocates almost universally attempt to avoid or, when pressed, downplay that reality, they must (and occasionally do) acknowledge that *something* is killed during a successful abortion. In order for pro-choice logic to avoid characterization as something utterly barbaric, the entity that is killed during an abortion *cannot* be a baby or even the moral equivalent of a baby. Nearly everyone in modern, Western society recognizes that intentionally killing a baby is morally wrong. So abortion cannot kill a baby or the moral equivalent of a baby if pro-choice logic is to stand.

Abortion must therefore kill *only a fetus.* Since the moral assumption underlying Balkin's arguments *requires* a fetus to be something morally inferior to a baby, and radically so (or else Balkin's logic is inherently barbaric), one can only assume that the moral assumption underlying Balkin's arguments is that a human fetus is definitely not the moral equivalent of a baby, even though Balkin never specifically makes this assertion. One can see evidence for this assumption, however, by examining the arguments he does make. Those arguments do not make sense if a fetus and a baby are morally the same thing. In rare moments of candor, other pro-choice advocates have blatantly appealed to that assumption, most notably Faye Wattleton who, in 1991, succinctly expressed that she does not accept that a "fetus is a baby; it is a fetus." In so many words, Justice Blackmun agrees, using the terms "meaningful life" and "persons in the whole sense" to contrast what he labels mere "potential life."

We can assume that Balkin would not characterize his own reasoning as barbaric. There seems to be no alternative, then, except that Balkin *assumes he is correct* in the unsupported notion that a fetus is not the moral equivalent of a baby. In fact, it is *critical* to Balkin's (and by extension pro-choice) arguments that this assumption be *the correct assumption*. This is the great flaw I find consistently running through the logic of nearly every pro-choice advocate. Like Blackmun before him, however, Balkin has no way of establishing that ultracritical assumption nor does he even attempt to. What is remarkable is the fact that many people with Balkin's mind-set rarely see any problem in proceeding with abortion on demand *in spite of* a glaring lack of evidence to back up *the most critical assumption* in their theory—an assumption that, if false, utterly ruins the rest of their case. It's as if they throw up their hands and sigh, "Oh well!" and move on as if nothing noteworthy has occurred.

Justice Blackmun asserts that "we need not resolve the difficult question of when human life begins." Pro-life proponents respond with: "Really? With all due respect. Mr. Justice Blackmun, what allows you to avoid the question? Does simply labeling it 'difficult' permit evasion?"

What makes the question so difficult, Blackmun suggests, is that doctors, philosophers, and theologians can't come to any consensus. Notably absent from Blackmun's list are biologists! It's unremarkable that theologians can't agree on a point in which the soul is instilled. Similarly, it is no great surprise that philosophers disagree about what constitutes a "person." But there is no question that biological science is well aware of the actual beginning of biological human life. There is no lack of consensus among biologists, only a lack of consensus from others on how to interpret the data.

Regardless, life is *clearly present* in the unborn child at the time of induced abortion since, in the absence of such life, *there is no need* for induced abortion to kill anything. Pro-life advocates object to the intentional *killing* of unborn humans, not the difficulty philosophers and theologians may or may not have in agreeing with one another. From that perspective, any debate over "when human life begins" is a charade. Clearly, life has begun by the time an induced abortion is required to kill it.

When Balkin writes that a "fetus is composed of human cells, so from conception we may assume that what is growing in the mother's womb is a potential member of the human species" (48), his logic is shaky to say the least. In the first place, human beings can only reproduce other human beings, so there is no "potential" species membership up for grabs. Human fetuses are card-carrying members of the "human species" right from the get-go. Eminent French geneticist, Jerome Lejeune, famous for discovering the cause of Down syndrome as well as several other genetic abnormalities, has stated:

I must say very simply, as a geneticist, I have never heard any specialist in husbandry of animals thinking about the "cattilisation" of cattle. They know that the embryo of a cow would be a calf.... From all the genetic laws that we have tried to summarize, we are entirely convinced that every embryo is, by itself, a human being. (Quoted in Patrick Lee, *Abortion & Unborn Human Life*, The Catholic University of America Press, 1996, 72)

That pro-abortion advocates often fail to come to terms with this basic biological concept is certainly perplexing.

Secondly, Balkin's use of the phrase "is growing" is an acknowledgment of the fact that abortion kills actual *living* humans rather than mere potential humans. Potential humans don't grow; actual humans do.

Finally, a human fetus is more than simply "composed of human cells." This seems to be a deliberate reductionist tactic on Balkin's part. It would be something like saying my four-year-old nephew is "composed of human cells," so he must be a potential member of the human species. When necessary to promote their agenda, pro-abortion proponents are masters of understatement. The fact is, a human fetus is a self-contained conglomerate of millions of complex cells that work together in a highly organized and coordinated manner to perform multifaceted functions which, in turn, are specifically designed to promote the overall health and growth of the whole organism—rather than the mother. In fact, the fetus draws nourishment from the mother in an effort to promote its own development—not the mother's.

To reduce the sheer miracle of human life and development to the notion of something that is "composed of human cells" with "potential membership in the human species" illustrates either biological ignorance or intentional avoidance of an inconvenient truth.

Nevertheless, Balkin's language reveals his bias. To suggest that a "fetus is composed of human cells, so from conception we may assume that what is growing in the mother's womb is a potential member of the human species" is consistent with the idea that a fetus is something *morally inferior* to a baby. If pressed, Balkin might happily accept the notion that his logic recognizes a fetus as a *potential* baby, and from that we might infer that a potential baby can morally be killed because of a fundamental right to privacy (according to Balkin's way of thinking), while an actual baby cannot. Here we see that if Balkin's underlying assumption *is correct*—that a fetus is something radically different from and inferior to a baby—then the rest of his pro-abortion logic would make sense. If not, his logic is in serious trouble.

Even granting the absurdity of the notion that a living human fetus is only a potential member of the species, what becomes obvious is that Balkin cannot (or at least does not) actually define what exactly might distinguish a "potential member of the human species," in the tangible form of a human fetus, from an actual member of the human species in the tangible form of a baby.

If Balkin were pressed on this issue it would be logically safer for him to take the "potential baby" approach rather than the "potential member of the human species" approach. Such an argument would mirror the *Roe* Court's use of "personhood." Balkin would then be free to argue that a baby is not an actual baby until birth (by definition), whereas a fetus ceases to be a fetus at birth (again, by definition). The result, then, would once again lead us to birth as the pivotal point separating potential vs. actual, unmeaningful vs. meaningful, nonperson vs. person. But this, of course, would merely be a definitional rather than a moral difference.

As Weddington had discovered decades earlier, birth is clearly the most convenient legal dividing line when logically attempting to defend pro-choice ideology. But birth is often too far along in the development of unborn children to sit well even with many pro-choice proponents, much less the public at large. Balkin seems to be no exception to this rule as he later explains that he wrote his opinion in anticipation that legislators, rather than judges, will wrestle with the question of identifying a specific "cutoff point" at which abortions should cease (presumably for moral reasons) (Balkin, 235). Conveniently, this allows Balkin to proceed as though there must be a rationally identifiable morally relevant point during pregnancy in which abortions should be "cut off" but without actually having to identify and rationally defend such a point.

He notes that his opinion "does not specify when the cutoff point for abortions must take place"; instead, it merely "requires that legislatures make findings about what period of time is sufficient to give pregnant women a fair and realistic chance to end their pregnancies" (Balkin, 235). Note the complete avoidance of the question of the status of and impact to the unborn child in any abortion decision. Balkin's emphasis is entirely on giving the woman a realistic opportunity to end her pregnancy while he is content to let legislators attempt to find the elusive but proper "cutoff point" for abortions.

One might ask Balkin why abortions should be "cut off" at any point in pregnancy. Is *time* the relevant moral factor? Should the "abortion right" cease merely because a certain amount of time has elapsed? Balkin's logic seems to reduce the abortion issue to the level of a timed sporting event wherein the contestant must complete a task before time runs out.

John Noonan informs us that moral decision making is essentially a matter of drawing lines:

> Line-drawing is the ordinary business of moralists and lawmakers. It says that up to a certain point such-and-such a value will be preserved, but after that point another value will have play. Line-drawing brings charges of inconsistency of principle only from a critic who believes that one value should not have any limits. The proper criticism of line-drawing, however, is not that it is inconsistent but that the line is drawn at the wrong place; usually, indeed, charges of "logical inconsistency" are simply disguises for real objections to where the line has been fixed. (John T. Noonan Jr., *The Morality of Abortion: Legal and Historical Perspectives*, Cambridge: Harvard University Press, 1970, 50)

Clearly Balkin is advancing *a moral* argument when he suggests that there is a proper "cutoff point" during pregnancy for abortions. But why? Refusing to draw the line himself, he suggests that if *Roe* would have followed his reasoning, then legislators in the states in the 1970s would likely have allowed abortion until "somewhere around twenty weeks, halfway through a normal pregnancy" (Balkin, 235). But Balkin never informs his readers what is so magical about the halfway point in pregnancy.

Is the fetus *becoming* an actual member of the human species *by degrees* as pregnancy progresses? This seems to be the conclusion Balkin's logic leads to. Can one *progress* toward actual membership in the human species? From a biological standpoint the answer is simply, no. But *Roe v. Wade* and derivative pro-abortion logic conveniently jettison the "well-known facts of fetal development" in favor of the variable and therefore more utilitarian concept of "personhood."

If one can progress toward personhood, however, does this alleged process of progression end in actualization at some critical point while the fetus is still in the mother's womb? Clearly Balkin does not wish to be encumbered with such trivialities. Simply taking the notion for granted, while never identifying any critical point during pregnancy, is much simpler. He is content to hope that legislators eventually stumble on a rational "cutoff point" for abortions. In the meantime, his mock rewrite of *Roe* would allow abortions without defining any critical point at which abortions should stop while simultaneously postulating that such a point must surely exist and that this point is critical to the morality of his position.

Pro-life advocates *logically* draw a line neatly at conception as the critical moral point, since before it *there is no* unique, living human being as clearly evidenced by the new and unique combination of chromosomes that genetically characterize the new individual. Balkin and the pro-choice logic he champions have no equally precise point to logically appeal to. Yet, he argues as though *there must be* a magical point in there, *somewhere*.

A line must be drawn at some point to enable the state to express its sincere and legitimate interest in the human potential of the fetus. But the line must not be drawn so early as to effectively extinguish the constitutional right to choose. *There is no magical formula for demarcating such a line with mathematical precision.* The balance between competing factors is essentially legislative, and must be drawn by legislatures themselves. (Balkin, 53, emphasis added)

At this point, if the reader is confused, he or she is not alone. One is at a loss to understand how on the one hand Balkin asserts that "a line must be drawn" while on the other he insists that "there is no magical formula for demarcating such a line with mathematical precision." Apparently Balkin believes a line is necessary (because the state needs "to express" its "interest in the human potential of the fetus") but can't quite figure out where to draw it.

While the concept of a compelling state interest in the form of "protecting" the unborn child goes back to *Roe,* Balkin's language appears to mask a rather superficial attempt at rhetorical appeasement. Like *Roe,* what Balkin's logic gives with one hand, it removes with the other. Pro-life proponents are not content to simply *express* their interests. They are instead dedicated to saving the actual lives of unborn children. If "the state" has a compelling interest in "protecting the unborn child," then a state has more than *a desire to express* its interest in that goal; rather, it has a desire *to act* on the compelling interest— which is pretty much what makes it compelling.

Moreover, pro-life proponents are not content to save only those lives that are threatened by abortion after twenty weeks. They do not see fetuses at 18 weeks, for example, as mere *potential* human beings, which again illustrates the real problem with Balkin's logic. If he is correct that human fetuses are merely potential human beings, then why legitimize halfway through pregnancy a "state interest" in what is still merely *potential*? Why would mere potential life trump a woman's right to terminate her actual pregnancy at *any* point in pregnancy?

Attempts to answer this question in terms of a *progressive* state interest in "potential life" tend to do more harm than good for the pro-choice cause. It's what led Justice Blackmun to create the arbitrary trimester framework that Balkin rejects. But Balkin does essentially the same thing only with much greater ambiguity with his notion of a mystery point hidden somewhere around twenty weeks:

> At the same time, a woman's right to abortion is not unlimited. The state has a legitimate interest in potential human life. Moreover, as the fetus develops during the later stages of pregnancy, abortion comes more and more to resemble infanticide. Thus, the state's interest in protecting unborn life becomes increasingly important to vindicate as the pregnancy proceeds, and it is strongest in the later stages of pregnancy. (Balkin, 52)

From this we see that Balkin recognizes a growing need to "vindicate" the state's interest in protecting unborn life because, according to Balkin, abortion in the later stages of pregnancy begins to "resemble infanticide." It remains unclear why abortion earlier in pregnancy apparently does not "resemble infanticide."

Be that as it may, Balkin clearly agrees that there is something morally wrong with killing a baby. It is equally clear that Balkin *believes* that killing a fetus is not the same thing as killing a baby. But why not? That crucial question is left unanswered. Regardless, Balkin's logic implies that *he believes* a fetus progresses toward becoming *an actual human being* during pregnancy. This belief, however, has no basis in real-world facts and, consequently, is not defended as fact by Balkin. He simply asserts that a line surely *must* exist but fails to identify where such a line *does* exist and ignores the consequences of guessing incorrectly.

Balkin recognizes this problem as a problem, but only when turning the same conundrum against anti-abortion laws that allow abortion in cases of rape and incest. Noting that the Georgia law under attack in *Doe v. Bolton* allowed abortion for just such cases, Balkin pounced:

> If Georgia is asserting an overriding interest in the life of human beings from the moment of their conception, it is not clear why fetuses conceived through rape are any less valuable to the state than fetuses conceived through consensual sex by adults. Surely the circumstances of pregnancy do not make these fetuses less human or less valuable as human beings. Compelling interests may be sacrificed to achieve other interests equally compelling, but Georgia has offered no equally compelling reason to permit the intentional destruction of what it understands to be human lives. (Balkin, 49)

Building on this argument, Balkin then underscores it with the assertion that he and his pro-choice colleagues suspect that the Georgia exception for rape suggests an inequitable application of law with respect to women, especially concerning the manner in which they become pregnant rather than a genuine concern for fetal life. Consequently, Balkin and his fellow (mock) pro-choice justices "do not think that Georgia has a compelling interest in forcing women who have sex to become mothers unless they have been raped" (Balkin, 49).

Without a doubt, this argument, skillfully stated, has an impact. What Balkin fails to point out is that the Georgia exception for rape was a recent invention (1968) put there by pro-abortion proponents. This was in response to the pro-abortion push for abortion law "reform" prior to *Roe v. Wade* that began to gain public sympathy in the wake of the Sherry Finkbine controversy (see chapter 5). The idea at the time was that nineteenth-century abortion laws (like that of Texas) that made no exception for cases of rape and incest were unduly burdensome in their lack of compassion for victims of rape or incest.

Exploiting the natural (and reasonable) compassion the average American feels for a victim of rape—especially when pregnancy results—the pro-abortion movement of the 1960s put pressure on several state legislatures like Georgia's to liberalize their abortion laws. At that point in time public sentiment was still opposed to abortion in most cases, so those in favor of abortion on demand were only pushing for mild reform of what they considered antiquated abortion laws rather than all-out repeal. The exceptions for rape and incest in Georgia's law were a direct response to this pro-abortion pressure and were modeled directly after the American Law Institute's Model Penal Code. No doubt reasonably expecting their law to last another century, Georgia legislators assumed they were doing the humane thing, while still keeping abortion illegal in most cases.

As if compassion for the pregnant victim of rape is the exclusive domain of pro-choice proponents, Balkin preempts any would-be pro-life sympathy for rape victims by suggesting that any exception in cases of rape renders pro-life logic inconsistent—even if the exceptions were put there as a direct result of pro-abortion "reform" pressure.

Balkin seems oblivious to the fact that his own logic would have us believe that abortion becomes incrementally more like infanticide as pregnancy progresses, while he is at a complete loss to identify and rationally defend any point during pregnancy at which abortion actually becomes immoral because of an inability to distinguish it from infanticide. Accepting Balkin's logic gives us a scale at which abortion (for any reason) is morally acceptable on one end, whereas on the other it is akin to infanticide while none of the intervening points are labeled.

Nevertheless, Balkin correctly observes that "the circumstances of the pregnancy do not make these fetuses less human or less valuable as human beings." That, of course, is what makes any concession by pro-life proponents in the cases of rape or incest so excruciating. When viewed without any consideration for the mother, one is certainly tempted (like Texas) to decline any allowance of abortion in cases of rape precisely because there is no difference in the value of human life conceived by rape or consensually.

But to do so is to simultaneously ignore the real trauma of rape. No woman should be raped. Pro-life advocates are not blind to the plight of a woman who becomes pregnant as a result of rape. They do not lack compassion for her. Ideally they hope that she would come to realize that the unborn child is also a victim, is as much her child as her attacker's, and should not be killed as a result of the sins and illegal behavior of the father—especially when adoption is so readily available. And yet due to the seriousness of rape, many Americans simply will not stand for abortion laws that do not allow exceptions for rape victims.

Indeed, Balkin's fellow pro-choice mock–Supreme Court justice, Jed Rubenfeld, attacks the Texas law for the alleged barbarity of *not* making an exception for rape:

> Texas makes abortion a crime from conception, unless "for the purpose of saving the life of the mother." Tex. Pen. Code arts. 1191, 1194. There are no exceptions. A man who rapes and impregnates a thirteen-year-old Texas girl can count on that state's officers to force her, under threat of prison, to carry his seed for nine months and then to mother his offspring. This barbarism has no place under our Constitution. (Balkin, 109–10)

From this we see that pro-life proponents can't win either way. Whether pro-life lawmakers show compassion for a rape victim and accordingly allow an exception in abortion law or not, either way, pro-choice proponents will criticize anti-abortion laws from both ends. Rubenfeld lambastes Texas for making no exception for rape, while Balkin labels the Georgia law inconsistent for doing so.

In general, however, many pro-life proponents are not willing to concede to pro-choice reasoning in cases of rape and incest. With the availability of adoption, most do not see it as unreasonable to require the mother to at least carry the baby to term and give the child up for adoption rather than consenting to the destruction of the baby before birth. The argument is succinctly stated in the form of a rhetorical question: Why kill the innocent child for the sins of the father? When considering the issue as an abstract principle, rather than a specific case, such a response seems reasonable.

On the other hand, some people within the pro-life movement could live (however uneasily) with a law (like Georgia's pre-*Roe* law) that makes an exception for rape and incest but that (like Pennsylvania's post-*Roe* law) also requires counseling in which the mother would be given information about the developing baby as well as contact information for organizations who can offer support both before and after delivery, as well as information on giving the child up for adoption. In effect, the freedom to choose abortion would be allowed in cases of rape or incest, but the mother would be strongly encouraged not to abort. The latter proviso, would, of course, be anathema to pro-abortion proponents, while the compromise itself would be extremely difficult for pro-life proponents.

The bottom line is that rape and incest are the most difficult ethical situations one can confront with regard to abortion, and there simply is no easy solution. Pro-choice proponents know this and, like Balkin and Rubenfeld, frequently exploit it. The resulting dilemma is a no-win situation for pro-life philosophy. If it is to remain true to principle, it must, like Texas, allow no exception to abortion in cases of rape, but doing so seems also to make it vulnerable to the inevitable emotional public response to forced pregnancies.

In the case of rape and the related problem of incest, choice wins an emotional rather than a logical victory precisely because a serious injustice has been forced on an innocent victim. What pro-choice proponents often fail to grasp is that when pregnancy results, there is no longer one but two victims. As Patrick Lee notes, in cases of rape one might "say that the woman has less responsibility to this child than in other types of pregnancy" (Lee, 121). Lee points out, however, that while this might be a relevant factor when considering whether to put the child up for adoption, "it does not warrant performing an action which would cause the child's death."

> Granted that it is extremely difficult for a woman or girl pregnant after rape to carry the baby to term, still, that difficulty is not in the same category as the harm that would be done to the child by causing his or her death. The difficulty for the mother which is unique to the pregnancy due to rape is the emotional distress she suffers by being reminded of the rape. But that emotional distress occasioned by the actual condition of pregnancy is temporary. The distress which would continue afterwards would exist in any case, and it can be alleviated or helped other than by causing the child's death. (Lee, 121)

Lee also observes that it is certainly not clear "that an abortion will help that emotional distress." Lee concludes by pointing out that "it is unjust to cause a person's death" in an effort to *possibly* alleviate emotional distress in another. The fact that an abortion is no guarantee that a rape victim's emotional distress will be alleviated cannot be understated. Abortion may—and quite likely will—contribute to and perpetuate the trauma and negative emotions confronting a rape victim.

Although abortion is touted by those who favor it as a reliable "cure" for unwanted pregnancy resulting from rape, there is an equal likelihood that abortion will simply add to the trauma instead of alleviating it. In light of this, Lee makes a convincing case that abortion due to rape is not morally acceptable, despite popular sentiment to the contrary.

The fact is, cases of rape and incest have gotten more mileage for the pro-choice cause than any other argument. Rape and incest is always brought up by pro-choice proponents when they want a guaranteed tactic to back pro-life advocates into a corner. It's a no-win situation from a pro-life perspective. Pro-choice proponents realize that the majority of Americans prefer to allow the option to choose abortion in the specific cases of rape and incest, and they also know how counterproductive a pro-life concession with regard to rape or incest can be for the pro-life cause.

The tactic is played out in a variety of ways, but the goal is always the same: Make the pro-life proponent squirm, hopefully in front of television cameras. Pro-abortion proponents have found it particularly effective to ask pro-life advocates specific but hypothetical questions about their own family members. For example: If your daughter came to you, Mr. Congressman, and informed you she had been brutally raped, impregnated, and desperately wanted an abortion, would you deny your own daughter the freedom to choose to terminate this unwanted pregnancy? They then enhance the developing guilt trip by adding even more traumatic details . . . the rape was a violent experience and the pregnancy reminds your daughter of the pain she was forced to endure. She had no desire to engage in sex and certainly no desire to become pregnant. She is an innocent victim. Maybe she is only fifteen. Are you so heartless that you are going to force her to endure nine months of pregnancy, every day of which she will be forced to relive this tragedy in her mind? And then bear and raise the child of her attacker? What kind of an uncaring brute are you?

There is no winning on such a one-sided playing field. The pro-life proponent is intentionally asked to deal with the most extreme situation imaginable and envision his or her own daughter caught in it. Most simply cannot formulate any kind of coherent response, and many of those who attempt one come across as either hypocritical or barbaric. A milder form of this tactic played out during the 2012 race to determine the GOP nominee to face Barack Obama in the general election for president. On the January 15 edition of the Mike Huckabee television show on the Fox News channel, then candidate former Utah Governor John Huntsman was asked the following question from a member of the audience:

Governor Huntsman, you are adamantly pro-life, however you place stipulations on the definition in cases of rape, incest or harm to the mother. If every single life is created by God, how do we place stipulations on these lives, and what would you do as president to protect them?

The governor responded as follows:

I'm very clear on my pro-life philosophy. I've always been pro-life and I always will be. And I have a daughter sitting right there in front of you. Her name is Gracie Ray. She's from China. She was born in a country where life isn't always valued. She was abandoned at two months of age in a vegetable market. We now have her in our family, and I thank her mother every day for giving her life. I have stipulations with rape and incest and health—uh, life of the mother. That's the conclusion that I have drawn after having looked at it, investigated it, and thought through it very, very carefully. That's where I am. It's where I always have been, and I hope it's good enough for you. Thank you (http://video.foxnews.com/v/1392761540001/jon-huntsman-on-defending-his-faith-beliefs).

Although the answer received polite applause, Governor Huntsman clearly dodged the question. And one can hardly blame him for doing so. There is no way to come out ahead when confronted with this question because the scenario itself is one in which all alternatives involve evil. Pro-life proponents correctly point out that the greater evil among the possible responses would be to kill an innocent unborn baby. It would be the most tragic end to a no-win situation. The fact is, when a woman is pregnant as a result of rape or incest, evil has already been done and nothing can undo it.

But the woman who is pregnant as a result of rape did not willingly engage in the act that caused the pregnancy. As pro-life proponents, we simply cannot ignore this crucial fact. Yet, it is she who must face nine months of pregnancy and then endure labor and delivery of a baby that was forced upon her and fathered by her attacker. It is a tragic situation from any perspective. Surely, this realization is what caused Governor Huntsman to allow for exceptions in cases of rape and incest while maintaining that he is pro-life.

Any such concession, however, is readily exploited by advocates of abortion as though it renders pro-life proponents hypocrites for merely expressing compassion for victims of rape. This is a tried and true tactic for astute pro-choice advocates. But a tactic it surely is. It's not that pro-choice proponents have any more inherent compassion for rape victims. To the contrary, they are the ones *exploiting* a tragic situation to further their agenda. And they are not content to use the tactic to justify only abortions resulting from rape. Instead they use the emotionalism of rape to justify all abortions. It is the pro-choice side that seeks to box pro-life philosophy into an absolute corner by using the tragic cases of rape and incest to achieve that goal. They would prefer that their pro-life opponents take a hard-line position that there should be virtually no exceptions for abortion. Such a position may appear "consistent" with pro-life philosophy but it is clearly out of touch with the rest of society.

When a pro-choice proponent can force a pro-life advocate into this no-win situation—especially in front of television cameras—it's a win-win for the pro-choice cause no matter how the pro-life advocate responds. This then feeds into the easily exploitable notion that pro-life proponents are either uncaring religious extremists who desire to force their unpopular views onto the rest of "normal" society or hypocrites who would not practice what they preach when their own daughters are faced with a dire situation like pregnancy resulting from rape.

The only rational approach to this is to acknowledge that cases of unwanted pregnancy as a result of rape or incest present a radically complex set of moral problems that simply cannot be neatly dealt with in a clear-cut, convenient way such that a straightforward, moral response clearly emerges. No matter what, we will be dealing with some sort of evil outcome. Even in the ideal situation where the mother wants to keep the baby, evil has still been done to her, and difficult consequences are inevitable. While it is true that human beings have a great capacity to heal and one can certainly hope and pray for that healing, we cannot ignore or downplay the trauma that results from these difficult situations. One would certainly hope that the woman who finds herself in such a situation would indeed come to bond with the child growing inside her and realize that he or she is also an innocent victim. This does occasionally happen but not always. Thankfully, pregnancies resulting from rape and incest are extremely rare, but they do occur.

Nevertheless, the Balkin and Rubenfeld attacks on both the Texas and Georgia laws illustrate that rape and incest are Catch-22 scenarios for pro-life proponents. If the state creates an abortion law that makes no exception for rape or incest, the Rubenfelds of the world will label it barbaric. And if a state creates an abortion law that makes exceptions for rape and incest, the Balkins of the world will assert that the law is inconsistent with pro-life philosophy.

CHAPTER 42

Acorns and Oaks

Nature never deceives us; it is we who deceive ourselves.
—Jean-Jacques Rousseau

While pro-life compassion for pregnant victims of rape in addition to compassion for the innocent unborn child is what leads to an exploitable situation, the philosophy of Rubenfeld and Balkin as well as Blackmun, Weddington, Means, Lucas, etc., suffers from an irreconcilable, inherent, fundamental flaw: namely, the notion that a fetus and a baby are radically different moral entities in spite of evidence to the contrary.

We've discussed several ways in which this unsubstantiated concept has been expressed. Here's how Rubenfeld puts it in *What Roe v. Wade Should Have Said:*

> . . . Texas argues that its abortion statute does not enact any distinctively religious articles of faith. Rather, the state argues, "advances in medical science" support the position that an independent human being, or person, comes into existence at the moment of conception. Texas bases this claim on three asserted facts: the fertilized egg is "genetically complete"; its natural development into a child has begun; and there is no other, non-arbitrary point in the course of gestation at which personhood could be said to begin.
>
> By this logic, a planted acorn is an oak tree. The acorn is genetically complete, its natural development into a tree has begun, and there is no non-arbitrary line that divides a planted acorn from a fully grown tree. (Balkin, 114)

The simple response to this is to agree. It would be a mistake to conclude that the above represents a refutation of either biological fact or pro-life logic. On the contrary, it highlights the inherent accuracy of pro-life philosophy. The fact is, a planted acorn *is* an oak in its earliest stages of development. Ironically, Rubenfeld's own words betray an erroneous motive while simultaneously revealing truth when he inadvertently acknowledges that there is "no non-arbitrary line that divides a planted acorn *from a fully grown tree*." By his own reasoning, then, a planted acorn *is indeed* an oak tree, just not "a fully grown tree." This, of course, is exactly the point pro-life proponents make with regard to the unborn child. No one is arguing that a fertilized egg *is a fully grown human*. Rather, a fertilized egg or zygote is a human individual in that individual's *earliest stages* of development. A related point that is nearly always overlooked is that no one is suggesting that a fertilized egg or zygote should be entitled to *the same rights* as a full-grown woman. Pro-life proponents merely assert that a fertilized egg or zygote should, at a minimum, be allowed to continue growing and developing.

Moreover, Rubenfeld also correctly points out that the Texas abortion statute ruled unconstitutional by the Supreme Court *does not* enact any distinctively religious articles of faith *precisely because* "advances in medical science" support the position that an independent human comes into existence at the moment of conception. Rather than refute this assertion by Texas, he avoids direct confrontation in favor of an analogy that backfires.

Implying uncertainty, Rubenfeld suggests that the claim of Texas is based on three "asserted facts." Yet, the very analogy he raises *supports* those asserted facts! What becomes clear is that removing and dissecting the fertilized acorn results in the death of the tree. Granted, the individual tree that is killed at that very early point is much smaller than when killed as a fully grown tree, but in either case, *the same biological entity* is killed. Again, this is exactly the point pro-life proponents wish to make. We might thank Rubenfeld for inadvertently stumbling into correct logic.

Perhaps sensing the weakness of his chosen position, Rubenfeld clarifies:

> To be sure, unlike an ordinary blood cell, the zygote is part of a human being's life cycle. This is a very important difference, but, again, it does not make the zygote a human being. A caterpillar is part of a butterfly's life cycle. It is not, however, a butterfly—any more than an acorn is an oak. (Balkin, 115)

Once again, Rubenfeld's own words reveal a faulty thesis. He frankly acknowledges that "the zygote is part of a human being's life cycle." This is obviously true. He then contradicts that correct observation with an incorrect assertion: "but, again, it does not make the zygote a human being." One is left to ponder how being a zygote could constitute a "part of the human being's life cycle" while, simultaneously, being a zygote "does not make the zygote a human being." The contradiction is mind numbing. What Rubenfeld is attempting to say is unclear. What Rubenfeld is evidently attempting *to avoid saying* is that being a zygote is simply one stage in the development of a human being, just as being a baby is another stage, as is being a toddler, a teenager, and a senior citizen. All are stages of development in the life of the same individual human.

Finally, Rubenfeld's second analogy fails with equal grandeur. In fact, a caterpillar *is indeed* the same individual insect as the butterfly that emerges from the cocoon. Once again, Rubenfeld confuses various stages of development in the same individual that may *appear* different with the erroneous notion that those stages actually do represent a different entity. Rather than supporting pro choice philosophy, the caterpillar analogy illustrates unawareness of both insect development and human development:

> All members of the order Lepidoptera, (butterflies and moths) progress through a four-stage life-cycle, or complete metamorphosis. Each stage: egg, larva, pupa and adult—serves a purpose in the insect's development and life. (insects.about.com/od/butterlfysmoths/p/lifecycle-leps.htm)

While a caterpillar may be a "potential butterfly," it is not a potential insect. The butterfly is, in fact, the same insect as the caterpillar was. In exactly the same manner, the human zygote, like the human baby, is a potential toddler, a potential teenager, a potential plumber, a potential doctor, a potential movie star, but it is not a potential human being. It is an actual human being at its earliest stage of development with a lot of potential.

If the baby ceases to exist, then none of its remaining potentialities can become actualized later in life. So it is with the caterpillar who ceases to exist; the butterfly stage will never be actualized for that individual caterpillar. The same is true for the potentialities resident in a human zygote. It is certainly true that a fertilized ovum doesn't *look like* a full-grown human. Nor would we expect it to. By the same token, a newborn baby doesn't look like Jennifer

Lopez. The human zygote looks exactly like a human being is supposed to look at that stage of development. There is no getting around this. That pro-choice advocates *want* their logic to be true does not make it so.

Now, the point here is not to deride pro-choice proponents for employing seriously flawed logic. Rather, the point is to illustrate how seriously flawed the logic is from the beginning, regardless of which advocate is making the case, and to suggest that the logic be dropped. It's not that Rubenfeld is lacking in intelligence. To the contrary, like Rubenfeld, many pro-choice people are highly intelligent. Rather the silliness of it all is expressed in a rigid, dogmatic adherence to a seriously flawed thesis *only because* one thinks women should have a fundamental right to terminate pregnancies they don't want. It is possible to hold that notion without reducing one's logic to the absurd but, as we will see in the coming chapters, doing so ultimately leads one into barbarity.

Rubenfeld is not alone in employing defective logic while arguing for alleged radical differences between human fetuses and human babies that supposedly diminish as pregnancy progresses. Writing in *Thornburgh v. American College of Obstetricians and Gynecologists,* Supreme Court Justice John Paul Stevens wrote:

> I should think it obvious that the State's interest in the protection of an embryo—even if that interest is defined as "protecting those who will be citizens"...—increases progressively and dramatically as the organism's capacity to feel pain, to experience pleasure, to survive, and to react to its surroundings increases day by day. The development of a fetus—and pregnancy itself—are not static conditions, and the assertion that the government's interest is static simply ignores this reality.... [U]nless the religious view that a fetus is a "person" is adopted ... there is a fundamental and well-recognized difference between a fetus and a human being...." (as quoted in Balkin, 87)

On the religious point, as we've already noted, the pro-choice position is carefully packaged and presented as though it is somehow devoid of religious or philosophical assumptions and dogma when, in fact, it isn't; whereas one supposedly cannot hold the notion that a "person" comes to be at conception without resting that notion on religion when, in fact, one can. This erroneous idea is repeated so often; many people now take it for granted. Like nearly all pro-choice proponents, Justice Stevens fails to explain how holding that the abstract notion of "personhood" begins at conception is any *more* a "religious view" than holding that "personhood" *is not present* until birth or at some other arbitrary point. As we will see, the problem in that conundrum lies in the definition of "personhood" and, more importantly, *who gets to define it* rather than in a hypothetical, radical moral difference between a fetus and a baby.

Justice Stevens's logic avoids the problem of suggesting that a state might have a compelling interest in protecting *potential life* by suggesting that what a state is actually protecting is an actual individual who has the potential to become a "citizen." While the absurdity of alleging a compelling interest in the protection of mere potential life is avoided, the problem of recognizing a living human who must be killed by abortion is raised. As with *Dred Scott*, the violation of human rights is morally justified on the basis of lack of citizenship. As if the precedent set by *Dred Scott* was not bad enough to indicate how fallacious such a line of thought is, it doesn't take a rocket scientist to conclude that killing illegal aliens merely because they are not citizens, as defined by the court, is unacceptable. By the same token, when the goal is justifying the morality of abortion, citizenship makes a lousy standard.

Nevertheless, Justice Stevens seems to imply that citizenship itself should hinge on "the organism's capacity to feel pain, to experience pleasure, to survive, and to react to its surroundings." While I find no such stipulation in the Constitution, Justice Stevens sees it as obvious that the state's interest in protecting unborn humans "increases progressively and dramatically" as the organism develops into a sentient being. One wonders about the moral implications of this line of thought for unconscious humans.

The flaw here occurs on at least three levels. First, development of sentience is progressive, so it is not possible to draw a line for which one side represents a nonsentient creature while the other represents a sentient creature. How then does one determine a morally acceptable point to cease abortions if such a line cannot be identified? In addition, the senses are not fully developed even at birth, so one could easily use this argument to promote infanticide. Finally, nonsentience can be induced by sleep or by drugs, yet we do not say that sleeping persons or drugged persons can morally be killed by virtue of temporary nonsentience. Similarly, even at its earliest stages the human embryo is only temporarily nonsentient, as even Justice Stevens acknowledges that the fetus is actively developing sentience.

Next Justice Stevens uses the words "to survive" as in, obviously, the viability of the fetus. This is also flawed logic because the fetus is quite capable of surviving in its natural environment: the mother's womb. Indeed, the problem is that the fetus is *too good* at surviving in its intended environment, which then perpetuates an unwanted pregnancy. Because the fetus is quite capable of surviving inside the womb, induced abortion must be employed to "solve" the resulting problem of unwanted pregnancy.

Justice Stevens then implies that the ability to "react" to one's "surroundings" is a key factor in the state's interest in protecting an individual's right to life. By this logic, so long as a victim is sufficiently bound, drugged, and gagged, it must be morally acceptable for a killer to kill. Nonetheless, it would be incorrect to assume that fetuses in the womb are incapable of reacting to their "surroundings."

Next, Justice Stevens asserts that the "development of a fetus—and pregnancy itself—are not static conditions, and the assertion that the government's interest is static simply ignores this reality." Mr. Justice Stevens is simply incorrect. While the development of a fetus is not "static" in the sense that changes do occur, it *is* static in the sense that the changes occur in the same (static) environment (the mother's womb) to the same (static) individual (the unborn child). Moreover, pregnancy is an all-or-nothing proposition. One cannot get progressively more pregnant. To assume so is to repeat Rubenfeld's blunder that naively assumes appearance equals reality. Certainly the outward signs that the mother *is* pregnant become more obvious to outside observers as pregnancy progresses, but the mother either is or is not pregnant. Pregnancy tests don't come with a "sort of" option. There is no middle ground.

Finally, as nearly all pro-choice proponents do, Justice Stevens attempts to paint the pro-life position as inherently religious: "Unless the religious view that a fetus is a 'person' is adopted . . . there is a fundamental and well-recognized difference between a fetus and a human being. . . ." Notice the clear implication: to hold that a fetus is a "person" is viewed by Justice Stevens as a "religious view." Yet he says nothing about the religious implications of holding that a baby *was not* a person while located inside the mother's womb.

Moreover, it turns out that this alleged "fundamental and well-recognized difference between a fetus and a human being" must be a closely guarded secret since, in decades of filtering through pro-choice literature, I have yet to discover it. Recently, however, I came across this:

> Rather than thinking of life as beginning at the moment of conception, biologists tend to think of it as existing on a continuum,

an image that is appropriate since no one can say for sure when life begins and ends. It is true that a genetic "blueprint," as biology professor Garrett Hardin preferred to call it, exists from the moment of conception, but much has to happen for that construction guide to become human enough to emerge from the mother's womb a fully developed person. (Faux, 148)

The quote above is found in Marian Faux's 2001 book titled: *Roe v. Wade: The Untold Story of the Landmark Supreme Court Decision That Made Abortion Legal.* Here, then, is a direct challenge to my central thesis. But Faux's challenge does not end with this paragraph. While I pleasantly note Faux's concession that "modern science has dispensed with the concept that a fetus is merely an appendage of a woman" (148), she nevertheless argues that science still "does not view it as a separate agent either" (148). Lack of "separate agency" under Faux's definition is hardly surprising given the physical attachment to the mother and location of the fetus inside her body. Comparatively, one wonders how much "separate agency" Faux might grant a newborn and whether the difference would be significant enough to justify killing the former and protecting the latter.

Citing "Christian feminist ethicist," Beverly Wildung Harrison, Faux asserts that Harrison:

... points out that all such comparisons and analogies of the fetus to a baby, although seemingly bathed in scientific fact, are actually ethical and moral arguments clothed in scientific language. The fetus may be like a baby in some respects, but it is emphatically not a baby. Although antiabortionists like to point out that the fetus is now a medical patient, we must realize that however wonderful these advances in medical treatment are, it is still the fetus and not a human baby that is being treated. The idea that the fetus is in fact a baby simply does not hold up scientifically, nor does the suggestion that the womb is a hostile environment for the fetus. Despite this, the analogies are highly seductive, and many jurists and physicians have fallen under their sway. (Faux, 149)

Obviously, either my assertions in this book are incorrect or Faux's are. Unless Faux is playing a semantic game, we both cannot be right. The key may lie in Faux's use of the word "baby," which is not a scientific term. The proper term, from a scientific standpoint, is "neonate." It is possible that Faux might suggest that a fetus "is emphatically not a baby" because, *by definition*, a baby exists outside the mother's womb, whereas a fetus does not. In that sense, of course, a fetus and a baby (neonate) are not technically the same thing. It seems clear from the arguments she presents, however, that she has more than a mere definitional difference based on location in mind, as do I.

There are, of course, some inconsequential differences between a fetus and a neonate. A fetus acquires nourishment through the umbilical cord, for example; a baby does so orally. My thesis is not that a fetus and a baby are exactly alike in virtually every conceivable aspect but that there is no *moral difference* that justifies the at-will killing of the former versus the legal protection of the latter. A fetus is unlike a baby in roughly the same ways a baby is unlike a teenager. The former is developmentally less mature than the latter but both are human beings and both merely represent stages in the life of the same individual human.

Obviously, a fetus takes in oxygen in a different manner than a baby does. Fetal lungs do not process oxygen the way a baby's lungs do. But this is a trivial difference. In both cases the organism takes in and processes oxygen. In both cases, the organism processing the oxygen is a living human. The fact that a fetus does not use lungs in the same way a baby does is inconsequential and is no justification for killing the fetus—any more than killing a scuba diver would be morally justified. Granted, there are trivial differences between a fetus and a neonate but nothing of any moral significance that would justify induced abortion in the absence of dire circumstances.

Faux's rhetoric is designed to sound authoritative, but a careful analysis reveals rhetorical tricks at play. First, Faux sets up a dichotomy, suggesting that one can either think of human life "as beginning at the moment of conception" or "as existing on a continuum." Given that Faux is writing in celebration of legal abortion, there is little doubt that this idea is intentionally borrowed from Weddington. Not surprisingly, Faux suggests that the correct way to think about life beginning is under the continuum framework because, according to Faux, this is how biologists "tend to think" of it. This "tendency" occurs, according to Faux, because "no one can say for sure when life begins and ends."

Faux's dichotomy is false. It is correct to think of life "as beginning at the moment of conception" *as well as* "existing on a continuum." One does not contradict the other as Faux implies. Dead organisms don't reproduce. One must have existing life in order for new life to be created (without supernatural intervention). But that does not mean that an individual biological life exists *at all points on the continuum!* On the contrary, individuals positively come into existence and cease to exist (at least in terms of being physically dead) at definite points on the continuum (whether Faux and her peers can accurately identify those points or not). So the premise Faux begins with is false. The continuum argument is simply a distraction, similar to the props an illusionist uses to refocus attention elsewhere.

Moreover, thinking of life as existing on a continuum does not relieve pro-choice proponents from acting in a morally responsible manner. Whether they prefer to think of life as existing "on a continuum" or coming into existence at a specific point is irrelevant to the fact that by the time elective abortion occurs the "continuum" ends for that individual unborn child.

Every effective deception will contain elements of truth. Faux accomplishes this by acknowledging that:

> It is true that a genetic "blueprint," as biology professor Garrett Hardin preferred to call it, exists from the moment of conception, but much has to happen for that construction guide to become human enough to emerge from the mother's womb a fully developed person. (Faux, 148)

Conceding the fact that the human genetic blueprint is fully intact at conception, Faux nevertheless rhetorically reduces the impact by suggesting it's still not human enough. The effect is that Faux begins by conceding to unavoidable biological fact and ends by asserting metaphysical dogma. The truth is, the newly formed zygote is not human enough *for Faux* under her biased and arbitrary criteria, but from a biological standpoint, a human zygote is both alive and fully human. Remarkably, Faux seems to agree with this, albeit apparently inadvertently:

> Biologists agree that human life starts out as a single cell, develops into a multicellular unit, and only gradually travels down the road toward becoming a full human being, and they also agree that along the way there are many wrong turns that can be taken, developmentally speaking. (Faux, 148)

While it is certainly not established that "biologists agree" that a zygote gradually travels "down the road toward becoming a full human being," Faux correctly notes that biologists do, in fact, agree "that human life starts out as a single cell," a concession calling into question her earlier assertion that, "rather than thinking of life as beginning at the moment of conception, biologists tend to think of it as existing on a continuum."

Faux then cites Beverly Wildung Harrison, who she describes as a "Christian feminist ethicist." While Harrison may argue from a religioethical perspective, her word on the matter is hardly authoritative from a biological standpoint. Without offering any specific quotes either within the text or even in her footnotes, Faux simply generically asserts that, according to Harrison, any:

> ... comparisons and analogies of the fetus to a baby, although seemingly bathed in scientific fact, are actually ethical and moral arguments clothed in scientific language. The fetus may be like a baby in some respects, but it is emphatically not a baby. (Faux, 149)

Given Faux's acknowledgment that "the fetus may be like a baby in some respects," one is left to wonder in what "emphatic" ways do a fetus and a baby differ such that it is morally acceptable to kill the former at will but not the latter. Faux suggests the answer lies in the concept of sentience.

CHAPTER 43

Sentience and Consciousness

We're all human, aren't we? Every human life is worth the same, and worth saving.
—J. K. ROWLING

A cknowledging that "fetal life was indisputably human," Faux nevertheless suggests that "it was not the same kind of human life that existed in a fully developed, sentient, already born person" (Faux, 147). What are the great moral distinguishing factors between a fetus and a baby according to Faux?

To understand why a fetus is not merely a small baby, one need only to consider the development of its organs, many of which are either absent or underdeveloped in the early stages or do not perform the same functions prior to birth that they will after birth. A fetus's liver, to take just one example, initially produces blood, a function that will later be taken over by its bone marrow. No matter how much a fetus may resemble a baby, its lungs do not breathe for it, nor do its stomach, intestines, bladder, and bowel digest and excrete for it as they will do later. These functions are performed by the placenta, an organ formed in the woman's uterus during pregnancy for the sole purpose of supporting the fetus.

Antiabortionists also made much of the fact that brain waves could be recorded at around eight weeks, as if that sign alone were incontrovertible proof that the fetus was a sentient being. But this analogy, too, is misleading. Before twenty-seven weeks, biologists tell us that brain function is a subcortical activity; that is to say, it is purely reflexive. Based on the best understandings of fetalogists [sic] and neonatologists, the young fetus does not feel pain, nor is it in any way a sentient being. (Faux, 147–8)

From this it is clear that Faux equates the possession of sentience with being "human enough" to qualify as a "fully developed person." Attempts to justify abortion using both sentience and consciousness as the key moral factors have become popular. The reason for the popularity is that the arguments seem to have a scientific and, consequently, an authoritative quality to them. Dissecting Faux's reasoning piece by piece reveals another story.

Faux suggests that one need only consider the development of fetal organs "to understand why a fetus is not merely a small baby." The absence of certain organs, or the fact that, when present, some organs perform different functions than they will at a later stage, Faux suggests, is enough to prove that a fetus is "not a small baby."

The term "baby" is defined by The American Heritage Dictionary as "a very young child; infant" (*The American Heritage Dictionary*, Second College Edition, 1983). The same dictionary defines "infant" as "a child in the earliest period of its life; baby," and a "fetus" is defined as "the unborn young from the end of the eighth week to the moment of birth as distinguished from the earlier embryo."

As implied in the definition, the distinction from "embryo" to "fetus" is indeed partly based on physiological development, with the idea that by the end of the eighth week, the child's development has reached a point where vital organs are intact and from that point on will simply mature. While Faux is correct to observe that some of those organs do not perform the same function as they will at a later stage in the child's life, the question of *why* organ functionality (or indeed multifunctionality!) should be a critical factor for determining the acquired vs. intrinsic value of a human being is raised but never satisfactorily answered. Instead, Faux seems to take it for granted that organ function is *critical* to assessing the value of human life, but she never explains either why that is or exactly what are the critical moral elements behind the assumption. Of course, if this were true it would be bad news for folks who have machines that perform the functions of biological organs for them. One would also wonder whether the recipients of organ transplants could be killed since their own organs are no longer useful. If one has a kidney failure, does this mean one is morally less of a person? Beyond this, common sense alone should be sufficient to conclude that organ functionality is not a proper moral indicator in determining whether a living human can be killed due to the circumstances of an older living human.

While such criteria might, to a limited extent, serve to technically distinguish fetal life from babies, they do not provide a moral basis for the killing of fetuses. Babies, for example, are not mature physiologically, mentally, or sexually, nor can a baby's legs, for example, function as they will later in life. These are not good reasons for allowing the killing of babies. We instinctively understand that while we may be dependent on the proper functioning of our organs, each organ function is designed to promote the growth, health, and ultimate fulfillment *of the individual,* and each performs an appropriate function to achieve that health and development at the proper time. It is the same individual that benefits at any given point in the process. Lungs that can breathe air directly, for example, would not be useful to a fetus when living in an airless environment. Consequently, oxygen is obtained in another manner, and lung development is not a priority in early pregnancy.

Moreover, we intuitively understand that our existence is greater than the sum of the functions our organs provide for us. Some organs are obviously more vital to continued existence than others. One can survive without one functioning kidney, for example, but the heart is crucial. As pro-life proponents emphasize, abortion stops a beating heart.

By focusing on organ development, Faux is not offering any scientific or moral justification for killing the whole human organism that is either actively developing vital organs and will soon put them to use or is already using them.

Faux's logic is hairsplitting for a reason that's fairly easy to miss when she asserts that many organs "are either absent or underdeveloped *in the early stages*" (emphasis added). What Faux doesn't say is what she considers to be the "early stages" or, more importantly, at what point do the "early stages" cease. Here again, we find the same practical ambiguity confronting Faux's expression of pro-choice logic that also plagues Balkin, Rubenfeld, Blackmun, Stevens, Weddington, and the rest. Using sentience as a critical criterion, Faux cannot positively identify and defend any one given point in fetal development such that prior to that point we have 100 percent nonsentient human life and afterward we have 100 percent sentient human life. The clear ramifications of this are that even by Faux's logic, abortion would still be the killing of *partially* sentient human beings, which would begin to be morally wrong at some point in pregnancy and become progressively *more wrong* with each passing minute. A critical problem under this thesis lies in never knowing exactly *how wrong* abortion is at *any* given moment.

Dr. Gerard Magill offers more insight into this conundrum:

> Consciousness and sentience is a function of the human brain. First of all, sentience is really about the nerve functioning in the body. Animals have sentience, I mean, a little worm, if you press it on the ground, has sentience.
>
> Consciousness is a very distinct function of the human condition where we are aware, through our cognitive activity, of our self and our surroundings.
>
> Sentience requires nerves to grow, being connected with the brain stem cell. So until the brain stem cell is formed, that's not possible; there is no sentience in a fertilized egg. As the egg multiplies within itself and divides, there is no sentience there until the brain stem forms, and that's a good bit into its development. And in the same way, consciousness, we're not quite sure when consciousness begins in the embryo. We now have enough evidence to suspect that it begins to occur in the womb, but we're not quite sure exactly when. We certainly know a newborn baby—we often question whether there is any consciousness there at all, other than just interactivity. We know there's enough brain function for it at least to be responsive, to be reactive. A baby will be reactive to heat and cold and pain upon birth. And the fact that both of those, sentience and consciousness, emerge in the development of the embryo is no argument at all about the meaning of human life.
>
> It's just, again, a function of science and it's just arbitrary. I mean, if you want to make an argument that sentience occurs on day 12 and consciousness occurs on day 30, therefore, up until day 12 and/or 30 you don't have human life, is like saying, well, the arms begin on day 14 and toes begin on day 17 so you don't have human life until your toes begin! I mean that's just random, arbitrary criteria that are being used there. That's privileging arbitrary standards. I mean, we know that consciousness and sentience are part of human development, and to just pick them out as being the standard of when human life begins is like picking out any aspect of human development and it's simply absurd.

As Dr. Magill indicates, the key problem with attempting to use sentience as a proper criterion to determine human worth is that it is an arbitrary standard. Patrick Lee further develops this point by suggesting that there are two basic ways of looking at it. To paraphrase Lee, one can conclude that the actual state of sentience itself is what is intrinsically valuable or that being capable of sentience is intrinsically valuable. According to Lee, this subtle distinction is important:

> On the first view, the physical organisms which are sentient are not intrinsically valuable, but are only the vehicles or perhaps the recipients of what really has intrinsic value. On the second view, the organisms themselves are intrinsically valuable. (Lee, 55)

Lee points out that the first view cannot be the correct view. One intriguing example he cites to illustrate this comes in the form of a thought experiment independently conducted by Robert Nozick and German Grisez with Russell Shaw in 1974. Lee quotes Nozick as follows:

> Suppose there were an experience machine that would give you any experience you desired. Super-duper neuropsychologists could stimulate your brain so that you would think and feel you were writing a great novel, or making a friend, or reading an interesting book. All the time you would be floating in a tank, with electrodes attached to your brain. Should you plug into this machine for life, preprogramming your life's experiences? (Lee, 51)

Lee points out that most of us would choose not to plug into the experience machine, even though it only offers positive experiences for the remainder of our lives. Lee suggests that:

> The very fact that we can choose an option other than one offering a life replete with positive experiences shows that what is intrinsically valuable is not experience alone.... As Nozick points out, the thought experiment shows that we care about actually *doing* certain things, and actually *being* in certain ways, as opposed to the mere experience of doing or being in certain ways. (Lee, 51–2, emphasis in original)

If perceptions and feelings are not intrinsically valuable in and of themselves, but sentience and/or consciousness is the moral basis for abortion, then it follows that the organisms themselves, having the capacity to experience and feel (sentience), are intrinsically valuable. Patrick Lee does not agree that sentience is the proper moral factor separating worthy and unworthy human life (nor do I), but asserts that:

> Even if the criterion of moral standing were sentience, nevertheless, we would still have to conclude that human embryos and fetuses have full moral standing. . . . If the thing itself is intrinsically valuable, then it is intrinsically valuable from the time it begins to be, not just when it acquires a state or property such as sentience. If X is in itself valuable, apart from any further features or relations not already included in just being X, then as soon as X comes to be, X must be intrinsically valuable: it cannot come to be at one time, and become intrinsically valuable at another time. So, even if sentience were the criterion of moral worth, it would remain true that human embryos or fetuses have intrinsic worth, because they are identical with entities who at a later time possess actual sentience. (Lee, 54, 55)

Lee's observations are especially salient. Many pro-choice advocates claim to have just as much respect for human life as their pro-life opponents do. They claim to recognize the intrinsic moral value of human life, but they dispute that the same value exists from the beginning of that individual's life as compared to later points in development. As Lee points out, such an assumption simply does not logically cohere.

Some people associate the development of a cerebral cortex in the brain at approximately 24 weeks with morally meaningful human life. The implication is that a person does not exist until the brain has sufficiently developed. But the precursors to brainwaves can be detected long before 24 weeks.

Dr. Gerster:

> The first brain waves can be recorded at 42 days. That doesn't mean they're not there before that but the fact is that we don't have the scientific equipment that can detect them.

If brain waves, neurological development, and brain development are to be the critical factors in determining the morality of abortion, they also do not offer much help since, once again, this development is a process taking place over time. How then can we know for sure when a person is present or not?

Dr. Magill:

For example, we know that the human soul is [present] in our life. We can argue that in a very different way from an embryo. But I can lose consciousness in an accident, and I can lose sentience through chemical use in surgery. I can be made absolutely nonsentient and unconscious by science. As soon as that happens on the surgery table, I *want* to be nonsentient and I *want* to be unconscious, but I think my soul is still there, surely! But, just as [with] lack of sentience when I'm on an operating table, I hope the doctor, when he's doing microsurgery on nerves in my neck, gets it right and doesn't make me paralyzed for life; but if he does make a mistake and does paralyze me for life and, you know, you become a quadriplegic through lack of sentience because the nerve endings have been shredded by an accident in surgery, that's not a justification for then killing the patient, surely.

In addition, the idea that brain activity is what constitutes "personhood" is simply that: an idea, not based on fact but rather conjecture made possible by the pliability of personhood in the first place. Complicating matters is the fact that human consciousness transcends the physical cells of our bodies. If a brain surgery requires the removal of brain tissue, we do not view the patient afterwards as less than a full person, but cognitive ability may indeed be temporarily or even permanently affected to varying degrees.

Even prior to brain development an embryo is still a living member of the human species, separate from, though dependent on and attached to the mother. If simply left alone, a mature brain will naturally develop over time while a successful abortion will end that and every other living process.

In the end, Faux's sentience-based assertions and those of pro-choice proponents like her are baseless. The idea that it "simply does not hold up scientifically," that a fetus is the moral equivalent of a baby is unsupported by factual, nonarbitrary evidence and is, instead, contradicted by it. The undeniable reality is that, irrespective of organ functionality or development of consciousness or sentience, induced abortion *kills* a human fetus and actively stops a very *actual* beating heart.

Faux's "logic" begins to hit concrete walls when she attempts to minimize advances in fetal surgery:

Although antiabortionists like to point out that the fetus is now a medical patient, we must realize that however wonderful these advances in medical treatment are, it is still the fetus and not a human baby that is being treated. (Faux, 149)

One can almost sympathize with Faux's plight when considering her task is to convince the public that what looks like a baby, moves like a baby, has a heart that sounds like a baby's, sucks her thumb like a baby, hiccups, sleeps, dreams, and squirms like a baby and, to top it off, is medically treated as a patient distinct from the mother, is not actually a baby. If Faux's rhetoric were not so threatening to the lives of millions of unborn babies, we might simply recognize her task as impossible, feel pity, and move on. As it is, too many people have swallowed this polemic uncritically, readily accepting the dismal consequences as inevitable.

CHAPTER 44

Dreams and Hiccups

I was stunned when I saw on the ultrasound a tiny, living creature
spinning around in my womb. Tap-dancing, I think.
Waving its tiny arms around and trying to suck its thumb.
I could have sworn I heard it laughing.
—MADONNA (QUOTED IN *WORLD*, OCTOBER 19, 1996)

M arian Faux introduced me to Beverly Wildung Harrison—not in a relational sense, of course, but in a literary sense. Faux cites Harrison in her book as authoritative. According to Faux, Harrison is a "Christian feminist ethicist who has perhaps thought and written more cogently on the subject of ethical behavior toward the fetus than anyone else" (Faux, 149).

Interestingly, Harrison agrees that human persons are intrinsically valuable:

> As a mixed theorist, I believe there are justifiable claims that some acts are morally dubious, consequences aside, because they violate intrinsic value—that which we ought to acknowledge as worthy apart from any functional or use relation to us. And within our human moral field, the human person most clearly and unambiguously may claim "intrinsic value." . . . Nothing in the moral defense of abortion that I offer here denies the supposition that persons have intrinsic value or that such an assumption is constitutive of the moral point of view." (Harrison, 191)

Harrison, like nearly every other pro-choice advocate, draws a distinction between what she labels "a form of human life" (i.e., a human fetus) and "the human person." She grants intrinsic value only to the "human person." This, of course, begs the question of what exactly is a "human person" and at what point does "a form of human life" existing as a living human fetus come to be one? It is the pro-choice side of the debate that has framed the argument in terms of hinging on a concept *they define* as "personhood"—or some variation thereof as in this case: "human person"—and since "personhood" is ambiguous, they argue that conclusions on the matter should be left up to each individual pregnant woman.

But this is simply irrational. The pro-choice side of the debate cannot satisfactorily agree on what personhood is, much less provide concrete evidence for when it comes into being. This is not the problem of the pro-life community. It is a problem entirely fabricated, enhanced, developed, and perpetuated by the pro-choice community for the express purpose of exploitation, motivated by a desire to be rid of unwanted but living human fetuses. Without the desire there would be no practical need to redefine unborn humans as nonpersons.

In short, if pro-choice advocates insist that being a "person" is the critical factor in determining the morality of abortion (as opposed to simply being alive and human), then, as with our earlier military general analogy, it is up to those same advocates to prove beyond a reasonable doubt that abortion *does not kill persons*. The problem is, attempts to do this are essentially metaphysical or philosophical in nature despite efforts to couch the arguments in scientific-sounding rhetoric.

The arguments Harrison employs in an effort to do this are certainly better than average from a purely rhetorical standpoint. Nonetheless, they are seriously flawed from a rational standpoint.

I'm going to resist the urge to quote Harrison's entire chapter on "Evaluating the Act of Abortion: The Debate about Fetal Life" (Harrison, 187–230). Harrison's arguments should be considered in some detail, however, since she offers logic in favor of abortion that seems, at first glance, to be convincing.

First, Harrison agrees that:

> The widespread consensus that human beings are to be treated as having intrinsic value grounds a further moral consensus—that killing human beings, without moral justification, is wrong. . . . The reason, then, that the debate about fetal life is so salient in the abortion discussion is that it is really a debate about *when* the notion

of "the intrinsic value of human life" should apply to developing fetal life; hence the debate about whether or when "the anti-killing ethic" should apply. (Harrison, 192)

Having established a common ethical starting point from which even pro-life proponents can agree ("that killing human beings, without moral justification, is wrong"), Harrison then suggests that:

> Even though moral consensus does exist about the intrinsic value of human life and the evil of unjustified killing, the evaluation of fetal life is complex. (Harrison, 193)

This sets the stage to claim that a radical difference exists between what is killed by abortion and what Harrison considers to be a "human being," which is apparently on par and interchangeable with Harrison's previous use of the term "human person." Harrison's logic necessarily begins to encounter logical difficulties as its assumptions begin to coalesce through articulation. Harrison asserts that:

> Because many Christian ethicists assume their tradition endorses "full hominization" from the earliest "justifiable" point onward, they bypass altogether the need for elaborated reason-giving with regard to fetal life. Rather, they embrace scientific species-continuity assumptions without requisite awareness that those who differ do not disagree with scientific data about the process of embryological development but remain unpersuaded that the presumption of species continuity warrants a moral valuation of a fetus either as individuated or as full human life, with the attendant implication that abortion is homicide. No one can speak meaningfully of the death of fetal life as *a human death* unless we have articulated reasons for believing that the fetus is a human life. (Harrison, 208, emphasis in original)

Harrison's choice of words, though surely intentional, is unfortunate since it can rather easily be demonstrated that a human fetus is, by definition, "a human life." Again, the argument that it is not is clearly refuted by the simple fact that humans can *only* reproduce other humans, and if the fetus were not alive, nothing would need to be killed by abortion. If Harrison would have added the qualifier "full human life" as she does elsewhere, then at least her logic would cohere well enough at this point. As stated, however, we can clearly "speak meaningfully of the death of fetal life as *a human death*" in regard to abortion precisely because a human fetus is both alive and human, and elective abortion intentionally kills it.

Harrison's assertions with regard to "species continuity" are more intriguing. Interestingly, she acknowledges that the pro-choice proponents she speaks for "do not disagree with scientific data about the process of embryological development." This is a rather remarkable concession in light of previously cited assertions by Marian Faux who, using Harrison as her authority, argues that "analogies of the fetus to a baby" are actually "ethical and moral arguments clothed in scientific language" (Faux, 149). By contrast, Harrison admits that pro-choice proponents "do not disagree with scientific data about the process of embryological development."

Perhaps inadvertently, Harrison effectively removes any possible claim that pro-choice philosophy rests on actual scientific data while pro-life philosophy rests on religious imposition. On the contrary, she concedes that the pro-choice community on whose behalf she speaks *agrees* with the "scientific data about the process of embryological development." Harrison does not dispute the embryological data. One might simply rest the case at this point.

Harrison does, however, "remain unpersuaded" about how to interpret the data. Clearly, then, what follows is a debate over *metaphysical concepts* rather than biological facts, which Harrison just agreed to. Essentially, Harrison agrees that human development is taking place because "a form of human life" resides in the womb, but she remains "unpersuaded" that the mere existence of a living human residing in the womb is sufficient to warrant "a moral valuation of a fetus either as individuated or as full human life, with the attendant implication that abortion is homicide." Thus, significantly, Harrison removes any potential of resting her case on empirical grounds. Instead, much like space-alien-believing cult members interpret observable, natural data in such a way that it conforms to preconceived dogma, Harrison must be *persuaded* that her interpretation of the raw embryological data is *incorrect*.

This is backward thinking. Harrison concedes that a fetus is alive, that a fetus is of the human species, and that abortion kills a fetus. She concedes that babies are human beings and that "killing human beings, without moral justification, is wrong." Since human fetuses emerge from the womb as babies, the burden of proof lies with Harrison (and her fellow pro-choice proponents) to *conclusively demonstrate* that a radical moral difference exists between the fetus that is killed by abortion and a baby.

Her *belief* that such a difference exists is not a satisfactory basis from which elective abortion can be morally grounded—especially when "the well-known facts of fetal development" seem to contradict her belief. The burden of proof does not lie with pro-life proponents to *persuade* Harrison that her interpretation of embryological data is incorrect; rather, because Harrison wishes to retain a right for women to choose to kill fetuses, the burden of proof lies with her and the pro-choice community to conclusively demonstrate beyond any reasonable doubt that what is killed by abortion is, in fact, *not* "a human being," given that she concedes that "killing human beings, without moral justification, is wrong." Proceeding with abortion on request *before* offering such conclusive proof is grossly irresponsible. Yet that is exactly what has occurred with *Roe v. Wade*.

Still, Harrison does attempt to portray the unborn human as not alive, not sufficiently complex, not autonomous, and not self-directed:

> The woman's body is the full, living life system not only sustaining but totally nourishing this as yet *very simple biological form*. We may call it *"the* fetus," but it is not yet in any sense *an actually alive organism* with human complexity. The applied logic of potentiality often goes unnoticed here, as does the degree of imputation of the concept "human" to the fetus. The analogy to an existent human life is very forced indeed; for, by anticipation, both autonomy and self-direction are projected back onto the fetus in its early development. (Harrison, 214, emphasis in original)

Harrison goes on to say that she doubts "the wisdom of imputing human agency to fetal life at all" (214) and that "predicating *any criteria derived from analogies to autonomous human beings* is dubious until fetal development approximates the necessary biological conditions for discrete human existence" (215, emphasis in original).

In addition to their speculative and agenda-driven nature, these suggestions are biologically incorrect. Contrary to Harrison's opinion, a developing human fetus is anything but "a very simple biological form." Complex processes are at work from the beginning and increase in complexity as pregnancy progresses.

Also contrary to Harrison, fetal development is indeed self-directed, just as child growth and development continues to be after birth.

One does not have to look far for examples of prenatal complexity. For instance, Sharon Begley of *Newsweek* magazine informs us that:

> By six weeks, the brain is visible and electrically active; by eight, it has the convoluted folds and shape of an adult brain. About 100,000 nerve cells sprout every minute until, by birth, there are 1 billion. Mother's movements stimulate the fetus's balance and motion detectors. Babies deprived of this movement, as when a high-risk woman is confined to bed, may lag behind in sensory-motor development. "Neural pathways that the child will use to think and remember are being laid down in the womb," says Dr. Mortimer Rosen of Columbia University College of Physicians and Surgeons. By the start of the last trimester the brain's neural circuits are as advanced as a newborn's, capable of paying attention and discriminating new from old. When a loudspeaker directs speech syllables at a mother-to-be's abdomen, the fetus's heart slows, a sign of attentiveness. The heartbeat speeds up as the fetus gets bored with the sounds, then slows again if new ones flow into the womb. (Sharon Begley, *Newsweek*, Special Issue, "How Kids Grow: Do You Hear What I Hear?" May 31, 1991, p. 14, hereafter "Begley")

In the same article, Begley reports that:

> Scientists have found hints of consciousness in 7-month-old fetuses and measured brain-wave patterns like those during dreaming in 8-month-olds. They have pushed sentience back to the end of the second trimester and shown that fetuses can learn. (Begley, 12)

After interviewing several fetal researchers Begley asserts that, "with no hype at all the fetus can rightly be called a marvel of cognition, consciousness and sentience" (Begley, 12). This simply does not gel well with pro-choice logic. Unconscious beings do not learn.

The universities of Fribourg, Lausanne, and Bern, Switzerland offer online courses for the convenience of students. Their human embryology course instructs students on the complexity of fetal development as follows:

The factors that, for example, determine the interactions between the tissues, the migration and differentiation of the cells, the proliferation of the cell colonies, as well as the apoptosis (programmed death of cells) are numerous. Embryonic development is a process of growth and differentiation in which the embryo becomes increasingly complex and is more and more enhanced with structures and functions.

The growth depends on the somatic multiplication of the cells through mitosis. In order to control the growth, certain restriction mechanisms are needed which are able to stop cell divisions at the right moment. The complexity of the structures is connected with morphogenesis and differentiation. One of the most fascinating aspects of embryonic development is the fact that out of a simple zygote (fertilized oocyte) an organism arises that consists of billions of cells. (Online course: "Human Embryology," Chapter 8.5 "Control of the Embryonic Development," The Swiss Virtual Campus, http://www.embryology.ch/anglais/iperiodembry/controlc01.html)

To suggest that a human fetus is "not yet in any sense *an actually alive organism* with human complexity" is simply outlandish. Dubbed the "Father of Modern Fetology," distinguished New Zealand surgeon and pioneer fetal researcher Sir William Liley has written:

Far from being an inert passenger in a pregnant mother, the foetus is very much in command of the pregnancy. It is the foetus who guarantees the endocrine success of pregnancy and induces all manner of changes in maternal physiology to make her a suitable host.... It is the foetus who determines the duration of pregnancy. It is the foetus who decides which way he will lie in pregnancy and which way he will present in labour. Even in labour the foetus is not entirely passive. (A. W. Liley, "The Foetus as a Personality," *Australian and New Zealand Journal of Psychiatry*, 1972, 6: 99, The Royal Australian and New Zealand College of Psychiatrists, 100; hereafter, "Liley")

In contrast to Harrison, who offers theoretical speculation of fetal life from the prejudiced perspective of a pro-abortion feminist, Liley provides actual insight into fetal life based on numerous observations in scientifically controlled environments. Those observations have revealed things like:

The foetus has been moving his limbs and trunk since about 8 weeks, but some 10 or more weeks elapse before these movements are strong enough to be transmitted to the abdominal wall. . . .

Foetal comfort determines foetal position, but comfort presents no problem in the first half of pregnancy when the foetus inhabits a relatively large and globular cavity. . . .

The mechanism by which the foetus changes ends in the uterus is simple—he propels himself around by his feet and legs. The mechanism by which he changes sides is more subtle—he employs an elegant longitudinal spiral roll and at the midpoint of his turn has a 180° twist in his spine. He first extends his head and rotates it, next his shoulders rotate and finally his lumbar spine and legs—in fact, he is using his long spinal reflexes. Insofar as this is the obvious way to turn over, there would be nothing remarkable about it except that according to textbooks of neonatal and infant locomotor function the baby does not roll over using his long spinal reflexes until 14 to 20 weeks of extrauterine life. However, we have unequivocal films of the foetus using this mechanism at least as early as 26 weeks gestation, and it is apparent that the reason we do not see this behaviour in the neonate is not that he lacks the neural co-ordination but that a trick which is simple in a state of neutral buoyancy becomes difficult under the new-found tyranny of gravity. . . .

The foetus is responsive to pressure and touch. Tickling the foetal scalp at surgical induction of labour provokes movement, stroking the palm of a prolapsed arm elicits a grasp reflex, and to plantar stimulation the footling breech obliges with an upgoing toe. (Liley, 100–1)

Liley has also observed fetal hiccups, swallowing, and sucking of fingers, toes, and thumbs.

But Liley is by no means the sole observer of fetal life. In fact, many researchers have observed similar prenatal activities. It was just these sorts of fetal discoveries that led Dr. Bernard Nathanson to a solidly pro-life position after having operated the largest abortion clinic in the world and even having performed numerous abortions. Nathanson had been a pro-choice repeal activist prior to *Roe v. Wade* but credits his newfound awareness of fetal development with his 180-degree turnaround. In contrast with Nathanson, however, other pro-choice proponents like Harrison and Faux apparently prefer to deny reality.

Writing in the *Journal of Medical Ethics* in 2001, Professor of Neonatal Pediatrics and Consultant Neonatal Pediatrician at University College in London, Dr. John Wyatt explained some of the complexities of fetal development he is experienced with:

> The development of ultrasound imaging has transformed the study of fetal physiology and behaviour. With modern equipment extraordinary detail, including rapid eye movements, breathing activity, fine motor patterns and cardiovascular responses can all be recorded and analysed. The first fetal movements are seen at seven weeks and over 20 different movement patterns have been described up to 16 weeks including hand-face contact, startle and sucking and swallowing movements. During the second trimester rest-activity cycles are observed and the development of rapid eye movement (REM) periods starts at 23 weeks. During the last three to four weeks complex and stable patterns of behaviour are apparent.
>
> The fetus first responds to sound at 20 weeks and subsequently develops more sophisticated auditory processing with the ability to discriminate different sounds. Towards the end of pregnancy the mother's voice can apparently be perceived clearly through the other sounds of the abdomen. Other responses include those to touch, changes in temperature and even the taste of the amniotic fluid. The newborn recognises its mother's smell and the taste of the breast milk immediately after birth. From 25 weeks the fetus tries to maintain its position in space, as the mother moves around. Complex cardiovascular and hormonal stress responses to invasive procedures have been detected from before 20 weeks gestation and there is continuing debate among fetal medicine specialists about the possibility of pain perception and whether the fetus should be anaesthetised prior to surgical and invasive procedures. (Dr. John Wyatt, "Medical paternalism and the fetus," *Journal of Medical Ethics*, 2001, Volume 27, Issue Suppl. 2., hereafter "Wyatt," http://jme.bmj.com/content/27/suppl_2/ii15.full)

Dr. Wyatt's direct, controlled and repeatable observations of fetal development in all its accompanying complexity has led him to conclude that:

> The "convenient fiction" that the fetus is a passive parasite within the mother's body cannot be sustained. Current scientific thinking is to regard the fetus not as a passive *tabula rasa*, but as a complex responsive organism interacting actively with its intrauterine environment. (Wyatt)

In his doctoral dissertation, Professor of Psychology at Caldwell University Dr. Stephen M. Maret quotes British Psychologist, Frank Lake, as concluding that fetal life is "not drifting on a cloud, [but as] eventful as the nine months that come after birth. The foetus is not unaware of itself, or of the emotional response of the mother to its presence, but acutely conscious of both and their interaction" ("Frank Lake's Maternal-Fetal Distress Syndrome—An Analysis," *Dissertation of Stephen M. Maret, Ph.D.,* Professor of Psychology Caldwell University, 41, http://primal-page.com/mf2menu.htm)

Researchers from the Institute of Reproductive and Developmental Biology at Imperial College in London inform us that:

> Fetal development is a very complex process. At different stages of development different aspects can be changed by specific outside influences. ("Fetal Programming," http://www.beginbeforebirth.org/in-the-womb/fetal-programming)

The same fetal researchers also state that:

> All of the fetus's senses will be stimulated naturally during the course of pregnancy, except for vision. The fetus has the ability to detect stimuli from as early as 8 weeks, in the case of touch. The environment of the fetus is not one of sensory deprivation. The older fetus learns, while in the womb, to recognize certain sounds or tastes, and this prepares them for life after birth. ("Fetal Development" http://www.beginbeforebirth.org/in-the-womb/fetal-development)

The Science Clarified website has this to say:

> An embryo is a living organism, like a full-grown rose bush, frog, or human. It has the same needs—food, oxygen, warmth, and protection—that the adult organism has. These needs are provided

for in a variety of ways by different kinds of organisms. ("Embryo and embryonic development," http://www.scienceclarified.com/El-Ex/Embryo-and-Embryonic-Development.html#b)

This same science-oriented website states that:

> During the eighth week, remarkable development occurs. Nerve cells in the brain form at a rate of about 100,000 a minute. The top of the head becomes more rounded and erect. Between day 52 and day 56, the fanshaped toes go from being webbed to separated. The fingers are entirely distinct. The eyelids close over the eyes and become fused shut until about the twenty-sixth week.

Contrary to Harrison's conclusions, a fetus not only looks like a baby but, according to Johns Hopkins University Psychologist Janet DiPietro, he or she starts acting like a newborn months before a normal week 40 delivery. Reporting on DiPietro's "highly sensitive and sophisticated" window-to-the-womb monitoring, Janet Hopson, reporter for *Psychology Today* writes:

> At 32 weeks of gestation—two months before a baby is considered fully prepared for the world, or "at term"—a fetus is behaving almost exactly as a newborn. And it continues to do so for the next 12 weeks. (*Psychology Today*, Sep/Oct 98, Vol. 31 Issue 5, 44, 6p, 4c.)

According to DiPietro, "Behaviorally speaking, there's little difference between a newborn baby and a 32-week-old fetus. A new wave of research suggests that the fetus can feel, dream, even enjoy *The Cat in the Hat*."

But the wonder doesn't begin at 32 weeks. According to Hopson, scientists are "creating a startling new picture of intelligent life in the womb" by simply observing and noting that:

- By nine weeks, a developing fetus can hiccup and react to loud noises. By the end of the second trimester it can hear.
- Just as adults do, the fetus experiences the rapid eye movement (REM) sleep of dreams.
- The fetus savors its mother's meals, first picking up the food tastes of a culture in the womb.
- Among other mental feats, the fetus can distinguish between the voice of Mom and that of a stranger, and respond to a familiar story read to it.

- Even a premature baby is aware, feels, responds, and adapts to its environment.
- Just because the fetus is responsive to certain stimuli doesn't mean that it should be the target of efforts to enhance development. Sensory stimulation of the fetus can in fact lead to bizarre patterns of adaptation later on.

DiPietro believes "that fetuses dream about what they know—the sensations they feel in the womb." It's difficult to conceive of an entity who, according to Harrison, is "not yet in any sense *an actually alive organism* with human complexity" who, nevertheless, manages to dream.

DiPietro and her colleagues have also observed unborn humans moving in all sorts of manners. Some of the more unusual fetal activities include: "licking the uterine wall and literally walking around the womb by pushing off with its feet." DiPietro has noticed that second- and third-born children tend to have "more room in the womb for such maneuvers than first babies" because the mother's uterus "is bigger and the umbilical cord longer, allowing more freedom of movement." She speculates that "second and subsequent children may develop more motor experience in utero and so may become more active infants."

A 2011 study observed facial expressions in fetuses:

> Before he or she is born, a fetus begins to move his or her face— parting lips, wrinkling a nose or lowering a brow for example— making movements that, when combined, will one day assemble expressions we all recognize in one another. A new study has shown that, as the fetus develops, these facial motions become increasingly complex. (Wynne Perry, "Facial Expressions Develop in the Womb," LiveScience, Sept. 7, 2011, http://www.livescience.com/15939-fetus-facial-expressions.html)

According to researcher Nadja Reissland, these facial expressions are "likely a form of practice, as the fetuses prepare to enter the social world, where they must form bonds with others." Reissland has also observed fetuses who "suck their thumbs in the womb and make breathing motions, both precursors for important activities once they are born."

According to Amber Canaan of Livestrong.com, a company that offers nutrients to pregnant mothers:

The nervous system of an unborn baby has begun to form often before the mother has even discovered that she is pregnant. Mothers need to eat a healthy and balanced diet in order to provide the necessary nutrients to their unborn baby. (Amber Canaan, "Nutrients for Human Fetal Brain Growth During Pregnancy," Nov. 2, 2010, http://www.livestrong.com/article/294481-nutrients-for-human-fetal-brain-growth-during-pregnancy/)

Despite the simple fact that fetuses in the womb have been observed doing the same things babies do, Harrison, Faux, and the pro-choice community they speak for resist the observed facts that indicate there is little significant developmental and no moral difference between the two entities in preference to the "'convenient fiction' that the fetus is a passive parasite within the mother's body." Like Justice Blackmun they choose to ignore or downplay the "well-known facts of fetal development."

Yet, remarkably, Harrison suggests that pro-life philosophy, resting on observable, biological facts (with which Harrison has agreed), is nevertheless, guilty of committing what she labels "the naturalistic fallacy" (Harrison, 206). She suggests that "*all* appeals to simple 'fact' as logically implying obligation or value are gross forms of this fallacy" (Harrison, 309, note 35, emphasis in original). In simple English, Harrison is suggesting that she believes it is fallacious to suggest that because she agrees that a fetus is both alive and biologically human, she is therefore morally obligated to treat the fetus as she would a living human being. To illustrate this alleged fallacy, she offers the following quote by Mary Meehan as an example:

> Yet it is biology, not faith, that tells us that a fertilized ovum is the earliest form of human life. Biology does not deal with the theological concept of "ensoulment"; but it need not deal with that concept in order to reach conclusions about when human life begins. This point is basic to the entire debate over abortion. . . . Juli Loesch, founder of an anti-nuclear weapons and anti-abortion group called Prolifers for Survival, says that it is the pro-choice people who make metaphysical statements about "potential life" and "meaningful life" and "personhood," while pro-lifers stick to "grubby little facts." Such facts include the time when the embryonic heart starts beating (two to four weeks of age), the time when the fetus has a clearly human

form (seven to eight weeks), and the fact that abortion usually tears apart the body of a tiny embryo and fetus. If more liberals were to study embryology books, they would understand that the debate can be resolved without reference to theology. (Harrison, 206)

This quote is serendipitously appropriate, considering that Harrison cites it as what she believes to be a clear violation of the "naturalistic fallacy," while I find nothing fallacious at all in Meehan's and Loesch's points. In fact, they are spot on. Harrison's response is to insist that the indisputable biological facts are open to moral evaluation:

> Meehan is right that theological justification is irrelevant, but her smug assurance that there can be only one side to the moral issue bespeaks the confusion that obtains whenever moral evaluation is suppressed by a refusal to distinguish between factual and moral claims. One can sympathize with the frustration of persons like Meehan and Loesch who believe that facts are so grubbily prosaic that they foreclose moral questions, but the result of this position is that the moral ground is cut out from under anyone who disputes the claims. Those of us who disagree are simply written off as "metaphysical speculators" who also, by implication, are both "unscientific" and resistant to confronting brute facts. (Harrison, 207)

By this point, Harrison's logic is beginning to unravel. While Harrison asserts that confusion obtains "whenever moral evaluation is suppressed by a refusal to distinguish between factual and moral claims," the reality is that any "confusion" introduced into the abortion discussion comes as a result of pro-choice proponents who wish to *redefine* existing biological human life as though it were less than fully human in order to maintain the illusion of moral acceptability in their desire to be rid of any obligation to it. *How much* less than fully human, they cannot say for certain, but sufficiently less to permit its at-will destruction. The logic used to excuse this intentional and unwarranted devaluation, in fact, amounts to metaphysical speculation based on, as Dr. Wyatt points out, what amounts to a conveniently fictitious misrepresentation of actual biological facts. It is essentially *religious dogma* in the sense that it must be accepted purely on faith—with no real-world support and in spite of contradictory evidence. Yet pro-choice proponents are rarely challenged directly in this regard while, at the same time, they hypocritically claim pro-life philosophy amounts to religious imposition.

"Grubby little facts" do indeed cut the moral ground out from under those who choose to argue that killing a human fetus is acceptable from a factually unsupportable standpoint. While Harrison alleges that she agrees with the "brute facts" of embryological development, she is nevertheless dogmatically attached to a "convenient fiction" that attempts to radically minimize the significance of the facts motivated by a desire to escape moral obligation. Harrison's logic not only appeals to dogma rather than "brute facts," it is also dubious as demonstrated by the fact that her justifications for abortion, if accepted, simultaneously justify infanticide.

While she disputes this due to her subjective assessment of what birth entails, the logic expressed in the quote above clearly supports infanticide if one accepts it as a valid defense of abortion. In short, Harrison would be appalled (one would hope) to think that mothers like Susan Smith might choose to argue that parents who believe their toddlers do not have a right to life "are simply written off as 'metaphysical speculators' who also, by implication, are both 'unscientific' and resistant to confronting brute facts." Yet such absurdity is exactly where Harrison's logic ends. The "brute fact" of the existence of toddlers does indeed bring with it certain moral implications regarding how one—especially a parent—may treat toddlers. If there is a vast moral difference between the fetus for which Harrison feels no compassion and Susan Smith's toddlers, it is not to be found in brute biological facts but rather in a "convenient fiction" born out of metaphysical speculation about those facts, which, in turn, is motivated out of a desire to be rid of moral obligation. Harrison attempts just such speculation.

Aware that thinking of this sort inevitably leads to justification of infanticide, Harrison attempts to preempt the connection by suggesting that her qualification of "personhood" as being morally dependent on "the discrete bodily existence achieved through birth" rules out "*any* presumption that infanticide is no more morally dubious than abortion" (Harrison, 220). Thus, Harrison believes her forced marriage of the metaphysical concept of "personhood" to the concrete event of birth insulates her logic from what would otherwise be its logical conclusion. But upon further investigation the marriage appears to be illegitimate. Paradoxically, Harrison's concept of personhood attainment is actually progressive:

> "Person" is a moral category, because in order to achieve full
> personhood we must intelligently reflect on our obligations to others,

our values, and decisions. In the absence of this understanding of the morality of personhood, neonates would be born into a world devoid of moral relations, in which the evolution of their personhood would be determined by the accident of their birth rather than by a community's collective striving to include them as beings like us. In ethics, "person" is a normative moral category not because philosophers arbitrarily wish to exclude the unborn but because they realize that our existing social relations must come under the sway of our intentionality and capacity to reason. If we reduce the category of "person" to sheer biological criteria or correlate it with highly complex organic forms of life, we suppress the moral dimension of existence as constitutive of humanity. (Harrison, 221)

This, of course, undermines her earlier assertion that a "presumption that infanticide is no more morally dubious than abortion" is ruled out by "the discrete bodily existence achieved through birth." If being a "human person" vs. not being a person is what makes infanticide immoral and abortion acceptable, then birth must be what makes one a person. If so, then personhood cannot be progressively attained after birth. Otherwise newborn infanticide is morally acceptable. To make rational sense of these assumptions, "full personhood"—or at least an amount sufficient to ensure one's right to continue living—cannot be achieved by an ability to "intelligently reflect on our obligations to others, our values, and decisions," as Harrison suggests. Rather, it must simply be achieved by the act of birth. In short, Harrison can't have it both ways. If being a "human person" is the critical difference, and birth confers personhood (on the basis of "discrete bodily existence"), then personhood is not a progressively attained quality. It is simply a convenient label arbitrarily associated with birth describing an equally arbitrary grouping of metaphysical stipulations.

On the other hand, if one *does* attain full "personhood" by "intelligently reflect[ing] on our obligations to others, our values, and decisions" then, obviously, full personhood is not achieved through the act of birth; which, in turn, renders infanticide morally permissible. Consequently, either newborn infanticide is acceptable under Harrison's logic, or personhood is not the critical factor separating the morality of abortion from the immorality of infanticide. If Harrison chooses to settle on her "discrete bodily existence" argument as the relevant moral factor while maintaining that "discrete bodily existence" does not instantaneously confer "personhood," she must scrap her previous moral assertion that "killing human beings, without moral justification, is wrong" (note: Harrison's inconsistent use of terminology confuses things, but she equates the term "human being" with the term "human person" or simply "person" and "full human life" at least insofar as she believes it is wrong to kill any one of them without moral justification) to something along the lines of: *Killing human beings without moral justification when those human beings are located outside the body of their mother is wrong.*

Either being "a human person" is what makes humans intrinsically valuable or not. If so, then "discrete bodily existence" must be what confers personhood if Harrison's logic is going to even get out of the starting gate. Yet "discrete bodily existence" cannot confer personhood, according to Harrison's own definition of personhood achievement. Something has to give. Harrison's logic cannot stand as articulated.

For Harrison, being human and alive is not sufficient moral ground in and of itself to guarantee even a basic right to continue living. Only "human persons" have that right, and pro-choice proponents get to decide who is admitted to the club and under what conditions they can apply. While Harrison suggests that "person" is a "normative moral category not because philosophers arbitrarily wish to exclude the unborn," coincidentally, her definition does, in fact, exclude the unborn. And while Harrison may feel confident that her logic precludes any advance into infanticide, her rather nebulous definition of "personhood" achievement as conditional upon intelligent reflection on "our obligations to others, our values, and decisions" certainly unlocks the gate and sets out the welcome mat.

CHAPTER 45

A Time to Live

*You can avoid reality, but you cannot avoid
the consequences of avoiding reality.*
—Ayn Rand

All pro-abortion arguments are prone to the inherent problem of identifying and rationally defending a specific point in time after which abortion is immoral. Consequently, nearly all pro-choice proponents speak in vague generalities that are not internally consistent with one another. The range of arbitrary "points" chosen as key moral dividing "lines" include but are not limited to the onset of quickening, viability, sentience, consciousness, birth, cognition, motor skills, and even the development of relationships. With the exception of birth, all of these points are arbitrary and inconsistent from individual to individual; even birth does not consistently occur at 40 weeks. The list of what, according to pro-choice logic, must be obtained before human life is "worthy" of simply not being killed is truly stunning.

Beverly Harrison agrees that qualities like sentience and consciousness are arbitrary. She attaches great moral significance to both viability and birth as key points at which a fetus gains autonomy from the mother. But exactly like Blackmun and Balkin, Harrison has difficulty finding an appropriate moral "cutoff" point for abortion, yet she seems to agree that such a point likely comes into existence at some point before birth:

> To argue that we may appropriately predicate to fetuses, in the late stages of gestation, "a right to life" does not mean, however, that the life of the pregnant woman should be overridden in decisions

about late-stage pregnancies. Rather, it means that abortions, at least in the second half of gestation, are not to be undertaken without serious justifications. My own belief is that the physical and emotional well-being of the pregnant woman, as a valuable existent person, still outweighs the incremental value of the fetus her life sustains. (Harrison, 225)

Logic such as this is what earns pro-choice philosophy a reputation of callous insensitivity to human life in the womb. It is precisely this sort of rigid lack of compassion that Naomi Wolf rightly condemns (see chapter 27, "Visualize Womb Peace") as an indication that the pro-choice movement has lost its soul.

Harrison's disregard for fetal life is emphasized by her inability to identify a morally significant point in fetal development or even to logically explain why "we may appropriately predicate to fetuses, in the late stages of gestation, 'a right to life.'" That seeming concession is an illusion, for just a few sentences earlier Harrison had stated that she does not believe "that even the highly developed fetus can yet be said to have 'an intrinsic right to life'" (224), but that extending such respect "de facto, to fetuses in late stages of gestation" is "morally wise" (224–5).

Harrison never indicates why so gracious an arbitrary extension of a highly qualified "right to life" is "morally wise." Like Weddington's logic before her, it seems that Harrison might also recognize "the emotional response to a late pregnancy" or, like Balkin, might acknowledge that abortion in late pregnancy "resembles infanticide." We are left simply to ponder why "abortions, at least in the second half of gestation, are not to be undertaken without serious justifications" while there is no moral problem with earlier abortions. And if Harrison can't explicitly state why late abortions are undesirable, like Balkin, she is equally unable or unwilling to draw a moral line in the sand identifying the proper boundary for the onset of an unborn's "right to life."

In short, for Harrison, even in the womb there is apparently a time to live but, exactly where it's hiding, is anyone's guess.

CHAPTER 46

After-Birth Abortion

As long as people believe in absurdities they will continue to commit atrocities.
—Voltaire

Faux's, Harrison's, and Weddington's dehumanizing logic exists to serve the broader political desire of unrestricted abortion on request. Without the desire to be rid of unwanted pregnancies, there would be no need to redefine unborn humans as less than fully human. Pro-abortion proponents who agree with prominent feminists on the question of abortion but rashly desire to take the logic even further illustrate why the innovations created to justify abortion are seriously flawed.

For Faux, at-will abortion is morally justified precisely because a fetus "is emphatically not a baby." In fact, Faux has structured her logic in such a way that it completely breaks down if it turns out that a fetus is, in fact, the moral equivalent of a baby. In that case, the thesis of her entire book, which is a celebration of how the abortion right came to be enshrined into law under *Roe v. Wade*, collapses and her heroine, Sarah Weddington, becomes a villain. In short, a fetus simply *cannot* be the moral equivalent of a baby if Faux's version of pro-choice logic is to remain out of the realms of barbarity.

But if the arguments of Alberto Guibilini and Francesca Minerva are rational, then Faux's thesis must collapse. In a highly controversial article first published online in the *Journal of Medical Ethics* on February 23, 2012, Guibilini and Minerva argue in favor of infanticide—which they refer to as "after-birth abortion"—*precisely because* there is no moral distinction between a fetus and a baby. The abstract of their paper states:

Abortion is largely accepted even for reasons that do not have anything to do with the fetus' health. By showing that (1) both fetuses and newborns do not have the same moral status as actual persons, (2) the fact that both are potential persons is morally irrelevant and (3) adoption is not always in the best interest of actual people, the authors argue that what we call "after-birth abortion" (killing a newborn) should be permissible in all the cases where abortion is, including cases where the newborn is not disabled. ("After-birth abortion: why should the baby live?", *Journal of Medical Ethics*, February 23, 2012, http://jme.bmj.com/content/early/2012/03/01/medethics-2011-100411.full)

Guibilini and Minerva's paper raised so many eyebrows, even in the first few weeks following its publication, that some observers speculated whether the whole thing was a (rather sick) joke. Others wondered whether the thesis was actually a pro-life spoof designed to shockingly illustrate the resulting savagery of taking pro-choice reasoning to its logical conclusion. But the article and its thesis were no joke. In fact, the logical flow from abortion to infanticide is neither a new nor incoherent concept, as Journal editor Julian Savulescu, notes in his defense of the decision to publish:

As Editor of the Journal, I would like to defend its publication. The arguments presented, in fact, are largely not new and have been presented repeatedly in the academic literature and public fora by the most eminent philosophers and bioethicists in the world, including Peter Singer, Michael Tooley and John Harris in defence of infanticide, which the authors call after-birth abortion.

The novel contribution of this paper is not an argument in favour of infanticide—the paper repeats the arguments made famous by Tooley and Singer—but rather their application in consideration of maternal and family interests. The paper also draws attention to the fact that infanticide is practised in the Netherlands. ("Liberals Are Disgusting": In Defense of the Publication of "After-Birth Abortion," Julian Savulescu, editor, *Journal of Medical Ethics*, Feb. 28, 2012, http://blogs.bmj.com/medical-ethics/2012/02/28/liberals-are-disgusting-in-defence-of-the-publication-of-after-birth-abortion/#comment-451456352)

While Savulescu may be correct to identify Guibilini and Minerva's unique application of Tooley's and Singer's (now apparently passé) barbarity as embodying the novelty in the current discussion, the cavalier logic used by Minerva and Guibilini to rationalize homicide is stunning. Contrary to Faux, Guibilini and Minerva push headlong into a brave new world, unafraid of the consequences of recognizing a right to abortion simultaneous to the moral equality of fetus and neonate:

> The fact that a fetus has the potential to become a person who will have an (at least) acceptable life is no reason for prohibiting abortion. Therefore, we argue that, when circumstances occur *after birth* such that they would have justified abortion, what we call *after-birth abortion* should be permissible.
>
> In spite of the oxymoron in the expression, we propose to call this practice "after-birth abortion," rather than "infanticide," to emphasise that the moral status of the individual killed is comparable with that of a fetus (on which "abortions" in the traditional sense are performed) rather than to that of a child. Therefore, we claim that killing a newborn could be ethically permissible in all the circumstances where abortion would be. Such circumstances include cases where the newborn has the potential to have an (at least) acceptable life, but the well-being of the family is at risk. Accordingly, a second terminological specification is that we call such a practice "after-birth abortion" rather than "euthanasia" because the best interest of the one who dies is not necessarily the primary criterion for the choice, contrary to what happens in the case of euthanasia.

How is one to respond to such "logic"? Reasonable conclusions are rarely achieved when one begins with a flawed premise. For Minerva and Guibilini the fact that a fetus "has the potential to become a person who will have an (at least) acceptable life is no reason for prohibiting abortion." Therefore, since "the moral status of the individual killed [after birth] is comparable with that of a fetus," infanticide logically follows abortion. In fact, the logical flow *is* sound. The premise, however, is hopelessly flawed from the outset.

Guibilini and Minerva could have easily concluded there might be a problem with society's acceptance of abortion *since it logically leads to infanticide!* Instead, they conclude that infanticide must also be acceptable. Since it isn't, however, they propose a name change.

The irony is that they do so *precisely because* they find no moral difference between a fetus and a baby, contrary to Faux's thesis. They suggest that, "failing to bring a new person into existence cannot be compared with the wrong caused by procuring the death of an existing person," a point on which most of us can agree. The problem, as in *Roe v. Wade*, is the criteria for determining when personhood begins. They suggest that:

> The moral status of an infant is equivalent to that of a fetus in the sense that both lack those properties that justify the attribution of a right to life to an individual.
>
> Both a fetus and a newborn certainly are human beings and potential persons, but neither is a 'person' in the sense of 'subject of a moral right to life'.

Since a baby is not a "person" as defined by Guibilini and Minerva, there is no moral reason to prohibit an opportunity for parents to kill their newborn babies. Thankfully, in the United States, the Fourteenth Amendment specifically defines born humans as "persons," so Guibilini and Minerva's logic finds a solid legal impediment here that prevents it from reaching its logical conclusion. Nevertheless, the radical philosophies of Guibilini and Minerva, Tooley and Singer continue to gain acceptability in liberal countries like the Netherlands.

That Guibilini and Minerva's logic flows directly from the logic expressed in the *Roe* majority opinion is obvious. In fact, despite its built-in barbarity, it is actually *more* coherent than the paradoxical conclusions expressed in *Roe*:

> The alleged right of individuals (such as fetuses and newborns) to develop their potentiality, which someone defends, is over-ridden by the interests of actual people (parents, family, society) to pursue their own well-being because, as we have just argued, merely potential people cannot be harmed by not being brought into existence.

There is a particularly biting irony in the stark, commonsense logic expressed here. If the premise were true, the conclusions would be watertight. Potential people cannot *actually* be harmed. Actual people can. The glaring problem, of course, is that actual humans *are* drastically harmed in both the case of abortion and infanticide. And in both cases, the idea that killing them is morally acceptable rests on the "convenient fiction" that they are not real *persons*.

So when do Guibilini and Minerva think a person begins to exist? The logic begins to sound like *Roe 2.0* when answering this question. In language vividly reminiscent of Blackmun, Guibilini and Minerva "do not put forward any claim about the moment at which after-birth abortion would no longer be permissible," but they *don't think* "more than a few days would be necessary for doctors to detect any abnormality in the child."

As if this failure to identify (and defend) a concrete point in development in which a person definitely resides inside a living human body were not suggestive enough of the mushy logic found in *Roe* and articulated by Sarah Weddington, Guibilini and Minerva recognize that what they are advocating is probably not a wonderful thing in and of itself:

> Second, we do not claim that after-birth abortions are good alternatives to abortion. Abortions at an early stage are the best option, for both psychological and physical reasons.

While Guibilini and Minerva are fantastically wrong when it comes to their conclusions about how to morally respond to the observation that a fetus and a baby *share the same moral status*, they are at least correct in that observation. This observation shatters the thesis of Marian Faux and her fellow pro-choice proponents.

CHAPTER 47

Aborting Motherhood

When motherhood becomes the fruit of a deep yearning,
not the result of ignorance or accident, its children will
become the foundation of a new race.
There will be no killing of babies in the womb by abortion,
nor through neglect in foundling homes, nor will there be infanticide.
—MARGARET SANGER, *WOMAN AND THE NEW RACE*

Jed Rubenfeld and Jack Balkin both further argue that restrictive abortion laws force a pregnant woman into unwanted motherhood, as if the state somehow rapes women. Rubenfeld suggests that:

> ...we deal with a law that would force a particular private life on particular private individuals; a law that would force on an unwilling woman what is likely to be a full-time, years-long occupation; a law whose purpose and effect is to make women bear children against their will. This the right of privacy does not allow. (Balkin, 119)

One is hard pressed to find a comparable assortment of equally egregious falsehoods clustered in so few words. First, the law forces nothing on anyone. Even in the tragic cases of rape, the woman can choose adoption, so unwanted occupational motherhood is in fact not being forced on an unwilling woman. While *continued* pregnancy *is* being forced, it is temporary and was not originally forced *by the law* as Rubenfeld suggests, but rather by a criminal. Unfortunately, reality is such that criminals tend to maintain a nasty habit of disregarding laws, which is what caused the problem in the first place.

In nonrape cases, the woman made a conscious decision to engage in an activity that contains the risk of pregnancy. The law did not force her to engage in sexual activity nor does it condemn her for doing so. It simply requires the natural consequence of that activity in lieu of killing a child.

Next, the purpose of anti-abortion laws are not "to make women bear children against their will." That is nonsense. The purpose is to prevent women from killing their children. That those children temporarily reside in the womb means that a by-product of preventing their intentional killing is that a woman must remain pregnant and eventually bear children against her will (assuming she has not changed her mind about wanting children after carrying and delivering them). A by-product of the law is not the same thing as the purpose of the law.

Finally, what is to prevent mothers like Susan Smith or Andrea Yates from adopting Rubenfeld's logic that, per Guibilini and Minerva, they should also be granted a right to a reasonable amount of time to decide whether to kill their born children on the grounds that they never really wanted to become mothers or that motherhood has become bothersome or disruptive of other goals or that they now realize they don't have the resources to properly care for children? Both Rubenfeld and Balkin argue that a "reasonable" amount of time should exist for a woman to realize she is pregnant and decide how she wants to respond to this information. Otherwise, they propose, the state is forcing motherhood on unwilling women. Rubenfeld suggests that:

> If, for example, a woman has the legal right to choose abortion until the twentieth week of pregnancy . . . she cannot reasonably complain afterward that the state forced motherhood upon her. (Balkin, 116)

If this is sound logic, then why can't mothers like Susan Smith argue that the realities of motherhood have now sunk in—realities that were not fully comprehended while her children were still in utero, and that, given the impact of this newly discovered reality, she wants out. Society should then be obligated to grant her a "reasonable" window of time to find the means and personnel capable of safely carrying out the destruction of her toddlers, thereby effectively eliminating her potential to "reasonably complain afterward that the state forced motherhood upon her" (Balkin/Rubenfeld, 116).

The argument might even be given more force, as Rubenfeld attempts to do, by adding factors that seem to weigh in favor of the woman's decision to kill her children. Perhaps pressure from societal expectations or her boyfriend, parents, husband, religion, peers, etc. forced her, against her will, to give birth, even though she wasn't technically raped. Perhaps she was unaware of the liberating abortion option Rubenfeld would have expected her to take advantage of ten months earlier. Or perhaps she was simply ignorant of what the true responsibilities of motherhood would actually entail. There are women who do kill their children. What is to prevent these women (or men for that matter) from adopting Rubenfeld's logic in defense of the killing of their children after birth? What if the stark realities of parenthood, once materialized, combine to convince the parent beyond any doubt that he or she does not desire a lifelong commitment to parenthood? What then? Is killing the child an acceptable solution? What reason would Rubenfeld give to overrule his own logic if it were used against him after birth?

One can only hope that he would point out something to the effect that: *Well, but you now have a living child who depends on you!* Suddenly (one would hope!), since Rubenfeld can no longer appeal to either Blackmun's or Balkin's ignorance as to where lines should be drawn (given that the child is now lying in a crib in front of him), he surely would belatedly recognize *the moral obligation* of the mother or father to the child. Moreover, he would now likely understand that that moral obligation *completely nullifies* virtually all of the arguments he just employed in his attempt to justify abortion. The implication is clear: The pivotal difference is that what Rubenfeld is willing to allow to be killed in the womb *cannot be the moral equivalent* of the child he (finally) recognizes as possessing a right to life that cannot be overruled by the parent's desires or unfortunate circumstances (convenience, whim, or caprice). But pro-choice logic has no way of establishing this crucial hypothetical factor.

Again, this is not applicable only to Rubenfeld's or Balkin's or Weddington's or Harrison's or Faux's articulation of pro-choice logic. It's not an articulation problem; rather, it's a fundamental flaw in the ideology itself that is solved only by recognizing the real problem. As we've seen, logical attempts to justify abortion nearly always end up logically justifying infanticide. This strongly suggests that there is something inherently wrong with the logic underlying abortion, *not* that infanticide must be morally acceptable.

CHAPTER 48

It's All in Your Mind

Not everything that counts can be counted,
and not everything that can be counted counts.
—Albert Einstein

The difficult but by now obvious truth boils down to this: Once pro-choice advocates are confronted with a living, breathing baby who can look back at them and smile or cry, they are, at that point, *forced* to come to grips with its right to continue living—unless they believe barbarity is rational. As long as that same individual remains out of sight, however, the immorality of abortion on demand remains out of mind.

This truth has been revealed on many occasions. One clear example took place in a simple conversation. I cite it here because I think it not only illustrates the point but also highlights the inevitable cognitive dissonance that results when pro-choice proponents are forced to honestly confront the implications of their logic.

The following is a transcript of a video interview that took place on July 23, 2009, in San Jose, California. It was captured and produced by a pro-life organization called Live Action, which was started by a then 15-year-old named Lila Rose. At the time of this writing, she's now in her early 20s. Lila has gained celebrity status for her undercover videos demonstrating, among other things, that Planned Parenthood engages in unethical and potentially illegal practices.

This particular video, however, was not a part of any sting operation. The camera was out in the open, and everyday people were simply asked for their opinions. The Live Action reporter was Ana Benderas. The conversation is spontaneous and moves very quickly, so the communication from both reporter and interviewee is informal. Here's how the conversation called, "I guess it's all in your mind" went: (LA = Live Action; YW = Young Woman)

LA: So do you think abortion is right or wrong?

YW: I think it depends on the mother or the mother's—like the child's carrier.

LA: So you think sometimes it's wrong and sometimes it's right?

YW: Yeah, it depends.

LA: When, when would it be wrong?

YW: It would be wrong if you're using abortion as uh, used like for birth control.

LA: Why is that wrong?

YW: Because then you're using, like you're killing a child because you've had unprotected sex when you should have used a condom or a birth contraceptive.

LA: Uh, you used the term "killing a child," are you referring to an abortion procedure?

YW: Yeah.

LA: So when is killing a child okay?

(Pause)

YW: When . . . you're bringing the child into the world where it isn't really fit for survival, like if you're . . .

LA: Like in the jungle?

YW: No. Not in the jungle. If you're in the jungle you're crazy having a child or whatever.

LA: What if a child is, is put under those same circumstances that it would be unfit but he's already born, is it okay to terminate the life of that child?

YW: What do you . . . I don't know what you mean. Like what do you . . .

LA: Uh, so you said abortion is killing a child. And you said that it is okay to do that when you would be bringing a baby in an unfit environment. So what if a baby, uh, that a born child is already in an unfit environment, would it be okay to terminate the life of that child?

YW: No, because it's already born, that would just be killing someone.

LA: What's the difference between born and preborn babies?

(Pause)

YW: I guess it's all in your mind.

LA: Do you have scientific evidence for that?

YW: No.

LA: Oh. Well, if I told you, if I gave you clear scientific facts that proves scientifically that a baby who is in the womb is already a human being would that change your mind about abortion?

YW: Uh, no.

LA: Why not?

YW: Because it's kind of like an out-of-sight-out-of-mind. . . . I know that sounds bad but if you're like sixteen and you have a child and you can't even, like pay for your own food how are you going to pay for that child? You're just putting your, what you did on other people and it's on, on the child.

LA: Very cool, thank you so much for your opinion.

(http://liveaction.org/perspectives/3.htm)

This conversation with its remarkable candor says a lot about the way many pro-choice people see the abortion controversy. The most glaring observation is that even if scientific facts demonstrate an unborn child "is already a human being," this young woman's mind would remain unchanged about abortion. When asked why that is, she frankly admits that the reason is because the child is out of sight, so the evil of abortion remains out of mind. She understands "that sounds bad," but she still thinks the child's mother should have the option to *kill her child* through abortion when the mother is young and can't afford to care for the child.

Remarkably she acknowledges that any differences between a fetus and a baby are "all in your mind" but, paradoxically, she thinks it is wrong to kill a "born child" even when that child is also in an unfit environment, yet finds it acceptable to kill the same child when that child resides in the womb.

It should be painfully obvious that there is something seriously wrong with this kind of logic. This young woman herself recognizes that when she admits it "sounds bad." Indeed it does! If it's wrong to kill a child after birth (and, thankfully, most of us still agree on that), then it must be wrong to kill the same child before birth unless truly dire circumstances threaten the life of the mother.

CHAPTER 49

Safe, Legal, and On Demand

Abortion should not only be safe and legal, it should be rare.
—BILL CLINTON, DNC SPEECH, AUGUST 29, 1996

Despite our differences, there are certain core beliefs and values that tie us together
and set us apart as Americans. And it is those beliefs that can guide us
in reaching our goal of keeping abortion safe, legal and rare into the next century.
—HILLARY CLINTON, SPEECH TO NARAL, JANUARY 22, 1999

The notion that abortion should be "safe, legal, and rare" became a mantra within the pro-choice community during the 1990s. The catchphrase originated with self-described pro-choice candidate and then President Bill Clinton. While still in use as late as 2008 when Clinton's wife Hillary was running for president, the phrase has recently fallen out of favor with most serious abortion advocates for a fairly obvious reason. While virtually all abortion advocates have no problem with the *safe* and *legal* aspects of the phrase, many have come to object to the notion that abortion should also be *rare*. Such an idea is (correctly) understood to imply that abortion is somehow not a desirable, public good. If abortion is a sacred and fundamental liberty protected by the Constitution on par with the rights of privacy and equal protection, if abortion truly empowers women and equalizes the playing field with men, if it frees women from a terrible burden they would otherwise be forced to bear, why should its occurrence be infrequent?

The resulting conundrum was obviously not immediately apparent to its advocates. The very notion that abortion should be rare is an indication that there might be something not entirely desirable about it, some negative factor that gives pause even to some of its most ardent supporters.

This is further illustrated by the observation that "choice" is nearly always promoted and sold to the public in lieu of "abortion." The blatant downplaying of the act of abortion in favor of the freedom to choose the act by the very community that should be championing the act itself reveals that community's basic understanding that what they are championing is not really a good or liberating medical procedure worth defending on its own merits. Instead, the option to choose the procedure is preferred over championing the merits of the procedure itself.

Here's how Sarah Weddington made the point in *Roe v. Wade*:

> MS. WEDDINGTON: We are not here to advocate abortion. We do not ask this Court to rule that abortion is good or desirable in any particular situation. We are here to advocate that the decision as to whether or not a particular woman will continue to carry or will terminate a pregnancy is a decision that should be made by that individual; that, in fact, she has a constitutional right to make that decision for herself; and that the state has shown no interest in interfering with that decision.

What are the implications when abortion's leading advocate bluntly states that she did not go to court "to advocate abortion"? What are we to conclude about a procedure whose most prominent proponent admits she was not asking the Court to rule on its desirability or goodness? Weddington's reluctance to openly advocate abortion in 1973 strongly suggests that even the most visible champion of abortion had misgivings about it. Regardless, the attempt to distance herself from abortion advocacy was shallow if not self-defeating.

Clearly, Weddington *was* advocating abortion as a viable option. If Weddington was not asking the Court to rule that abortion is "good or desirable," then how would she prefer the Court to characterize it? Bad? Undesirable? A "necessary evil"? Of course, she was advocating that abortion is both desirable and good in comparison to what she saw as the alternative. It was desirable enough *for her* to choose even though it was illegal at the time.

Abortion was desirable to Weddington because it eliminated any obligation she would otherwise have to the child growing in her womb. The choice in favor of abortion (which Weddington obviously had despite its illegality) was more desirable to Sarah Weddington than remaining a mother.

The notion that one can separate advocacy of an action from advocacy of the option to choose the action, while certainly a novel tactic, was anything but accurate. A similar argument could be made by anyone desiring to avoid the stigma of any kind of negative behavior. An advocate of unrestricted speed limits might argue that he's not advocating for the goodness or desirability of speeding, just the option to choose to speed. The meth user can insist he's not asking the public to think of meth as good or desirable, he merely wants the option to choose meth.

Given the difficulty of rhetorically extricating the act of killing from the concept of abortion, Weddington and other pro-abortion proponents recognized a clear need to distance themselves from barefaced abortion promotion while reinforcing the idea that they were, instead, the champions of "choice." Instinctively if not candidly, they understood that the action of abortion was anything but inherently desirable. Pro-choice writer Connie Paige accordingly states: "Nobody likes abortion. It is bloody" (Paige, 29). University of California Professor, Ernest Partridge notes that:

> Furthermore, no one is, strictly speaking, "pro-abortion"—that is to say, no one seriously contends that abortion is *prima facie* a "nice thing" to happen to a woman. Instead, the pro-choice position regards abortion as a "necessary evil." How "necessary" and how "evil"?— that moral perception varies with each individual. (Ernest Partridge, Ph.D., *The Gadfly Bytes*, "The Paradoxical Right to Life," October 1999, http://gadfly.igc.org/liberal/abortion.htm)

Necessary evil? In the rare cases where the life of the mother is genuinely threatened, Dr. Partridge might gain nearly universal agreement on his assessment. But what of the other 99 percent of abortions? Are they also *necessary* evils?

Even Barack Obama jumped on the "abortion is not a good thing" bandwagon when he was campaigning for the Catholic vote in 2008:

> No one is pro-abortion, and I respect that people of good faith will disagree on this issue. I strongly support a woman's right to

choose. I also firmly believe that women do not make these decisions casually and that they are ultimately in the best position to make this decision with their family, their doctor, and their pastor. (Talking Points, *A U.S. Catholic Interview: "*The presidential candidates make their case for the Catholic Vote," September 15, 2008, http://www. uscatholic.org/culture/social-justice/2008/09/talking-points)

Sarah Weddington likens abortion to divorce, indicating that "no one says 'I'm pro-divorce'" (Weddington, 238).

What Weddington, Paige, Obama, and others of the same mind-set fail to come to grips with is that the general inclination to avoid describing oneself as "pro-divorce," to use Weddington's analogy, is an indication that there is something inherently negative and undesirable about divorce and, by association, advocating for it. While society may indeed recognize divorce as a "necessary evil," it nevertheless holds divorce in a negative context and something to be avoided if at all possible. That negative context is what allows Weddington to use divorce as analogous to abortion. Even the one whose dire circumstances have culminated in a desire for divorce still typically understands it to be the lesser evil rather than an inherently good thing. And while divorce certainly is a negative event, it does not require that one of the parties must end up dead. By contrast, abortion is always fatal for the unborn child.

It is this inherent realization that abortion is not a public good to be desired and championed that allowed the notion that abortion *should be rare* to temporarily resonate with many pro-choice constituents during the 1990s. That idea, however, was self-contradictory if the underlying but critical premise of fetal inferiority or "nonpersonhood" was also correct. In short, the pro-choice slogan that abortion should be rare undercut the very basis of pro-choice philosophy. If a fetus is the moral equivalent of a tonsil, for example, then why should abortion be rare? Especially when coupled with the popular argument pro-choice advocates are fond of making that abortion, especially during the early months of pregnancy, is safe. Moreover, if abortion gives a woman equality with men, why shouldn't it be performed any time she desires such equality?

Surprisingly, it took a few years for the realization of a contradiction to sink in. Many pro-abortion proponents did not immediately recognize the logical inconsistency of resting abortion justification on the fragile notion that there is no moral difference between a fetus and an appendix and that abortion is the great equalizing, fundamental right of women, while simultaneously advocating for the infrequency of the procedure.

The idea that abortion should be rare seems to have been a momentary aberration among those calling themselves pro-choice, something akin to temporary amnesia. Leading abortion reform advocates in the 1950s and 60s instinctively rejected it. Reporting on the surprising ease with which a pre-*Roe* less-restrictive abortion reform law was passed on April 25, 1967, in Colorado, pro-choice historian David Garrow informs his readers that the jubilation of reform proponents at that time,

> . . . over their amazingly quick and obstacle-free victory was somewhat tempered by the realization that only a modest percentage of women seeking abortions would qualify for legal ones under the provisions of the new Colorado statute. (Garrow, 325)

A similar realization developed among abortion advocates nationwide after it became apparent that the modest "gains" made in states like Colorado, North Carolina, and California had actually legalized only about 5 percent of the total number of abortions that were *desired* (Garrow, 332). After the initial success of these and similar reform efforts, the argument for still increased legal availability of abortion was then being framed in terms of how many women *desired* it rather than finding themselves in a situation where abortion was a necessary but evil response.

In the years leading up to *Roe*, several states had liberalized their laws, but most of those reforms merely legalized abortion in the hard cases of rape, incest, and fetal deformities—previous unofficial "therapeutic" exceptions which, in any case, had rarely been prosecuted. Expressing the frustration of abortion proponents in the years leading up to *Roe*, Howard Moody of the Clergy Consultation Service on Abortion summed up the problem in terms of its frequency, "Our day to day work taught us how few women wanted abortions for the reasons most liberals conceded were justifiable" (Garrow, 351).

That abortions in these states were only taking place in cases where the public was most likely to think of abortion as "morally justified" was apparently not satisfactory for abortion proponents. There were simply *not enough* abortions occurring to please abortion advocates, even under newly enacted "reform" statutes, in comparison to the number of women who desired them. Stated another way, the realization that reform laws actually resulted in abortion being a *rare* procedure was unacceptable. This led to a shift in policy among abortion proponents during the years leading up to *Roe v. Wade*. Modest liberalization of existing laws was dropped as a tactic in favor of complete repeal.

CHAPTER 50

The Right to Remain Uninformed

*I am pro-choice, but I find that abortion is a failure of the feminist establishment.
With every kind of birth control available in the world, abortion is not something
to be proud of. If you need an abortion, you've failed.*
—Tammy Bruce, speech at Columbia University, April 6, 2005

*I have met thousands and thousands of pro-choice men and women.
I have never met anyone who is pro-abortion. Being pro-choice is not being pro-abortion.*
—Hillary Clinton, Speech to NARAL, January 22, 1999

P *lanned Parenthood v. Casey* was another Supreme Court decision involving abortion. Many on the pro-life side hoped it would be the case to overturn *Roe v. Wade.* While the 1992 decision left the basic liberty of abortion as defined in *Roe* intact, the pro-life community did not view the decision as a complete loss. The Court upheld a Pennsylvania requirement that women must be given information through counseling prior to undergoing an abortion, which constituted "informed consent."

Although the Court concluded that this requirement to provide women with detailed information about the development of an unborn child, especially through photographs, was not an "undue burden" for pregnant women, several feminist groups passionately disagreed. Enraged defenders of abortion, like Feminist Majority leader Eleanor Smeal, described the requirements as "the right to harass women" with "state based propaganda" (www.c-spanvideo. org/program/26815-1).

Planned Parenthood President, Gloria Feldt, also complained about the "informed consent" requirement in *Casey*:

> The mandatory counseling materials vary from state to state, but often include photographs and videos of fetuses at various stages of development, lists of abortion alternatives and adoption agencies, and sensationalistic misinformation about the risks of abortion. Typically biased, inflammatory, graphic and medically inaccurate, the materials are designed to deter women from seeking abortion. (Feldt, 157)

Although pro-choice groups passionately claim to be advocates of choice rather than the desirability of abortion, and even though the rarity of abortion was, at least for a time, advocated by prominent pro-choice proponents, it seems that any attempt to "deter" abortion is met with ridicule and scorn from those same groups. In the process of accusing the materials which included "photographs and videos of fetuses at various stages of development" of bias, Feldt readily expresses her own. In lieu of pointing to specific inaccuracies in a genuine effort to correct what she describes as "inflammatory, graphic and medically inaccurate," Feldt prefers to simply heap generic ad hominem attacks on the material as though using enough adjectives will bring her characterization to pass.

For Feldt, the choice for abortion was apparently the only politically correct choice.

Even with the limited requirements of some states to provide a minimum amount of pre-abortion counseling and information, most women who experienced post-abortion complications say they weren't given *enough* information about the risks involved. According to the Elliot Institute, over 90 percent said they weren't given enough information to make an informed choice. Over 80 percent said it was very unlikely they would have aborted if they had not been so strongly encouraged to abort by others, including their abortion counselors. And 83 percent said they would have carried to term if they had received support from boyfriends, families, or other important people in their lives (as reported in Alcorn, 74–5).

Dr. Jefferson:

> You cannot face the fact that you're talking about a living human being; the youngest member of our own families. And the only way

you can just allow the willful destruction of these lives is to pretend they aren't there.

Dr. Brennan:

This is a perversion of the first order because it exploits the language of rights as a pretext for taking away the most fundamental right to life itself. It is an arrogant, elitist assumption of the awesome power to destroy those who cannot defend themselves, an extreme manifestation of the strong victimizing the helpless. It is also a blatant sham because the victims, the ones most drastically affected, are the very ones who do not have the right to select or choose. It is death at someone else's selection or choice. This is not freedom but the worst kind of tyranny.

The ruse of advocating choice over abortion, while often obvious to pro-life advocates, is rarely acknowledged by their pro-abortion counterparts. One exception, however, is Lauren Sabina Kneisly, who worries that her opposition to the use of the term "choice" will instantly identify her as a pro-life advocate when nothing could be further from the truth. While Kneisly unequivocally supports unrestricted access to abortion, she nevertheless agrees with the pro-life community that the term "choice" is an overused euphemism designed and implemented to obscure the true goal of the pro-abortion movement. On her website, Kneisly bluntly states that:

The only conclusion I can come to, is that for a large portion of those who argue in favor of abortion, the very word "pro-abortion" does not represent their image of themselves. Rather than arguing for abortion all these 26 years, they argue instead for "choice."

Thus they argue not for the service itself, but instead for the "option," the "right," or the "liberty" to buy the service of abortion! It has become unfashionable to demand the service itself, instead we argue for the ability to decide to "choose" the service.

By taking up the term "choice" as synonymous with abortion, the movement now argues for the option of buying a product rather than explaining and standing up for the product itself.

Leaving no room for doubt about where she stands on the question of abortion she further states:

I also feel that rather than hiding behind the easily appropriated word "choice," it's time to begin asking for what we really want and need, which is full and unrestricted access to abortion. (Lauren Sabina Kneisly, "Choice: An Obsolete Strategy," www.barf.org/articles/0035/, originally published January 20, 1999)

Yet, Kneisly's candor is a rare thing indeed. As she grudgingly acknowledges in her article, her negative attitude toward "choice" and positive attitude toward abortion is met with raised eyebrows among her less candid pro-abortion peers who clearly understand the dangers of promoting an unfiltered pro-abortion agenda to the general public. But if, as pro-choice advocates insist, there is no moral difference between a fetus and an appendix, this should not be the case. There should be no controversy.

In the decades after *Roe*, many support groups for post-abortive women have come into existence. Groups with names such as "Women Exploited by Abortion," "Victims of Choice," "Abortion Trauma Services," and "American Victims of Abortion," offer support and counseling for thousands of women who regret their "choice" and live with feelings of guilt an emotional trauma.

One is left to wonder where are the support groups for post-appendectomy women? Do women suffer from guilt over the removal of tumors? If a fetus is the equivalent of a tonsil, why would women feel guilty after having an abortion? Yet they often do. To combat those feelings, pro-abortion proponents now often describe unwanted pregnancy in terms of a disease or affliction attacking the woman's body with abortion being the only cure.

CHAPTER 51

No Reverse?

Certainly most of the pro-choice arguments make sense within the context of reducing the fetus to a subhuman status. However, would recognizing the humanity and right to life of the fetus nullify all pro-choice arguments?

Here again, not everything is clear cut. The arguments most often used to justify abortion are the exceptional or hard cases. Should abortion be legal, even recognizing the fetus's right to life, in the case of rape or incest? Should abortion be legal in the case of severe fetal abnormalities? Should abortion be legal when the mother's life is in jeopardy or perhaps when the mother's health could be in jeopardy? Can any of these factors override the fetus's right to life, even granting fetal personhood?

There certainly is widespread disagreement over these questions. In general, those who are pro-life tend to see almost no valid exceptions to allowing abortion apart from situations where the mother's life is in genuine danger. And those who are pro-choice tend to see no valid reasons to limit a woman's access to abortion.

Dr. Jim Thorp:

> I consider myself pro-life. On the other hand, some people might not view me as being a pro-life physician because I do and I have performed indicated terminations of pregnancy, in fact, terminations of pregnancy that I believe are indicated in terms of

saving the mother's life. And I think there are several situations that a very, very difficult decision has to be made and a fetus, a fetal life terminated; a fetal life killed for the benefit of the mother's life. And I think that that's a very unfortunate situation, but I think it should be emphasized that that is probably an extremely small minority of the number of terminations, but, nonetheless, it is an occurrence and, you know, especially in my specialty.

And if you look at various scenarios where that occurs and, you know, for example if you take a patient who has a life-threatening hemorrhage from a placenta which is implanted very close to the cervix, and that occurs at a gestational age which is less than the gestational age which is viable, say that occurs at 18 to 21 weeks gestation, and you need to evacuate the uterus and you need to terminate the life of the fetus and induce that pregnancy, labor and delivery in order to save the mother's life. That may occur in a situation where there is rupture of membranes. Membranes have ruptured at 18 to 22 weeks gestation and there is a significant life-threatening infection in the mother, and if that uterus is not evacuated then mother could most certainly die of a life-threatening sepsis.

Other more difficult situations are, for example, severe preeclampsia. It's unusual for severe preeclampsia to occur at those very early gestational ages but they do occur. I am aware of a case in which there was what is called a partial mole, and the patient presented with a significant amount of neoplastic molar tissue in the uterus coexisting with a fetus at 16 weeks' gestation with a life-threatening hemorrhage. Unfortunately, those are situations in which pregnancy needs to be terminated. And from my perspective that's a very difficult situation, but I believe that there is a pretty clear indication for a termination of pregnancy in a situation like that. And I would say that in those situations I still believe it's taking the life of the fetus or killing a fetus to be more blunt, and I don't try to couch those terms. I think that, unfortunately, sometimes a life has to be taken in certain situations. I think that, ethically, that there are different situations in which it may be right to take a life, and I think this is one of them.

Now, in all fairness to the debate, there are a whole set of other situations that are probably not as black and white as the situations that I just described, where it's a gray area. And I think that these are areas and situations that are extremely unfortunate.

A common pro-choice tactic when the debate reaches these questions is to argue that if the fetus were granted legal personhood with a nonviolable right to life, there would then be no reason to ever permit abortion, which would inevitably result in the death of those women whose lives are threatened by pregnancy. In making their case, they almost always center around the concept of the problems created by granting equal rights to both fetus and mother.

But essentially, this is a false dichotomy. The fetus would not need to be granted equal rights in order to have a right to continue living. In fact, it would be somewhat ridiculous to attempt to argue that a fetus has rights equal to that of the mother. We instantly recognize that neither a baby nor a toddler nor a teenager has equal rights with those of a full-grown adult. Additional rights such as driving or voting are granted as the individual ages. So, despite what the pro-choice community claims, reversing *Roe* would not mean a huge loss of fundamental rights for women. In fact, the only loss would be the right to legally kill the fetus, and even then with exceptions like those mentioned by Dr. Thorp. The woman would still retain the right to choose whether to raise the child as her own or to give the child to someone else who can provide a better environment.

CHAPTER 52

Rome Wasn't Built in a Day

Our lives begin to end the day we become silent about things that matter.
—DR. MARTIN LUTHER KING JR.

Is there any solution that will satisfy the majority of Americans and put an end to the abortion war?

Randy Alcorn:

> I'm not optimistic about it. I would hope a time would come in the same way that somebody in the 1850s, if they were asked, you know, do you think that slavery will ever be overturned, it might be pretty hard to imagine but it was. Yet, so many things have to change in order for that to happen, I think, in terms of . . . it's more than the Supreme Court. The Supreme Court so much reflects what the citizenry is willing to tolerate and what they believe. So, I mean, I certainly hope and pray for a day when *Roe v. Wade* is overturned. I'm not going to predict that that's going to happen in five years, ten years, or twenty years, though.

Dr. Brennan:

> I think, ultimately, we have to have a constitutional amendment which will protect unborn children just as the Fourteenth Amendment protected black people and Native Americans in the past. It's a formidable task but something that we have to keep working on. Keep in mind that Rome wasn't built in a day. It took centuries

before black people were recognized as persons and also Native Americans. I hope it doesn't take that long before we recognize the unborn as persons under the Fourteenth Amendment or some other appropriate amendment and also those after birth who are also in jeopardy in terms of being defined as nonpersons.

I think we have to insist that the only legitimate role for a physician in a truly civilized society is to protect, heal, and care for human life despite its status, condition, or stage of development. We have to call upon members of the medical profession to cease their war on the unborn and their escalating assaults against those defined as post-natal discards, and return to the "do no harm" ethic embodied in the Hippocratic oath, an ethic which explicitly condemns killing both inside and outside the womb.

Dr. Jefferson:

You can't kill people constantly without it having some effect; from violating the basic and the critically important premise of the Hippocratic tradition, the separation of killing and curing functions of the doctor, and the obligation of society not to ask the doctor to kill.

As passionate as both sides are and as deeply held as their beliefs run, it is difficult to imagine any situation that could satisfy both sides of this debate. Identifying a problem is nearly always easier than inventing a workable solution. That the United States government is spending more money than it takes in, for example, is obvious. The resulting 16 trillion-dollar debt (and counting) is clearly a problem. Finding a workable solution to that problem is another matter.

In the same way, I hope this book has at least identified a problem in American society. I hope, at least, that readers will come away with a realization that the "logic" used to "justify" legalized abortion was faulty, and the logic currently used to sustain it is equally flawed. Unfortunately, many people are becoming complacent. The problem has been with us since 1973 and, though slightly altered, remains intact.

After pondering and studying the issue for decades, I am convinced that there simply are no easy, generic solutions that work in each individual situation. There are general principles, but one can always find heart-rending exceptions. It is perhaps true that the best we can hope for in a societal response to the problem of unwanted pregnancies is the lesser of the available evil responses. Except for those rare circumstances in which a pregnant woman's life is at stake, I cannot envision a scenario in which an option that entails saving the life of the unborn child is not the lesser evil.

I am convinced America has not reached a morally satisfactory point with *Roe v. Wade* and subsequent abortion rulings. Most Americans don't like the idea or topic of abortion but feel that there are certain but rare times in which it is a necessary option. But they are also overwhelmingly opposed to abortion on demand. They are opposed to women using abortion simply as a method of birth control. And in an era where birth control is both legal and readily accessible, as Margaret Sanger, founder of Planned Parenthood suggested, abortion should be a useless crime.

In the end, no matter what occurs in the coming years, *Roe v. Wade* has permanently changed the American legal landscape. At present, the gulf that separates each side of the debate is still wide, but there are the beginnings of signs that possibly indicate a move in the direction of pro-life thinking. Education can help. People need to know the facts about fetal development and need to understand the "convenient fiction" of pro-choice "logic" that has brought about the incongruity and discord we experience today. When enough Americans begin to understand the faulty, deceptive, self-serving, and unjust arguments used to "justify" abortion on demand and keep its nearly unrestricted practice legal, a campaign for positive change will inevitably result.

Dr. Brennan:

This war will never end until far more people become aware of how closely today's corruption of language and thought resembles the legacy and name-calling that dominated the public mind-set in past atrocities. Today's proponents of abortion, euthanasia, and physician-assisted suicide, embryonic and fetal research, and research cloning must become aware that the language and rhetoric they are using to justify these destructive practices are the very same words and rationalizations constructed to defend the annihilation and experimental exploitation of people throughout history. Only when we become aware of the atrocities of the past and challenge their continuation into the present can there be hope for the future.

CHAPTER 53

Conclusion

Tell the truth and then run.

—Unknown

The basis for abortion on demand as proclaimed by Sarah Weddington in *Roe v. Wade* was that the pregnant woman has a fundamental constitutional right to decide whether or not to continue her pregnancy and that the state had no moral grounds for interfering with that decision. The focus of Weddington's argument involved a decision made by a pregnant woman. But the choice itself involved only two possible outcomes: either life or death for the fetus she carried.

No need to worry about that, declared the Supreme Court; *it turns out that fetuses are not fully human beings.* Not only would the *Roe* Supreme Court and the pro-choice logic it created have us unquestioningly accept the idea that it is possible for human nonpersons to exist, they would also have us stop demanding proof for the real existence of such hypothetical entities. To modern day pro-choice proponents, the morality of abortion is a question answered decades ago when abortion orthodoxy was first revealed by the men in black.

In this book, I have argued that the history of abortion as presented in *Roe* was inaccurate and lopsided; the rhetoric used in the effort to excuse abortion on demand was irrational and inconsistent. The perpetuation of that "convenient fiction" over the ensuing years has been accomplished through the popularization of what amounts to dogmatic adherence to a necessary but false and unsupportable premise based on the metaphysical idea that there exists a radical and significant moral difference between a human fetus and a human baby.

Here's the problem:

- Although this dogma is fanatically held and promulgated by disciples with enough zeal and devotion to make any cult leader green with envy;
- although it lacks essential fact-based support and is, in fact, contradicted by real-world evidence;
- although its underlying premise cannot be openly discussed without ending in either inconsistency or barbarity;
- although no images can be mustered to support its crucial premise, and, in fact, undoctored images must be censored;
- although it was necessary to install, update, and reboot the latest version of acceptable pro-abortion language into popular culture;
- although none of its prominent defenders (with rare exceptions like Naomi Wolf) can afford to speak honestly about what actually happens in an abortion "procedure";
- although it cannot appeal to the "well-known facts of fetal development" but instead must divert attention elsewhere;
- although it was necessary to rewrite history;
- although its frequency was disparaged while its alleged gender-equalizing capacity was hyped;
- although it faced potential extermination by the same Court that had created it; pro-choice philosophy is still packaged and peddled by the media, academia, and pop culture as the only conceivable nonpartisan position to take with respect to abortion.

In spite of this, accurate information as well as raw graphic images serve to rapidly break down these false premises no matter how dogmatically and zealously they may be held. Clearly, there is a war for hearts and minds. That war began long before *Roe v. Wade*, but *Roe* amounted to a decisive victory for the pro-abortion cause. Although the effects of that victory have lasted for a generation, polls now indicate things are changing. No one is quite sure exactly why the majority is shifting away from pro-choice philosophy, but it might have something to do with the fact that the first images of today's young activists are sonograms.

As we move beyond the fortieth anniversary of *Roe v. Wade*, there is hope.

Groups like Live Action are making an impact, and fetal research continues to shed new light on the complexities of fetal development. If the trend toward pro-life philosophy continues, *Roe* and its aging supporters may wake up one day to find their liberty fatally lacking in popular support.

RESOURCES CITED

Books

Alcorn, Randy. *Why Pro-life?* Colorado Springs: Multnomah Publishers, 2004.

Baird, Robert M. and Stuart E. Rosenbaum. *The Ethics of Abortion*. Prometheus, 2001.

Balkin, Jack M. *What Roe v. Wade Should Have Said.* New York University Press, 2005.

Brennan, William. *The Abortion Holocaust.* St. Louis: Landmark Press.

Carlson, Bruce M. *Patten's Foundations of Embryology.* 6th edition. New York: McGraw-Hill, 1996.

Considine, Douglas. ed. *Van Nostrand's Scientific Encyclopedia.* 5th edition,. New York: Van Nostrand Reinhold Company, 1976.

Coulter, Ann. *Godless.* New York: Three Rivers Press, Random House, 2007.

Cox, Archibald. *The Role of the Supreme Court in American Government.* Oxford University Press, 1976.

Dellapenna, Joseph W. *Dispelling the Myths of Abortion History.* Carolina Academic Press, 2006.

Edelstien, Ludwig. *The Hippocratic Oath: Text, Translation, and Interpretation.* Baltimore: Johns Hopkins University Press, 1943.

Faux, Marian. *Roe v. Wade: The Untold Story of the Landmark Supreme Court Decision That Made Abortion Legal.* First Cooper Square Press, 2001.

Feldt, Gloria. *The War on Choice: The Right Wing Attack on Women's Rights and How to Fight Back.* Bantam, 2004.

Garrow, David J. *Liberty and Sexuality: The Right to Privacy and the Making of Roe v. Wade.* Macmillan Publishing Company, 1994.

Harrison, Beverly Wildung. *Our Right to Choose: Toward a New Ethic of Abortion.* Boston: Beacon Press, 1983.

Hepper, Peter, Alan Slater, and Michael Lewis, eds. *Introduction to Infant Development.* Oxford University Press, 2006.

Hodge, Hugh Lenox. *Foeticide, or Criminal Abortion: A Lecture Introductory to the Course on Obstetrics and Disease of Women and Children, University of Pennsylvania, Session 1838-40.* Philadelphia: Lindsay and Blakiston, 1869.

Hull, N. E. H., and Peter Charles Hoffer. *Roe v. Wade: The Abortion Rights Controversy in American History.* University Press of Kansas, 2001.

Langman, Jan. *Medical Embryology.* 3rd edition. Baltimore: Williams and Wilkins, 1975.

Lee, Patrick. *Abortion and Unborn Human Life.* Washington, DC: The Catholic University of America Press, 1996.

McCorvey, Norma. *I Am Roe: My Life, Roe v. Wade, and Freedom of Choice.* HarperCollins, 1994.

Mohr, James C. *Abortion in America: The Origin and Evolution of National Policy, 1800-1900.* Oxford University Press, Inc., 1978.

Moore, Keith L. *Essentials of Human Embryology.* Toronto: B. C. Decker, Inc., 1988.

Moore, Keith L., and T. V. N. Persaud. *Before We Are Born: Essentials of Embryology and Birth Defects.* 4th edition. Philadelphia: W. B. Saunders Company, 1993.

Noonan, John T., Jr. *The Morality of Abortion: Legal and Historical Perspectives.* Cambridge: Harvard University Press, 1970.

———. *A Private Choice.* The Free Press, 1979.

O'Rahilly, Ronan and Fabiola Müller. *Human Embryology & Teratology.* 2nd edition. New York: Wiley-Liss, 1996.

Paige, Connie. *The Right to Lifers, Who They Are, How They Operate, Where They Get Their Money.* New York: Summit Books, 1983.

Sanger, Margaret. *An Autobiography*, 1938.

———. *The Case for Birth Control*. 1917.

———. *Women and the New Race*, 1920.

Shaver, Jessica. *Gianna: Aborted and Lived to Tell About It.* Colorado Springs: Focus on the Family Publishing, 1995.

Shettles, Landrum B., and David Rorvik. *Rites of Life.* Grand Rapids: Zondervan, 1983.

Stevens, John V., Sr. *The Abortion Controversy.* Founders Freedom Press, 2008.

Storer, David. *Duties, Trials and Rewards of the Student of Midwifery*. 1855.

Storer, Horatio Robinson. *Why Not? A Book for Every Woman.* American Medical Association, 1868.

Weddington, Sarah, *A Question of Choice*. Penguin Books, 1993.

Court Cases and Commentaries

Blackstone, William. *Commentaries on the Laws of England.* London, 1765.

Griswold v. Connecticut, 381 U.S. 479, 1965.

Roe v. Wade, 410 U.S. 113, 1973.

Scott v. Sandford, 60 U.S., 1857.

Essays, Articles and Testimony

American Medical Association. *12 Transactions of the American Medical Association, Report on Criminal Abortion.* 1859.

Begley, Sharon. "How Kids Grow: Do You Hear What I Hear?" *Newsweek. Special Issue.* May 31, 1991.

Gianelli, Diane M. "Second Trimester Abortion: An Interview with W. Martin Haskell, M.D." *Cincinnati Medicine*, Fall 1993.

———. "Shock-Tactic Ads Target Late-Term Abortion Procedure." *American Medical News*, July 5, 1993.

Hopson, Janet. "Embryo and Embryonic Development." *Psychology Today*, 31, no. 5, (Sept./Oct. 1998): 44, 6p, 4c.

Johnson, Douglas. "Testimony of Douglas Johnson Legislative Director, National Right to Life Committee on the Partial-Birth Abortion Ban Act [H.R. 929, S. 6] at a Joint Hearing Before the U.S. Senate Judiciary Committee and the Constitution Subcommittee of the U.S. House Judiciary Committee." March 11, 1997, http://www.nrlc.org/abortion/pba/test.htm.

Leonard, John Preston. "Quackery and Abortion." *Boston Medical and Surgical Journal* 43 (January 15, 1851): 447–81.

Liley, William. "The Foetus as a Personality." *Australian and New Zealand Journal of Psychiatry* 6 (1972): 99-105.

Lucas, Roy. "Federal Constitutional Limitations on the Enforcement and Administration of the State Abortion Statutes." *North Carolina Law Review* 46 (June, 1968).

Maret, Stephen M. "Frank Lake's Maternal-Fetal Distress Syndrome—An Analysis." PhD diss., Caldwell University. http://primal-page.com/mf2menu. htm.

McConnell, Michael W. "*Roe v. Wade* at 25: Still Illegitimate."

Means, Cyril, Jr. "The Law of New York Concerning Abortion and the Status of the Foetus, 1664–1968: A Case of Cessation of Constitutionality," *New York Law Forum* 19, num. 3 (1968).

Means, Cyril, Jr. "The Phoenix of Abortional Freedom: Is a Penumbral or Ninth-Amendment Right About to Arise From the Nineteenth-Century Legislative Ashes of a Fourteenth-Century Common-Law Liberty?" *New York Law Forum* 17, num. 2 (1971).

Nathan, Debbie. *Texas Observer,* Sept. 25, 1995 as quoted in Norma McCorvey. *Won by Love.* Thomas Nelson, Inc., 1998.

Olivarez, Grace. "Separate Statement." Rockefeller Commission Report, *Population and the American Future.* 1972, 161.

Planned Parenthood of NW & NE Indiana, The Munster, Indiana *Sunday Times,* March 1, 1992

Rivenburg, Roy. *A Decision between a Woman and God, Human Life Review* 22, no. 3 (Summer 1996): 59.

Tribe, Laurence H. "Foreword to the Supreme Court—1972 Term: Toward a Model of Roles in the Due Process of Life and Law," *Harvard Law Review* 87 (1973): 20–23.

Various. "Effects of Anesthesia During a Partial-Birth Abortion." Hearing Before the Subcommittee on the Constitution of the House Judiciary Committee, March 21, 1996, Serial no. 73.

Watts, Malcom. "A New Ethic for Medicine and Society." *California Medicine,* 1970, 68.

Wolf, Naomi. "Our Bodies, Our Souls." *New Republic,* October 16, 1996, 26.

Wyatt, John. "Medical Paternalism and the Fetus." *Journal of Medical Ethics* 27, suppl. 2.

Web Articles, Blogs, and Videos

Banderas, Anna. "It's all in your mind." Live Action Video.

http://liveaction.org/perspectives/3.htm.

Begin before Birth. "Fetal Development." http://www.beginbeforebirth.org/ in-the-womb/fetal-development.

Canaan, Amber, "Nutrients for Human Fetal Brain Growth During Pregnancy," Livestrong.com. Nov. 2, 2010. http://www.livestrong.com/article/294481-nutrients-for-human-fetal-brain-growth-during-pregnancy/.

Guibilini, Alberto and Francesca Minerva. "After-birth abortion: why should the baby live?" *Journal of Medical Ethics,* February 23, 2012 http://jme.bmj.com/content/early/2012/03/01/medethics-2011-100411.full.

Kneisly, Lauren Sabina. "Choice: An Obsolete Strategy." Biblical America Resistance Front, January, 1999. www.barf.org/articles/0035/.

Kurtz, Howard. "There's No Question the Media Forced the Komen Apology." The Daily Beast video, 3:54. February 6, 2012. http://www.thedailybeast.com/videos/2012/02/06/there-s-no-question-the-media-forced-the-komen-apology.html.

Leslie, Katie. "Handel Resigns from Komen." *Atlanta Journal Constitution,* February 7, 2012. http://www.ajc.com/news/handel-resigns-from-komen-1337241.html.

Mitchell, Andrea. "Andrea Mitchell Interviews Susan G. Komen's Nancy Brinker" MSNBC video, 11:34. Feb. 2, 2012. http://firstread.msnbc.msn.com/_news/2012/02/02/10303379-andrea-mitchell-interviews-susan-g-komens-nancy-brinker.

Partridge, Ernest, PhD. "The Paradoxical Right to Life." *The Gadfly Bytes,* October, 1999. http://gadfly.igc.org/liberal/abortion.htm.

Perry, Wynne, "Facial Expressions Develop in the Womb." LiveScience, Sept. 7, 2011. http://www.livescience.com/15939-fetus-facial-expressions.html.

Planned Parenthood, "Plan Your Children for Health and Happiness," Planned Parenthood Publication, Aug. 1963. Online photocopy at http://i81.photobucket.com/albums/j214/yodavater/PPPlanYourFamily63.jpg.

Savulescu, Julian. "'Liberals Are Disgusting': In Defence of the Publication of 'After-Birth Abortion.'" *Journal of Medical Ethics blog,* Feb. 28, 2012. http://blogs.bmj.com/medical-ethics/2012/02/28/liberals-are-disgusting-in-defence-of-the-publication-of-after-birth-abortion/#comment-451456352.

Science Clarified, "Embryo and embryonic development.; http://www.scienceclarified.com/El-Ex/Embryo-and-Embryonic-Development.html#b.

Smith, Wesley J. "Abortion Matters More Than Fighting Breast Cancer to Liberals?" *Human Exceptionalism* (blog), *National Review Online,* February 1, 2012. http://www.nationalreview.com/human-exceptionalism/322583/abortion-matters-more-fighting-breast-cancer-liberals.

———. "Pyrrhic Victory for Planned Parenthood as Komen Kisses the Abortion Ring" *Human Exceptionalism* (blog), *National Review Online,* February 3, 2012. http://www.nationalreview.com/human-exceptionalism/322586/pyrrhic-victory-planned-parenthood-komen-kisses-abortion-ring.

Swiss Virtual Campus. "Control of the Embryonic Development." Chapter 8.5, *Human Embryology.* http://www.embryology.ch/anglais/iperiodembry/controle01.html.

Taranto, James. "Komen Get It: The Abortion Protection Racket." *Wall Street Journal,* Feb. 2, 2012. http://online.wsj.com/article/SB10001424052970203889904577199110913604418.html?mod=WSJ_Opinion_MIDDLETopOpinion.

U.S. Catholic, "Talking Points: A U.S. Catholic Interview." *U.S. Catholic,* September 15, 2008. http://www.uscatholic.org/culture/social-justice/2008/09/talking-points.

INDEX